Automatic Vaudeville

AUTOMATIC VAUDEVILLE

Essays on Star Turns

JOHN LAHR

METHUEN : LONDON

First published in Great Britain in 1984 by
William Heinemann. This paperback edition first published
as a Methuen Paperback in 1985 by Methuen London Ltd,
11 New Fetter Lane, London EC4P 4EE.

SBN 413 55960 2

The essays on Stephen Sondheim, Studs Terkel, Noël Coward, and
Notes on Fame were first published in different form in *Harper's*.
The Beatles essay appeared in the *New Republic*, and a shorter
version of the Joan Didion-John Gregory Dunne essay was published
in *Horizon*. The pieces on Sam Shepard, Edna Everage and Hunter
Thompson are from *New Society*. The essay on Leiber & Stoller was
the introduction to *Baby, That Was Rock 'n Roll: The Legendary
Leiber & Stoller*. And the Joe Orton essay was the introduction to
The Complete Plays.

Printed in Great Britain by
Biddles Ltd, Guildford, Surrey

For Anthea & Christopher

To see you through
Till you're everything you want to be . . .
This time the dream's on me.
JOHNNY MERCER

Contents

Acknowledgments

Automatic Vaudeville was a popular penny arcade on New York's Lower East Side at the turn of the century. Through the viewfinders of its wrought-iron machines, cranked by hand, passed a variety of diversions: low comedy, dance routines, melodramas, travelogues, documentary history.

Writers often collude in the romance of individualism by making a myth of the isolation out of which their work emerges. But life is collaboration, especially for the writer. Fortunately I have friends who talk me out of my worst ideas and edit my best ones into more lucid shape. These essays, which cover the period from 1975 to the present, owe a lot to a number of fine professional editors. Bob Gottlieb of Knopf and David Godwin of William Heinemann have been generous with their enthusiasm and insightful with their criticism. Accordingly, the essays on Noël Coward, Eugene O'Neill, and Woody Allen have been greatly expanded, and those on Stephen Sondheim and on fame rewritten in part. Much of my American writing in recent years has appeared in *Harper's,* a blessing I owe entirely to its then Associate Editor, Helen Rogan, who has also edited my pieces with the grace and wit that distinguish her own prose. Rick Hertzberg, editor of the *New Republic,* had the happy idea of the Beatles piece. In London, Tony Gould of *New Society,* where I write a monthly column on drama, showed me how to do my American dance with English style. Mary-Kay Wilmers of the *London Review of Books* did some fine filagree work on the first part of the Coward essay, which she originally commissioned. A critic is someone who has the job; and for giving me that opportunity on their pages, I'd like to thank Lewis Lapham, editor of *Harper's;* Paul Barker, editor of *New Society;* and Rhoda Koenig, literary editor and resident *chanteuse* of *New York.*

But it is to Anthea Lahr, to whom all my books are dedicated, that these essays owe their existence. Our journey together these last eighteen years has been one of constant intellectual excitement and discovery. Our daily debate inevitably finds its way onto these pages. Besides being the best of companions, she remains the best of editors, a brute with her red pencil and her logical mind.

London
February 1983

Automatic Vaudeville

I

1

Stephen Sondheim

How is it you sing anything?
How is it you sing?

SWEENEY TODD

Musicals celebrate two things: abundance and vindictive triumph. Tall tales of the urban middle class, musicals revel in the spectacle of material well-being. They cajole the audience that if you don't have a dream, how you gonna have a dream come true? In its combination of script, song, and comic turn, the musical's formula meets the restless need of the American public for action and enchantment. The musical is mythic. People don't walk, they dance. Problems exist only to be sung or hitch-kicked away.

Until the mid-sixties, the best popular songs came out of the American musical. The confections of the Gershwins, Cole Porter, Irving Berlin, Frank Loesser, Richard Rodgers and Lorenz Hart and Oscar Hammerstein II, Harold Arlen with E. Y. Harburg were the backbeat of American progress. Their songs created a climate of confidence and promise. These songs played a dramatic part in molding the myths of modern America. For nearly half a century, the musical has been refurbishing with new words and rhythms the well-worn clichés of the middle class. Social comment is as unwelcome to most Broadway producers as syphilis is to a whore. Yet, although its creators never admit it, the musical's fierce and mischievous commitment to the status

5

quo has made it unwittingly the nation's most effective political theatre.

The form itself is an endangered species. In 1929, there were about eighty new musicals on Broadway; in 1978, there were fewer than fifteen. The writing is on the fourth wall. Spiraling cost is one of the culprits in killing off the art form, but economics is only an accomplice to the crime. The musical has not been able to adapt to the changing social and psychological mood of America. Over the past two decades the musical's comforting faith in the nation's goodness has been betrayed by public events; and it has found itself with nothing to sing about. Almost all the "new" hit shows (*Annie, Cabaret, Fiddler on the Roof, My Fair Lady, Hello, Dolly!, Irene, Funny Girl,* et cetera) are set in the past, where the complications of contemporary life can't shake an implacable hopefulness. Most of the smash hits of the past twenty years have been nostalgic for the elegance, innocence, lavishness, and values of earlier times. As America's Dream becomes increasingly threadbare, so has the art form that best promoted it. In this, at least, the musical remains the perfect metaphor for the time.

Much of the hope for the musical's survival resides in the acerbic intelligence of Stephen Sondheim. In collaboration with his director/producer Hal Prince, Sondheim has given a sense of occasion back to the musical and moved it away from the Shubert Alley formula of "No girls, no gags, no chance." At fifty-three, he is young enough to hanker for radical reform of the musical yet old enough to have absorbed professional expertise from the master craftsmen with whom he's worked: Oscar Hammerstein, Leonard Bernstein, Jerome Robbins, Richard Rodgers, and Jule Styne. Lyricist and composer of *A Funny Thing Happened on the Way to the Forum, Anyone Can Whistle, Company, Follies, A Little Night Music,* and *Pacific Overtures,* and grudging wordsmith to such great shows as *Gypsy* and *West Side Story,* Sondheim has become the American musical: a king on a field of corpses.

Traditional musicals dramatize the triumph of hope over experience. Characteristic of their flirtation with modernism, Sondheim's shows make a cult of blasted joys and jubilant despairs. He admits that joy escapes him. "If I consciously sat down and said

I wanted to write something that would send people out of the theater *really* happy, I wouldn't know how to do it." His mature musicals sing about a new American excellence: desolation.

Very few of the great Broadway songwriters grew up poor. Except for Berlin and Harburg, the majority were middle-class kids whose sense of the good life was part of their optimism. They'd always known abundance, and their songs registered a sense of wonder and excitement at the blessings of the material world. The truth of that magical well-being was proved by their fame and astronomic royalty statements. Sondheim, heir apparent to their stardom, shares, if not their world view, then this intimacy with affluence. The differences are generational. The sense of blessing has given way to boredom, the innocence to irony.

The precocious son of a dress manufacturer, Sondheim was educated at private schools in New York City and Bucks County, Pennsylvania, where he moved with his mother at the age of ten after his parents divorced. His ambition to write musicals was fired by the friendship and tutelage of Oscar Hammerstein II, who lived nearby. Sondheim wrote his first musical at fifteen. After graduating from Williams College as a music major, he won a two-year fellowship to study modern music with the avant-garde composer Milton Babbitt. Sondheim's mind and his training were more sophisticated than those of many of his musical comedy mentors, but he moved in their swank milieu. In Craig Zadan's *Sondheim & Co.*, Milton Babbitt remembers: "He had a very nimble mind and he was very musical. . . . He was also constantly diverted with parties. His social world . . . was very Park Avenue. . . . He was terribly bright and one could only wonder how serious he could afford to be. He had money, he was accustomed to frivolity, he was *not* accustomed to working terribly hard in a serious composer's sense."

No wonder that Sondheim's early lyrics mined the familiar mainstream vein of hope and attainment, and gave the musical eloquent expressions of its bourgeois dream. The sense of anticipation—that peculiarly American expectation of a magical insulation from life (true love, fame, money)—was superbly defined in "Something's Coming" from Sondheim's first Broadway show, *West Side Story* (1957):

> Could it be?
> Yes, it could.
> Something's coming,
> Something good—
> If I can wait.

On the eve of the sixties, *Gypsy* gave voice to the mythology of pluck and luck that show business acts out. With the hyperbole of Kennedy's New Frontier about to race the heart of the nation, skepticism was as "un-American" in the theatre as it was in the society. Whatever small irony the songs gave to the characterization of Rose and her girls in their uphill battle to show-biz fame and fortune, their message was clear: "Everything's Coming Up Roses." Rose—who early in the show expresses the familiar democratic longing for mobility and success: "All the sights that I gotta see yet/All the places I gotta play"—is crazed in her ambitions for her daughters. In fact, as the song's shift of pronouns makes clear, she is a backstage mother with nowhere to go and nowhere to play. Rose assumes the "father" role to her daughters and suffers the same fate as the rejected father. Her pride and self-fulfillment depend on her daughters leaving her behind and "doing better" than she. In "Rose's Turn," Sondheim dramatizes the pathos of her vicarious life. Rose pretends she's a performer on the empty stage and spews out her anger and longing:

> Why did I do it?
> What did it get me?
> Scrapbooks full of me in the background.
> Give 'em love and what does it get you?

The Broadway musical can never bring itself to deny completely the ethic that sustains it. In *Gypsy*, the end justifies the means: an attitude the star system has made irresistible. Sondheim, in 1959 a would-be star, concurs with that selfishness. "Rose's Turn" ends with Rose nearly shouting:

This time for me,
For me!
For me!

Rose and her daughter Gypsy Rose Lee reach some understanding at the finale. The audience gets its happy ending, its
world view very much intact. The boldness of "Rose's Turn"—
one of Sondheim's great numbers—is compromised. The victim's moment is show-stopping. Rose's crazed energy is gorgeous. Success may be punishing, but on Broadway it's never
really questioned. Instead, the waste of life is justified and forgiven in the thrilling moment of vindictive triumph the song
provides. Whatever loss or impoverishment Rose feels, the audience knows that this whole million-dollar enterprise, with all its
creative energy and star performers, is memorializing her vain
obsession, and theirs.

This spirit of aggrandizement links Sondheim emotionally
and technically to the traditional musical. "I believe *Gypsy* is one
of the two or three best shows ever written," Sondheim has
said. "The last good one in the Rodgers-and-Hammerstein tradition."

After *Gypsy*, Sondheim's next three musicals, although experimental in lyric technique, were still very much part of the Broadway mainstream. *A Funny Thing Happened on the Way to the Forum*
(1962), a smash hit, used songs as respites from hilarious action;
Anyone Can Whistle (1964) was a legendary mess that tried to make
songs comment on the action; and *Do I Hear a Waltz?* (1965), his
uninspired collaboration with the granddaddy of the traditional
musical, Richard Rodgers, left Sondheim wondering why such
musicals needed to be mounted and Rodgers wondering why
he'd worked with Sondheim (Rodgers: "I watched him grow from
an attractive little boy into a monster").

Sondheim sat out the turmoil of the late sixties in his Manhattan
townhouse, reemerging in 1970 with *Company*, a musical in tune
with the new, winded, post-protest times. Sondheim had come of

age: his own diminished sense of life and guarded emotions were now shared by a nation obsessed with its despair. Sondheim's glib toughness echoed the mood of the unromantic era. He became a phenomenon new to the Broadway musical, a laureate of disillusion.

A society that feels itself irredeemably lost requires a legend of defeat. And Sondheim's shows are in the vanguard of this atmosphere of collapse. He shares both the culture's sense of impotence and its new habit of wrenching vitality from madness (*Sweeney Todd* revels in murder). Sondheim's musicals do not abandon the notion of abundance, only adapt it. They show Americans a world still big, but in death-dealing, not well-being.

Sondheim's mature scores mythologize desolation. *Company* chronicles the deadening isolation of city life. *Follies* (1971) records in pastiche the death of the musical and dramatizes the folly of aspiration by staging the theatrical "ghosts" of the past. *A Little Night Music* (1973)—more attenuated and bitter than Ingmar Bergman's film *Smiles of a Summer Night*, on which it is based—depicts love among the ruins of a decadent and rootless Swedish aristocracy. *Pacific Overtures* (1976) shows the destruction of Japanese culture through the encroachment of the West. And *Merrily We Roll Along* (1981), which deals with the corruption, betrayals, and soured ambition of a successful songwriter, is a study of gloom at the top.

"All writing is autobiographical," Sondheim has said. "You find something of yourself that fits the character." Most of Sondheim's characters are numbed survivors whose songs examine fear, loss, betrayal, and anger. At the finale of *Company*, the central figure realizes he needs to make a human connection, that "alone is alone not alive":

> Somebody hurt me too deep,
> Somebody sit in my chair
> And ruin my sleep
> And make me aware
> Of being alive . . .

It is a passive climax. The spirit doesn't soar, it surrenders. Life is no longer dramatized as an adventure but as a capitulation. Impotence reigns, and all that is left to man's abused freedom is to justify its debasement. Typically, "Being Alive" lets the public applaud its emptiness: "Somebody force me to care,/Somebody let me come through."

The theme of the dead heart trying to resuscitate itself dominates much of Sondheim's work. As Alexis Smith sang in *Follies:* "How can you wipe tears away/When your eyes are dry?" The heart is so well defended from hurt that little can penetrate it. Instead of celebrating the ease and spontaneity of emotion that was the stock-in-trade of the traditional musical responding to a world it insisted was benign, Sondheim's songs report the difficulty of feeling in a world where, as his song says, there's "so little to be sure of." In *Anyone Can Whistle,* he first obliquely confronted the inhibitions that give his later scores their strained and haunting sense of incompleteness:

> Maybe you could show me
> How to let go,
> Lower my guard,
> Learn to be free.
> Maybe if you whistle,
> Whistle for me.

As Sondheim dramatizes again and again, commitment is something in which he has no faith. He is at a loss for compelling words about love. He has publicly denounced "I Feel Pretty" from *West Side Story,* pointing out the lie of its alliteration ("I feel fizzy and funny and fine"): "Somebody doesn't have something to say." Sondheim's judgment of his song could be leveled at the emotional impoverishment of a great deal of his work. In his large and impressive catalogue, most of the love songs are written in collaboration with other composers, such as Bernstein ("Maria," "Somewhere"), Styne ("Small World," "You'll Never Get Away from Me"), and Rodgers ("Do I Hear a Waltz?"), whose music has a melodic grace Sondheim's music lacks. Sondheim can be brilliant in his diagnosis of the failure of relationships, but never quite believable about their success. Romance, once the bread and butter of the musical, is now only stale crumbs on Sondheim's table.

While words for passion fail him, those for rage come easily. In the loveless and faithless worlds he writes about, anger is the surest test of feeling. Sondheim's scores bristle with the bitchy irony of deep-dish journalism. (Both make profit in exploiting pain.) Sondheim uses wit to sell his anger. In a superb song like "The Ladies Who Lunch," from *Company*, he lets mockery have a field day. With her checklist of the various bourgeois pastimes, the sozzled singer uses anger to stir things up and create the illusion of movement in a stalled life:

> And here's to the girls who just watch:
> Aren't they the best?
> When they get depressed, it's a bottle of Scotch
> Plus a little jest.
> Another chance to disapprove,
> Another brilliant zinger.
> Another reason not to move,
> Another vodka stinger.

Mockery is disillusion in action; but by the time Sondheim brought it to Broadway, it had been accepted in American life. For a decade Pop Art had been throwing back at the public as fine art the detritus of industrial society—soup cans, beer cans, billboards, comic books. The youth culture made mockery a "lifestyle," and *Hair* (1968) brought it into show business. Even Hollywood, sniffing the winds of change, managed *M*A*S*H*, a send-up of the war effort. In literature, satirists such as Joseph Heller (*Catch-22*), Kurt Vonnegut (*Slaughterhouse-Five*), Tom Wolfe (*Radical Chic*), Jules Feiffer, and Lenny Bruce found a wide new audience. Their satire identified the social cancer. But Sondheim never lets his maliciousness go beyond the wisecrack. The jeers at marriage in "The Little Things You Do Together" (from *Company*) are as facile as they are smug. By making delightful his disgust with family, Sondheim sells the sickness while others before him sold the antidote:

> The concerts you enjoy together,
> Neighbors you annoy together,
> Children you destroy together
> That keep marriage intact.

The metaphor for *Company*, Sondheim wrote in *The Dramatists Guild Quarterly*, was New York City: "We were making a comparison between a contemporary marriage and the island of Manhattan." The traditional musical made the city into a playground, from which the characters emerged undaunted and invigorated by New York's obstacles. Manhattan, *Company* suggests, is a lethal, suffocating battlefield where survival hardens the heart and infects all contact with desperation. Now, the battle is shown as hardly worth the prize. Sondheim put it brilliantly in "Another Hundred People":

> And they meet at parties
> Thru the friends of friends
> Who they never know.
> Will you pick me up,
> Or do I meet you there,
> Or shall we let it go?

This song captures New York as the contemporary middle-class audience experiences it. The answering service, the television, the intercom, the beeper—all the devices that keep urban dwellers "in touch" also help them hide. They magnify the citizens' terrifying isolation. As Sondheim's song says, New York is "a city of strangers," its frantic pace at once a distraction and a destiny. If there is no peace here, at least there is exhaustion—a state of collapse in which neither the dead heart nor a death-dealing society matters. *Company* exalts fatigue; *Follies* exploits its cultural manifestation, nostalgia.

In discussing Hal Prince's concept for staging *Follies*, Sondheim is quoted as saying: "The Roxy opened in the late '20s with a picture called *The Loves of Sunya*, a film which starred Gloria Swanson, and when it was torn down in 1960, she posed in the ruins with her arms outstretched. And Hal said that *that's* what the show should be about—rubble in the daylight.''

Conceived as a show-biz reunion on the *Follies* stage, which is soon to be demolished for a parking lot, the show sets the musical dreams of the past against the brutal actualities of the performers' present lives. It is an extravaganza of irony. In its delectation of decay, *Follies* put older stars like Gene Nelson, Alexis Smith, Fifi D'Orsay, Ethel Shutta, Dorothy Collins back on the boards. This crude juxtaposition traded on nostalgia to make a point about it, and them. But *Follies'* appetite for carrion is at once breathtaking and sinister. Ghosts of Broadway's past are symbolically as well as literally materialized on the *Follies* stage. Of course, sculptors like George Segal and Edward Kienholz have been creating brilliant and ghostly environments since the early sixties. Their worlds are unrelenting and silent. In making death the subject of story and song, *Follies* also makes it spectacular. The audience is asked not only to watch decay, but to *love* it. Sondheim's "I'm Still Here," sung by Yvonne De Carlo (!), turns devastation into delight:

> I've been through Reno,
> I've been through Beverly Hills,
> And I'm here.
> Reefers and vino,
> Rest cures, religion, and pills,
> And I'm here.

The show is full of Sondheim's smart pastiche numbers, which convey the dreams of fulfillment and success. At the finale —when, as the record notes report, "The cacophony becomes a fever and all the stops are let out as the nightmare fills the stage" —a character in white tie and tails tries to put over the old Broadway bravado. He can't finish the song.

> What's the point of shovin' your way to the top?
> Live 'n' laugh 'n' you're never a flop. . . .

Follies' disenchantment isn't convincing because it hungers for traditional success. The show's numbers take their energy not from what they ironically reveal about their characters, but from their vision of the old mythic forms dusted off and lovingly put before an audience. "It's a schizophrenic piece," Sondheim said. "And it's supposed to be." But the split in the show's consciousness is deeper than he realizes. *Follies* is paralyzed by the nostalgia it wants to expose. "Hope doesn't grow on trees," a character says at the end. "You make your own." That's what the musical has always believed. *Follies* wants to detach itself from the form and content of the traditional musical, but manages only to return to the status quo ante.

In *Merrily We Roll Along,* Sondheim rages at success while enjoying the benefits of it. In Sondheim's fable of irony-ever-after, the Broadway composer and film producer Frank Shepard sings, flashing back over his career while addressing the graduating class of his former high school:

> ALL: Best of all, we don't stop dreaming
>   Just because we're rich—
> FRANK: And famous—
> ALL: And suntanned—
> FRANK: And on the covers of magazines
>   And in the columns and on the screens
>   And giving interviews
>   Being photographed
>   Making all the important scenes . . .

By going back in time, Sondheim lets the audience know the characters' futures before they do. In this way their dreams are stripped of enchantment. Sondheim gets both to exploit the traditional Broadway song motifs of anticipation, love, accomplishment, friendship and to piss on them from a great height.

Before it was art, the musical was fun. In trying to push the musical toward greater artiness, Sondheim's shows have lost much of their fun. As a lyricist, Sondheim disdains the enchant-ers. "I cannot resist the temptation to add my choice for the most overrated lyricist," he wrote with typical acerbity in *The Dramatists Guild Quarterly*'s poll of favorite lyricists. "Lorenz Hart, whose work has always struck me as being occasionally graceful, touching, but mostly, technically sloppy, unfelt and silly ('Lover, when I'm near you/And I hear you/Speak my name/Softly in my ear you/Breathe a flame')." But in their technical expertness, Sondheim's own songs often lose in resonance what they try to gain in statement. "The danger of argument in verse," Auden warns in *The Dyer's Hand*, "is that verse makes ideas too clear and distinct." Sondheim polishes every idea; the result is lucid and cold:

> Every day a little death . . .
> Every day a little sting
> In the heart and in the head.
> Every move and every breath,
> And you hardly feel a thing,
> Brings a perfect little death.
> (*A Little Night Music*)

"Anybody can rhyme 'excelsior' and 'Chelsea or,'" Sondheim has said. "I'd rather have an ear-catching thought than an eye-catching rhyme." This is more clever than clear. Sondheim speaks proudly of how his songs define and advance the characters in his musicals. But what distinguishes the characters in most of his later work is that they have no character. As he himself has pointed out, "In *Company* we were up against one of the oldest dramatic problems in the world: how do you write about a cipher without making him a cipher? In *Follies* we deliberately decided not to create characters with warts and all. Everybody would be, not a type, but an essence. . . . *Pacific Overtures* was an attempt to tell a story that has no characters at all." Sondheim makes an asset out of a liability and calls it a breakthrough.

The very nature of the lyric holds the musical back from taking issue with its society. Verse, Auden writes in *The Dyer's Hand*,

> is unsuited for controversy, to proving some truth or belief which is not universally accepted, because its formal nature cannot but

convey a certain skepticism about its conclusions. "Thirty days hath September/April, June, and November" is valid because nobody doubts its truth. Were there, however, a party who passionately denied it, the lines would be powerless to convince him because, formally, it would make no difference if the lines ran: "Thirty days hath September/August, May, and December."

Pacific Overtures falls into this trap. When Sondheim's lyrics tell a story with no didactic purpose, as in his account of Admiral Perry's treaty-signing with the Shogun, "Someone in a Tree," the song can be astonishing. But at the finale, when the show strains for significance and lectures the audience about the perils of industrialization by showing modern Japan, the lyric is woefully inept. The form of "Next" belies the seriousness of its message:

> Streams are dying,
> Mix a potion.
> Streams are dying,
> Try the ocean—
> Brilliant notion—
> Next!

"I'm essentially a cult figure," Sondheim wrote in *The Dramatists Guild Quarterly* in 1979. "My kind of work is caviar to the general [public]." Sondheim has set himself up as an avant-gardist in an avowedly popular form. His shows aspire to be mass entertainment while remaining suspicious of the mass. "You have to remember that the average audience for a musical is by definition more traditionalist than for a straight play," he told *The Times* (London). "In America they still regard Kurt Weill as highly avant-garde. . . . But you must go on breaking down old musical forms and creating new ones, otherwise there's nothing but repetition."

But musical comedy is to music what Ping-Pong is to tennis. Only on Broadway could Sondheim's music sound radical. He uses a harmonic language developed in France between 1895 and 1910, notably in the art songs of Ravel. *A Little Night Music*, a show whose libretto confirms Voltaire's dictum that anything too silly to be said can always be sung, is musically Sondheim's most interesting score. It contains moments of uncommon interest: the roving harmonies in "You Must Meet My Wife"; the metrical modulation in "The Miller's Son," in which the rhythm is constant and the meter changes; great lyrics matched to a memorable melody in "Send In the Clowns." Too often in his music, rhythmic monotony is overlooked because of the vivaciousness of his lyrics. Unlike Gershwin, who began his songs with introductions, Sondheim's songs begin with vamps—an approach that restricts his melodic invention and gives away to the audience what follows. The boldness of the initial musical gesture becomes monotonous because of this imposed pattern.

Of all Sondheim's shows, *Company* is the most successful if not the most ambitious. The limitations in Sondheim's music—its cold technique, its nervousness with emotion, its stylish defensiveness—match the brittle world *Company* describes. It is not the absence of hits—"Send In the Clowns" is one of his few—but the lack of heart in Sondheim's music that has been his real nemesis. His music never risks embarrassment. Instead, he hides his deepest feelings behind style, which keeps both his music and his musicals from as yet reaching their fullness. In *Sondheim & Co.*, Leonard Bernstein speaks perceptively about Sondheim's inhibitedness, his fear of direct, subjective expression:

> Nothing must be straight out subjectively because it's dangerous, because it reveals your insides. The fear usually takes the form of the fear of corniness, of being platitudinous, or whatever. Steve has very strong feelings and therefore must invent correspondingly strong defenses to guard against those feelings. . . . He's always been a little bit afraid of the word "beautiful," except as it can be reinterpreted as charming, decorative, odd, sweet, touching—touching in some oblique way.

To many people, including Bernstein, "Send In the Clowns" augured a breakthrough, the emergence of a personal language at once passionate and penetrating. But this now seems unlikely. *Pacific Overtures* followed *A Little Night Music*, another "smart" idea that allowed Sondheim to dodge deep personal feelings in a virtuoso display of technique. *Sweeney Todd* (1979) updates Sondheim's appetite for disillusion in one ferocious metaphor of revenge, which turns his emotional limitation into an asset. It is not love but laceration that is the popular delirium; and Sondheim makes a dazzling opera of cannibalism and gore, but without a shudder.

> Swing your razor high, Sweeney!
> Hold it to the skies!
> Freely flows the blood of those
> Who moralize!

Even before the play begins, the audience is submerged in a nether world where life is in retreat. An organ's funereal wheeze, a grave, gravediggers, a pile of dirt, "the deafeningly shrill" sound of a factory—all establish a dark and brutalizing world. A gourmand of griefs, Sondheim's first number, the brilliant "Ballad of Sweeney Todd," sets the stage for the production's boulevard nihilism, praising at once terror *and* technique:

> He kept a shop in London town,
> Of fancy clients and good renown.
> And what if none of their souls were saved?
> They went to their Maker impeccably shaved. . . .

A visionary of death ("Sweeney heard music that nobody heard"), Todd is a demon barber, that is, he has a genius for killing. The ballad hymns his professionalism. A stickler for detail, Sweeney shares with the show a capacity for making emptiness elegant:

> Sweeney pondered and Sweeney planned,
> Like a perfect machine 'e planned.

Framed by a lecherous judge who plans to despoil his wife and later lay siege to his daughter, Sweeney is deported and returns to London many years later under his new name to look for his family. Convinced that his wife is dead and his daughter lost,

Sweeney sets about administering his rough justice from the barber's chair. *Sweeney Todd* allows Sondheim to make the dead heart heroic. Revenge, after all, is impotence in action.

Sweeney is quick to register his hatred of life and the hierarchical English class system that has victimized him:

> At the top of the hole
> Sit the privileged few,
> Making mock of the vermin
> In the lower zoo . . .

By making Sweeney part of the walking wounded of both the class war and the corruptions of capitalism, the show justifies Sondheim's flexing his misanthropic muscle. Eugene Lee's brooding industrial set makes alienation beautiful. The production huffs and puffs to give the gory tale some political resonance; but there is nothing more hollow than a lecture on poverty by the well-fed Broadway elite, idealists with servants. The real issue of the play is hate, and hate alone.

In Todd, Sondheim has found his perfect hero. Although a nineteenth-century figure, Todd expresses a contemporary infatuation. In the absence of a destiny, revenge becomes his mission. Rage gives the illusion of strength to the powerless; and the ambitiousness of hate hides the sense of a stalled life. It is not in love but in murder that Todd approaches pure emotion. For Todd (and Sondheim), anger makes him feel alive. As Todd slits his first victim's throat, he is exalted. "I'm alive at last," he sings. "And I'm full of joy."

Other writers as various as Joe Orton and Tom Lehrer have exploited the macabre to satirize the rapacity of mankind, but with a difference. Behind their fury is a moral impulse. Their worlds admit a sense of sin; and their unrelenting laughter is essentially forgiving. But Sondheim simply fulminates. (In the play's epilogue, Sweeney rises from the dead and at the final beat stares malevolently at the audience, then exits slamming the door in its face.) The show merely gives Sondheim's anger an outing. Inevitably, the love interest in *Sweeney Todd* is flat, unconvincing and uninspired; but when Sondheim is scoring the moments of revenge, the music bubbles with energy and confidence. Death is resolutely Sondheim's dominion. Yet even his appetite for blood is bloodless. Death, what Henry James called "that distinguished thing," is turned into a shallow camp in a world where evil holds no odium and life no significance. In the show's epilogue, Sondheim scolds the audience for clinging to dreams he helped mold, and so gets even for his own lyric past:

COMPANY:	Sweeney wishes the world away,
	Sweeney's weeping for yesterday,
	Is Sweeney!
	Sweeney, Sweeney!
	(*Pointing around theatre*)
	There! There! There! There! . . .
TODD:	To seek revenge may lead to hell,
MRS. LOVETT:	But everyone does it, and seldom as well
BOTH:	As Sweeney . . .

Are we all murderers? But if you call everyone murderers, then what do you call a murderer? Too chic to acknowledge blame or apportion guilt, *Sweeney Todd* celebrates the only value its creators believe in: expertise. The show is wonderful to watch, but the implications behind it are monstrous. In cheering the psychopathic style, *Sweeney Todd* is as traditional a piece of American fare as apple pie.

From My-Lai to El Salvador, the American public has become casual about absorbing catastrophe. And Sondheim has turned this numbed anguish into a mass product. His musicals claim victory for themselves as new departures, but they are the end of the musical's glorious tradition of trivialization. Sondheim's cold elegance matches the spiritual pall that has settled over American life. His musicals are chronicles in song of the society's growing decrepitude. They foreshadow the newest barbarism—a nation that has no faith in the peace it seeks or the pleasure it finds.

2

Noël Coward

Mr. Coward is his own invention and
contribution to this century.

JOHN OSBORNE

Noël Coward never believed he had just a talent to amuse. A man
who spent a lifetime merchandising his de-luxe persona, Coward
liked to make a distinction between accomplishment and vanity:
"I am bursting with pride, which is why I have absolutely no
vanity." A performer's job is to be sensational; and in his songs,
plays, and public performances, Coward lived up to the responsibility of making a proper spectacle of himself. His peers had
difficulty in fathoming this phenomenon. T. E. Lawrence thought
Coward had "a hasty kind of genius." Sean O'Casey spat spiders
at the mention of his name: "Mr. Coward hasn't yet even shaken
a baby-rattle of life in the face of one watching audience." J. B.
Priestley, as late as 1964, taxed him mischievously: "What is all
this nonsense about being called the Master?" Shaw, who prophesied success for the fledgling playwright in 1921, warned him
"never to fall into a breach of essential good manners." He
didn't.

A star is his own greatest invention. Coward's plays and songs
were primarily vehicles to launch his elegant persona on the
world. In his clipped, bright, confident style, Coward irresistibly
combined reserve and high camp. He became the merry-andrew

of moderation, warning mothers to keep their daughters off the stage, confiding, in *Present Laughter* (1942), that sex was "vastly overrated," and sardonically pleading: "Don't let's be beastly to the Germans." Coward was a performer who wrote, not a writer who happened to perform. He wrote his svelte, wan good looks into the role of Nicky Lancaster in *The Vortex* (1924): *"He is extremely well-dressed,"* explain the stage directions. *"He is tall and pale, with nervous hands."* The play made Coward a sensation both as an actor and as a playwright. Coward was his own hero; and the parts he created for himself were, in general, slices of his legendary life. Leo *(Design for Living)*, Charles Condomine *(Blithe Spirit)*, Hugo Latymer *(A Song at Twilight)* are all smooth, successful writers. Garry Essendine *(Present Laughter)*, George Pepper ("Red Peppers" from one of the cameos in *To-Night at 8:30*), and Elyot Chase, a man of no apparent métier in *Private Lives* who nonetheless manages a dance and a few songs at the piano, all exploited Coward's theatrical past. Even in World War II, when he hoped his writing talent could be put to some serious use, it was Coward's presence that was valued. "Go out and sing 'Mad Dogs and Englishmen' while the guns are firing—that's your job," Churchill told him. Coward's massive output (sixty produced plays, over three hundred published songs, plus screenplays, volumes of short stories, autobiography, and fiction) contributes to his legend. His work was so successful an advertisement for himself that Kenneth Tynan, I think rightly, observed: "even the youngest of us will know in fifty years' time what we meant by 'a very Noël Coward sort of person.'"

Like all great entertainers, Coward knew how to exploit his moment. In the thirties, Cyril Connolly was complaining that his plays were "written in the most topical and perishable way imaginable, the cream in them turns sour overnight." The American critic Alexander Woollcott dubbed Coward "Destiny's Tot," but he was England's solid gold jazz-baby who later turned into an international glamour-puss. Coward swung with the times and suavely teased them. "I am never out of opium dens, cocaine dens, and other evil places. My mind is a mass of corruption," he told the *Evening Standard* in 1925. Every new-fangled idiom found its way into his dialogue, even if he didn't always fully grasp its meaning: "You're psychoanalytic neurotics the both of you," complains one of the characters in *Fallen Angels* (1925). *The Vortex* exploited the clash between Victorian and modern mores, the old and the young idea. *Fallen Angels* and *Easy Virtue* (1925) mined the mother lode of sex, scandal, and pseudosophistication. *Cavalcade* (1931) and *This Happy Breed* (1942) spoke directly to the political chauvinism of the day. All these plays had great commercial success, and the last two were considered serious patriotic statements about England and her fighting spirit. But Coward was not a thinker (at the mere suggestion, O'Casey exclaimed: "Mother o' God!"). His genius was for style. When his plays aspired to seriousness, the result was always slick (O'Casey compares the sketchy characters in *Cavalcade* to "a tiny monogram on a huge bedspread"); and when he wrote himself into the role of ardent heterosexual lover (*Still Life,* which he himself called the "most mature" of the one-act plays in *To-Night at 8:30*) or ordinary working-class bloke (*This Happy Breed*), the characterization is wooden. The master of the comic throwaway becomes too loquacious when he gets serious, and his fine words ring false. Only when Coward is frivolous does he become in any sense profound.

Frivolity, as Coward embodied it, was an act of freedom, of disenchantment. He had been among the first popular entertainers to give a shape to his generation's sense of absence. His frivolity celebrates a metaphysical stalemate, calling it quits with meanings and certainties. "We none of us ever mean *anything,*" says Sorel Bliss amid the put-ons at the Bliss house party in *Hay Fever* (1925). The homosexual sense of the capriciousness of life is matched by a capricious style. "I think very few people are completely normal really, deep down in their private lives. It all depends on a combination of circumstances. If all the various cosmic thingummys fuse at the same moment," says Amanda in *Private Lives* (1930). This high-camp style, of which Coward was the theatrical master, worked as a kind of sympathetic magic to dispel both self-hatred and public scorn. "Has it ever struck you that flippancy might cover a very real embarrassment?" someone asks, again in *Private Lives*. The most gossamer of his good plays, *Private Lives* is adamant on the subject of frivolity.

ELYOT *(seriously):* You mustn't be serious, my dear one, it's just what they want.

AMANDA: Who's they?

ELYOT: All the futile moralists who try to make life unbearable. Laugh at them. Be flippant. Laugh at everything, all their sacred shibboleths. Flippancy brings out the acid in their damned sweetness and light.

AMANDA: If I laugh at everything, I must laugh at us too.

ELYOT: Certainly you must. We're figures of fun all right.

In *Design for Living* (1932), the laughter of the *ménage à trois* reunited at the finale ("they groan and weep with laughter; their laughter is still echoing down the walls as the curtain falls") is frivolity's refusal to suffer. Even as she leaves her third husband, aptly named Ernest, Gilda, like Elyot Chase, insists that she is not serious. The battle in Coward's best comedies is not between license and control but between gravity and high spirits. At least three times in *Private Lives* people shout at Elyot (Coward's role) to be serious. "I fail to see what humour there is in incessant trivial flippancy," says Victor, sounding like one of Coward's critics. Like James Agate, for instance, who wrote in the *Sunday Times:* "Mr. Coward is credited with the capacity for turning out these highly-polished pieces of writing in an incredibly short time, and if rumour and the illustrated weeklies are to be believed, he writes his plays in a flowered dressing-gown and before breakfast. But what I want to know is what kind of work he intends to do after breakfast, when he is clothed and in his right mind." Elyot, Coward's spokesman, lives in the world of appearances, the world of the moment, and he celebrates it: "Let's be superficial and pity the poor Philosophers. Let's blow trumpets and squeakers, and enjoy the party as much as we can, like very small, quite idiotic school-children. Let's savour the delight of the moment. . . ."

Coward's best work follows, more or less, this recipe for

chaos. His reputation as a playwright rests on *Hay Fever, Private Lives, Design for Living, Present Laughter, Blithe Spirit* (1941), and the brilliant one-act *Hands Across the Sea* (1936). In all these comedies of bad manners, the characters are grown-up adolescents. There is no family life to speak of, no children, no commitment except to pleasure. The characters do no real work; and money, in a time of world depression, hunger marches, and war, is taken for granted. Monsters of vanity and selfishness, they appeal to the audience because their frivolity has a kind of stoic dignity. Written fast and in full, confident flow (*Hay Fever* in five days; *Private Lives* in four days; *Present Laughter* and *Blithe Spirit* each in six days), Coward's best work has the aggressive edge of his high spirits (even his bookplates show him winking). And when, in the fifties, his plays no longer found favor, he took frivolity's message to the public in person as a cabaret turn, brilliantly mocking his audiences' appetite for anxiety with such impish songs as "Why Must the Show Go On?" and "There Are Bad Times Just Around the Corner":

> With a scowl and a frown
> We'll keep our peckers down
> And prepare for depression and doom and dread,
> We're going to *un*pack our troubles from our old kit bag
> And wait until we drop down dead . . .

"It's all a question of masks," explains Leo in *Design for Living*. "Brittle, painted masks. We all wear them as a form of protection; modern life forces us to." But Coward's acute awareness of and insistence on the performing self comes out of a homosexual world where disguise is crucial for survival.

In *Present Laughter*, Garry Essendine (a successful actor and another Coward star turn) is trapped in his performance. "I'm always acting—watching myself go by—that's what's so horrible—I see myself all the time, eating, drinking, loving, suffering—sometimes I think I'm going mad." Essendine is another of Coward's irresistible heterosexual postures: "Everyone worships me, it's nauseating." Garry is fantastically successful—and success can be the most effective mask of all. The jokes in the play belie concerns of a different nature. Although elsewhere Coward sang about following his secret heart and being mad about the boy, he didn't push it on stage. His plays tread cautiously around his deeper meanings. The comedies hurry the audience past issues that the dialogue tries tentatively to raise.

Only in *Semi-Monde* (unpublished, 1929) does Coward find a successful metaphor for the sexual complications that lie behind his posturing. *Semi-Monde* is easily the most visually daring of his comedies, and the most intellectually startling. Set in a swank Paris hotel lobby and bar over the years 1924 to 1926, with dozens of lovers continually making their predatory exits and entrances, *Semi-Monde* is made up of sexually mischievous tableaux vivants and gets much nearer the homosexual knuckle than Coward's public image allowed. The play was never produced in Coward's lifetime. In *Semi-Monde*, Coward's camp sensibility has a field day. "My dear—where did you find that?" says Albert to Beverley, meaning his traveling companion, Cyril. "It's divine." And when Beverley goes to buy *Vanity Fair* at the newsstand, Albert pipes up: "Do get *La Vie Parisienne*, it's so defiantly normal." In this play, where everyone is on the make, there is no need for Coward's statements about role-playing, the transience of relationships, the need to be lighthearted—his usual comic hobbyhorses—because here the game is shown in action. "I'm going to be awfully true to you," says Tanis to her husband, Owen, on their honeymoon in 1924. "I've got a tremendous ideal about it." But by the third act (1926) she is having an affair with a successful writer, Jerome Kennedy. Owen is smitten by Kennedy's daughter, Norma. It is to the writer, as usual, that Coward allows a few closing moments of articulate disgust: "We're all silly animals," he says, when the affair is finally out in the open, "gratifying our beastly desires, covering them with a veneer of decency and good behaviour. Lies . . . lies . . . complete rottenness. . . ." But Jerome, like the others, can't and won't change. "There's nothing to be done, you know—nothing at all." The only thing left is to put on a good show.

Coward's most vivacious playwrighting is about what Preston Sturges liked to call "Topic A." Yet his official theatrical line on sex is not to laugh the issues off the stage, but to treat them with distant superiority. As Garry Essendine admits in *Present Laughter*, "I enjoy it for what it's worth and fully intend to go on doing so for as long as anybody's interested and when the time comes that they're not, I shall be perfectly content to settle down with an apple and a good book!" Coward's wit fights no battles in his plays except to endear him to his public. "Consider the public" were the first words of advice to the brash New Wave in 1961. "Treat it with tact and courtesy. Never fear or despise it. . . . Never, never, never bore the living hell out of it." Coward's laughter is always reassuring, which is why it is still commercial.

Coward has an immense reputation for wit, but unlike the rest of the high-camp brotherhood, Wilde, Firbank, and Orton, he rarely essays epigrams or sports directly with ideas in his plays. "To me," he maintained, "the essence of good comedy writing is that perfectly ordinary phrases such as 'Just fancy!' should, by virtue of their context, achieve greater laughs than the most literate epigrams. Some of the biggest laughs in *Hay Fever* occur on such lines as 'Go on,' 'No there isn't, is there?' and 'This haddock's disgusting.' There are many other glittering examples of my sophistication in the same vein. . . ." Such famous Coward-isms as "Very flat, Norfolk," "Don't quibble, Sybil," "Certain women should be struck regularly like gongs" have the delightful silliness of an agile mind which was never as bold on stage as it was in life. "Dear 338171," Coward wrote to the shy T. E. Law-rence in the RAF. "May I call you 338?" Nor are Coward's theat-rical put-downs (AMANDA: Heaven preserve me from nice women. SYBIL: Your reputation will do that) as bitchy as some of the real-life improvisations like "Keir Dullea, gone tomorrow."

Where Coward's humor is incomparable is in his chronicling of the strut and swagger of certain society ladies:

> It was in the fresh air
> And we went as we were
> And we stayed as we were
> Which was Hell . . .
> ("I've Been to a Marvellous Party")

It was not the situations of English life (except for *Blithe Spirit,* his comedies have no substantial plots) but the sounds of it that interested Coward. When, in *Hay Fever,* Simon Bliss admits to his mother that he hasn't washed, Judith says: "You should, darling, really. It's so bad for your skin to leave things about on it." Coward loves such fluting vagueness and he has left modern theatre a number of cunning pen portraits of an endangered species. In *Hands Across the Sea,* from *To-Night at 8:30,* Lady Maureen "Piggie" Gilpin is faced with the unexpected arrival of the Wadhursts, a colonial couple with whom she once stayed while traveling in the Far East. Her own breathless social whirl makes it impossible for her ever to get to know them:

> PIGGIE: . . . *(The telephone rings)* I've got millions of questions to ask you, what happened to that darling old native who did a dance with a sword?—*(At telephone)* Hallo—*(Continuing to everyone in general)* It was the most exciting thing I've ever seen, all the villagers sat round in torchlight and they beat—*(At telephone)* Hallo—yes, speaking—*(Continuing)* beat drums and the—*(At telephone)* hallo—darling, I'd no idea you were back—*(To everybody)* and the old man tore himself to shreds in the middle, it was marvellous— . . .

In his memorial to Coward, Kenneth Tynan remarked that Coward "took the fat off English comic dialogue." Tynan tried to float the notion that the elliptical patter characteristic of Harold Pinter's plays originated in Noël Coward's. In support, he quoted a line out of context from *Shadow Play* (1935): "Small talk, a lot of small talk, with other thoughts going on behind." But Coward's characters live nervily on the surface of life, and say pretty much what they mean. The reticence in the comedies comes not from the characters holding back, but from the author. He defends his artifice to the end. "Equally bigoted," he wrote in his diatribe against the New Wave, "is the assumption that reasonably educated people who behave with restraint are necessarily 'clipped,' 'arid,' 'bloodless' and 'unreal.' "

Tynan called Coward "a virtuoso of linguistic nuance." But it is a disservice to the splendid energy Coward gave to his half

century to put him so elegantly on the literary shelf. His triumph
was noisier and, thankfully, more vulgar. He ventilated life with
his persona. And it is the frivolity in his plays which has proved
timeless. The reason is simple. Frivolity acknowledges the futility
of life while adding flavor to it.

II

Once, when asked how he would be remembered by future generations, Noël Coward shrewdly replied: "By my charm."

Charm was Coward's main theme both on and off the stage.
"I have taken a lot of trouble with my public face," he said.
Coward wanted his public to be enchanted; he wanted not simply
triumph but total surrender. "Lose yourself," he commented
about acting, "and you lose your audience." Coward kept himself
and his public under tight control. "You've got to control the
audience," he remarked of killing the ripples of small laughs to
get the waves. "They've got to do what I tell them." Charm made
this tyrannical willfulness seem like good manners. "This extra
politeness is not entirely real." But then nothing about Coward
was entirely real, except his allegiance to his talent and to the
public that kept him a "great celebrated cookie" from 1925 to his
death in 1973. Charm was the outward and visible sign of the
boulevard desire to please—a desire to which Coward dedicated
and finally surrendered his life.

Coward's theatrical impulse came from a sense of his persona,
not a sense of life. From his first produced play, *I'll Leave It to You*
(1920), to his last, *A Song at Twilight* (1966) from *Suite in Three
Keys,* his obsession remained his performing self. Where his stage
frivolity announced a philosophical detachment, his charm
broadcast a craving for affection. It was a potent mix.

The word "charming" appears in the first entry of *The Noël
Coward Diaries,* which cover his postwar years until his knighthood
in 1970, and echoes like a lost soul through his day-by-day account of the life he made legendary. Churchill was "so ineffably
charming, that I forgave him all his trespasses and melted into

hero worship." At the Royal Command Performance (1954), the Queen was "very charming, everyone was very charming." The wedding of Princess Elizabeth to Prince Philip is "pictorially, dramatically and spiritually enchanting." Even the gangsters who ran the Las Vegas hotels where, in the mid-fifties, Coward's sagging stage career got an unexpected new lease on life, were "all urbane and charming."

To Coward, charm was virtue, and its own reward. After reading a debunking biography of T. E. Lawrence, Coward dismissed it in his diary in spite of its truth: "[Lawrence] was charming to me anyhow, with a charm that could only be repaid by affection and a certain arid loyalty."

The name of charm's game is omnipotence. Charm is a performance that negotiates a truce with reality, manipulating the world but keeping one's individuality well defended. "It's wonderful what a little determined charm will do," Coward confided to his diary, and he put it to the test when Vivien Leigh, staying at Coward's Swiss home in 1959, was deluged with reporters pursuing the story of her rumored break with Laurence Olivier. "I received [the press] politely, gave them a pre-lunch drink, and utterly cowed them with excessive good manners. They were too cowed to ask Vivien a single embarrassing question about the marriage."

Charm teases boundaries without overstepping them: the delicacy of the dissimulation requires constant vigilance. From the first, Coward examined his role-playing in both songs and plays. His twenties lyrics directly expressed the notion of life as charade: "Life is nothing but a game of make-believe" ("When My Ship Comes Home"); "I treat my whole existence as a game" ("Cosmopolitan Lady"). *The Young Idea* (1922) dramatized the power of charm to create harmony; *The Vortex* was about the terror of losing enchantment; *Hay Fever,* Coward's finest light comedy, was about being as role-playing, and the charm of talent that makes monstrous egotism forgivable. Insofar as it hides pain and promotes good feeling, Coward saw charm as a kind of moral courage—an idea he staged in *Easy Virtue* (1925). The display of good manners under difficult circumstances always moved him.

"Vivien [Leigh], with great sadness in her heart and for one fleeting moment tears in her eyes, behaved gaily and charmingly and never for one instant allowed her private unhappiness to spill over," Coward wrote of his house guest's behavior. "This quite remarkable exhibition of good manners touched me very much. . . . There is always hope for people with that amount of courage and consideration for others."

Coward had learned early that a good offense is the best defense. He used charm to mask his insecurity and admit to his high-spirited ambition. "It is important not to let the public have a loophole to lampoon you," he told Cecil Beaton in 1930, as one phenomenon to another. Beaton recounted the conversation in his diary:

> That, [Coward] explained, was why he studied his own "facade." Now take his voice: it was definite, harsh, rugged. He moved firmly and solidly, dressed quietly. . . . "You should appraise yourself," he went on. "Your sleeves are too tight, your voice is too high and too precise. You mustn't do it. It closes so many doors. It limits you unnecessarily. . . . I take ruthless stock of myself in the mirror before going out. A polo jumper or unfortunate tie exposes one to danger."

"Danger" seems a strange word for the most famous young man of his generation to apply to the public. But there were so many things about Coward that the English might misconstrue as a bad show. He was brash and driven. He was hardworking and infuriatingly precocious. He was homosexual. He was also largely self-educated and raised "in circumstances which were liable to degenerate into refined gentility unless watched carefully." Coward watched himself like a hawk.

"On Monday I attended a gargantuan cocktail party given by the publishers in honour of my new paper-bound book," Coward wrote in his 1955 diary. "I shook hands with hundreds of people, was tirelessly charming, and made cheerful, modest little jokes." No one else could work a room with as much sensational modesty. Coward made his success as charming as his persona. Even jokes at his own expense somehow broadcast his stature. "I was incredibly unspoilt by my success," he wrote in the first volume of his autobiography, *Present Indicative*.

In public, Coward's charm worked a treat; in private, his panic sometimes showed through. Dame Sybil Thorndike remembered that Coward "could play these nervous, strange people, hysterical people, which is very rare. He was absolutely wonderful. It's only people who are hysterical who can play hysterical parts. You see he could scream!" Coward was an upstart. To Edith Sitwell, whom he lampooned unmercifully in *London Calling!* (1923), he was "little Coward." He had to work hard at masking his ambitious self-involvement. Sir Henry ("Chips") Channon recounts having tea with him in 1945:

> He was flattering (he is an arch-flatterer), insinuating, pathetic and nice. I have never liked him so much, though he talked mainly about himself. At length, after many compliments and vows of eternal friendship, he left.

Always one step ahead of his generation, Coward was born on December 16, 1899. "Up until the actual moment when I was deposited," he wrote in his diary, "[Mum] hadn't really wanted me. The tragedy of Russell's death at the age of six and a half had broken her heart and she dreaded further maternal anxieties." Violet Coward cosseted her second boy and encouraged his ambitions, but Coward's unrelenting hunger for acceptance comes back to this primitive desire to win parental affection finally and forever. By the time he was twenty, he'd been earning applause on the stage for a decade. His coming of age coincided with the emergence of Youth as a new, demanding force in English society. Newspapers continually mulled over "the question of Youth." As one *Evening Standard* editorial of 1924 had it: "Post-War Youth won the war. . . . Youth ought to make the peace . . . but mere noise, high-spirited defiance, is no substitute for service." Coward combined a Victorian work ethic with the high

jinks of the young. He was industry in cap and bells. He laid siege
to the public as songwriter, actor, and playwright. He wanted to
be everywhere. And because of his talent and the changing times,
he largely succeeded. He *was* the young idea of the twenties—
gaiety, courage, pain concealed, amusing malice. In him, Youth
found a symbol and a boulevard spokesman: someone equal to
their elders in sophistication, yet who made their impudent disenchantment a star turn. "I was," Coward observed, "the belle
of the ball."

Having worked up an irresistible persona, he turned his
quick-witted, scintillating charm into dramatic legend in the
thirties, at once teasing and condoning his self-involvement.
As an observer of the world at large, Coward was hopeless; as a
social reporter of his class and the de-luxe isolation of his consciousness, he could be brilliant. With its chic dressing gowns
and bitchy dressing downs, *Private Lives* winked at Coward's
emotional underinvolvement and abnormal sexuality. A self-
confessed "celebrity snob," in *Design for Living* Coward sported
with his great success and the defiantly private, self-obsessed
talentocracy of postwar England of which he was a charter member. At the end of the decade, *Present Laughter* (written in 1939,
produced in 1942) celebrated the politics of charm, admitting the
artificiality of the persona only to make its charm triumphant.
"Garry Essendine is me," Coward told the BBC years later,
speaking of the play's romantic comedian, who dissimulates so
eagerly that he has forgotten who he is.

Occasionally, Coward's friends took him to task for this. "She
told me that for the last three years I had been becoming so
unbearably arrogant that it's grotesque," Coward wrote, airily
dismissing one heart-to-heart the following day. "The reason
Pacific 1860 is so bad is that I have no longer any touch or contact
with people and events. . . ." But the diary shows that the man
who staged himself as Frank Gibbons, the spokesman for the
ordinary patriotic English working bloke in *This Happy Breed*, had
no rapport with ordinary people, and, worse, no way of imagining
their suffering. "There can be no doubt about it," Coward wrote

in 1942, the year the play was produced, "I have no real rapport with the 'workers,' in fact I actively detest them *en masse.* They grumble and strike and behave abominably." Talent set him apart from the mass. "I have at least a few months in hand before I resume singing and acting and showing off and being a fascinating public legend," he wrote in 1954, with tongue only half in cheek.

"People," Coward had noted in 1926, when he was recuperating from a nervous collapse, "were the danger. People were greedy and predatory and if you gave them the chance they would steal unscrupulously the heart and soul of you without really wanting to or even meaning to. From now on there was going to be very little vitality spilled unnecessarily." Charm was Coward's camouflage that hardened into armor. Onstage, it excused private inadequacies by making them delightful; offstage, it was a form of public reticence that also straight-armed public scrutiny. Charm kept the public engaged and the performer aloof.

Present Laughter makes light of this transformation. To elude his fans, Essendine, polite to the end, tiptoes out of his house at the finale, leaving the fans inside. Coward ends all his major comedies (*Hay Fever, Private Lives, Blithe Spirit*) with the image of characters tiptoeing away from chaos. The stage pictures give shape to the mission of his laughter: frivolity aspires not so much to evade the issue as to escape it. But, as the diaries show, Coward never did. The spellbinder is also trapped by the spell he casts.

On rereading his diaries, Coward thought his life "one long extravaganza," like living inside a Fabergé egg. "Its no use imagining that I can escape the consequence of my own fame," he wrote. "I am bound to be set on and exploited by people wherever I go." But he never tried to abandon fame. "I have had screaming rave notices and the news has flashed round the world," he wrote of his Las Vegas cabaret debut in 1955. "I am told continually, verbally and in print, that I am the greatest attraction that Las Vegas has ever had and that I am the greatest performer in the world, etc., etc. It is all very, very exciting."

Attention was his fix; and the rich and famous confirmed and extended the charm that sustained the illusion of omnipotence.

Coward socialized with no one but the rich and famous; he traveled nowhere except first class. (August 29, 1961: "The Mellons sent their private jet plane for us and we were whisked to Osterville on Cape Cod . . . where we had lunch with the President and Mrs. Kennedy, both of whom were charming.") Coward spent the postwar years shuttling between the watering holes of Los Angeles, New York, the Riviera, Jamaica, and Switzerland. And even when he followed his secret heart to Marrakesh, he still longed for the Ritz. "To hell with local colour. I'd go mad if I spent one night in the ever so fascinating native quarter and that's that."

Coward imposed as sharp and disarming a sense of form on his life as he did on his art. He required his life, as well as his recounting of it, to have an enchanting symmetry. As a result, the diaries are remarkable for their lack of observation and detail about the rarefied world he inhabited. The rough edges go unseen and the raw words go mostly unreported, a formula in keeping with Coward's faith in niceness, which he associated with good taste. "Taste," he said, "can be vulgar, but it must never be embarrassing." Occasionally, as when the Beatles refused to meet the Master because of something he'd been quoted as saying about them in the press, Coward let his guard drop:

> I thought this graceless in the extreme, but decided to play it with firmness and dignity. I asked Wendy [the publicist] to go and fetch one of them and she finally reappeared with Paul McCartney and I explained gently but firmly that one did *not* pay much attention to the statements of newspaper reporters . . . I sent messages of congratulation to his colleagues, although the message I would have liked to send them was that they were bad-mannered little shits.

In recording his rigorous work routine, his social whirl, and the endless series of successful public engagements, Coward's diary betrays a man obsessed with being distracted from himself.

Inevitably, this led to the attenuation of his spirit and his talent, something that Coward feared as early as 1946, when he reminds himself in his diary: "If I forget these feelings [about the war] or allow them to be obscured because they are uncomfortable, I shall be lost." In the end, shunning change and seeking comfort, he was lost.

Later, in postwar England, when priorities were being drastically overhauled, Coward was flummoxed. Frivolity, which is skepticism on holiday, had little to say to a society obsessed with rebuilding itself. Coward's late work aggressively trivialized the major aesthetic and social shifts of his day. *Nude With Violin* (1956) treated modern art as just a con. At a time when England was divesting herself of her colonial interests, *South Sea Bubble* (1956) was an imperialist fantasy in which a colony eschews independence and reform. "Believe me," says the island potentate, "we are too young yet for such brave experiments. Too young and gay and irresponsible to be about to do without our Nanny." And on the issue of democracy, *Relative Values* (1951) jokes staunchly for the status quo ante. "I drink," says the butler Crestwell, raising his glass at the finale, "to the final inglorious disintegration of the most unlikely dream that ever troubled the foolish heart of man—Social Equality." Coward knew how to be popular, but he was no longer pertinent. "I have never felt the necessity of being 'with it,' " he said, with a characteristic smug twinkle. "I'm all for staying in my place."

Coward's eleven postwar plays brought home the bacon, but no glory. He was booed onstage after the opening of his musical *Ace of Clubs* (1950). The New Wave wanted disenchantment; Coward's charm cultivated reassurance and enchantment, which served the status quo. In the class war being waged, Coward fought with the old guard. The tuxedo and the teacup were his coat of arms. "[I] cannot understand," he wrote in 1957, "why the younger generation, instead of knocking at the door, should bash the fuck out of it." But except when Coward took the stage himself as a cabaret turn, his charm was losing its potency. "Oh dear," he wrote in his diary in 1950, "I really seem quite unable to please." His instinct was for retreat. As the title song from *Sail Away* (1961) counseled:

> When the storm clouds are riding through a winter sky
> Sail away—sail away.

In 1956, Coward went into tax exile, first to Bermuda; then in 1959 he shifted base to Switzerland. His plays, too, moved away from contemporary English life. He was drawn primarily to period musicals and romantic comedies that looked to a past whose manners and meanings he could fathom and stage. As Coward's idea of England ossified, so did his antic spirit. Bitterness seeped into his diaries, if not into his plays. "Our history except for stupid, squalid, social scandals is over," he wrote in 1963. "I despise the young, who see no quality in our great past and who spit, with phoney Left-Wing disdain, on all that we, as a race, have contributed to the living world."

Coward's best postwar play, *Waiting in the Wings* (1960), used the metaphor of an old-age home for former music-hall stars to show off the gallantry of the performers' charm while exploring their fear of losing it. The notion of stars being forgotten, of performers' "magic" no longer being able to protect them from the vagaries of life, touched something deep in Coward. But this shrewd and moving play, like almost all of his postwar work, was dismissed by the critics.

In his last West End offering, *Suite in Three Keys* (1966), three one-acts, of which *A Song at Twilight* was the best, Coward returned to the theme of charm and dissimulation, which for the young man promised harmony and for the old man had created a wasteland. Coward played Hugo Latymer, who, like himself, had sacrificed his life for his reputation. "Latymer," wrote one critic, "is Garry Essendine thirty soul-sapping years on." Coward's makeup suggested a connection with Somerset Maugham, which put the public off the scent of *A Song at Twilight*'s essentially autobiographical nature.

In the play, the well-known writer is threatened with being exposed as a homosexual. Letters from him have come into the hands of a woman who was ill treated by Latymer in an early affair. "Your book," says Carlotta, speaking of Latymer's autobiography, "may have been an assessment of the outward experience of your life, but I cannot feel that you were entirely honest about your inner one." Later she takes him to task for his lack of moral courage and his dishonesty, in words for which there is no comeback. "You might have been a greater writer instead of a merely successful one," she says, voicing Coward's autumnal thoughts, "and you also might have been far happier." Latymer survives with his public image intact, but the play ends in a tableau of isolation and regret. *A Song at Twilight* came as close as Coward ever could to admitting the price he'd had to pay for his legendary life.

Coward, like Latymer, had steadfastly dodged the issue of homosexuality in his writing. "Any sexual activities when overstated are tasteless," he wrote in his diary. When he fell in love, he could only muster a coy, inadequate sentiment: "I fear that Old Black Magic has reared itself up again." As he once admitted in poetry, Coward was no good at love. Unable to sustain a love relationship, his only enduring commitment was to the public. He had posed as a romantic comedian and turned his fantasy of heterosexuality into show-biz legend. Instead of being explorations of consciousness, the majority of his plays remain explorations of his self-consciousness. Popularity only intensified the masquerade. His burnished charm won him a wide following but trapped him into a perpetual star performance. He rationalized this alienation as duty. "If you're a star, you have to behave like one," he said. "The public is very demanding. They have a right to be."

The man's diary, like his career, ends on a note of smug triumph. Coward referred to the revival of his stock as a playwright in the mid-sixties as "Dad's Renaissance." And in his last diary entry (December 31, 1969), he described attending the National Film Theatre, which was presenting a season of his films; a birthday party thrown by the BBC in his honor; and then a birthday lunch given by the Queen Mother, at which the Queen asked Coward if he'd accept a knighthood. "Apart from all this," he wrote, "my seventieth birthday was uneventful." He died three years later, on March 26, 1973. His public facade remains rock solid. Having dedicated his life to a glamorous success, Coward left no hint of his impoverishment. For that, as with all professional charmers, the public must read between the lines.

3

Sam Shepard

Sam Shepard caught the first wave of the Off-Broadway revolution in 1964 and rode it further than any of his American contemporaries. Nearly two decades on, Shepard, one of the hors d'oeuvres of the avant-garde, has become a main course on the American and English repertory menus.

I first met Shepard in 1970, when the king of downtown drama went uptown with an astonishing play called *Operation Sidewinder*. The Vivian Beaumont Theatre (of which I was then literary manager) was at Lincoln Center, a ghetto of established culture on New York's West Side whose budget for running the open-air fountain ($25,000 a year) and patrolling the buildings ($400,000 a year) could have bankrolled many seasons of plays at La Mama Experimental Theatre Club and Theatre Genesis, where Shepard, like many of the new young writers, got started. *Operation Sidewinder* was to me, and still is, the only American play that found a proper metaphor for the oppression and optimism of those demented times. But it was as much a risk for the Beaumont to do Sam Shepard as it was for Shepard to venture above 14th Street.

Shepard was a man of few words, most of them mumbled. A

lean, romantic, handsome figure, he trod the maroon carpets of Lincoln Center in cowboy boots and a high-school windbreaker. Once during rehearsals, after I'd written a parody column in the *Village Voice* suggesting Samuel Johnson of London's *The Rambler* would be the next critic of the *New York Times* and reporting the reaction of New York's local critics to the idea, Shepard took me aside. "Hey, man," he said. "What's the story on this Johnson?"

"I am an American," said Shepard's tormented spokesman in *Operation Sidewinder,* as alien and as insular as Shepard himself. "I was made in America. Born, bred and raised in America. I have American scars on my brain . . . I bleed American blood. I dream American dreams . . . I devour the planet. I'm an earth eater."

Shepard then may not have known much about European culture; but he explored the American landscape like a pathfinder. His greatest asset as a playwright was his voracious curiosity about America. He was not a city playwright but a Mid-western wanderer who had driven the back roads of the land, tramped the wilderness, scored on its main streets. He dredged the detritus of the society for the pure gold of its diction and its daydreams. Out of his distinctive and audacious work came a very special sense of America's deliriums.

At the first preview, standing nervously in front of the thirty-foot marble slab of bar in the Beaumont lobby, Shepard and his moon-faced actress wife, O-Lan, giggled a lot. The Vivian Beaumont Theatre's audience was part of the other America, the one that sipped five-dollar glasses of champagne in the interval, wore furs and three-piece suits on a night out. They were uptown people buying official culture; and to Shepard, uptown was still the enemy. Uptown was where President Nixon had a home, where the "pigs" went to sleep at night dreaming of domino theories and still hoping for victory in Vietnam. According to my diary, the Lincoln Center bartender didn't like the sight of us:

Bartender tries to shoo us away because we look too scruffy. I have a tennis ball and throw it to Sam who drops it. He's funny and playful and affectionate to O-Lan who is very pregnant. At the beginning of the performance Sam says, "Gee, it's not like Theatre Genesis. I don't know anybody in the audience." At intermission, obviously disgruntled, Sam says, "Don't you think it's too smooth?" Talking about the audience he says, "I'm not worried about the old people. I'm worried about the young ones." The audience laughs at the Hopi ritual. Sam really spooked by this. Leaves after the show without talking to anybody.

Up to *Operation Sidewinder*, Shepard's plays were written to fit the postage-stamp stages and beer-money budgets of Off-Off-Broadway. Small cast, one set, minimum props, the plays were one-act epiphanies of paranoia told in startling stage pictures and an idiom that began in naturalism and ended in allegory.

The early plays were metaphysical melodramas (one is even called *Melodrama Play*, 1967) in which Shepard tried by surrealistic means to convey the experience of fear instead of explaining it. In *Red Cross* (1966), a man's flesh is disintegrating as he talks; in *Icarus's Mother* (1966), a plane strafes a beach barbecue and brings intimations of the apocalypse; in *Chicago* (1966), primarily a monologue delivered in a bathtub, Shepard meditates on mortality. *Operation Sidewinder* extended these obsessions in a stage language that was at once more scenic and more coherent than his early plays.

The play dramatized not only the suffocation of a death-dealing society, but the search for new symbols to transcend the terror. Outrageous and threatening, the plot was a typical Shepard dreamscape of the society. A six-foot rattlesnake turns out to be an escaped military computer; black, white, and Indian renegades scheme to capture Air Force planes by putting dope in the military reservoir; and a Hopi snake-dance ritual transforms the sidewinder computer from military property to religious icon.

At the finale, soldiers fire into the crowd of Indians, who clutch the snake. No one falls. Finally a soldier wrestles the snake away. He rips off its head—his victory is the destruction of the world. The Indians, untouched, move toward their salvation; the soldiers writhe in violent death. Smoke fills the theatre. This final poetic image, which so confounded the Lincoln Center audience, brought together the destinies of two cultures: the sacred and the profane.

Shepard's proliferating imagination was at odds with the arrogance of his avant-garde aesthetic. He was in the business of public entertainment, but he didn't like, or really even want, a public. He hated the lavishness of Lincoln Center, but had written a play which required a behemoth snake, a '57 Chevy, a garage car rack, a Hopi wikkiup, and a rock-'n'-roll band.

Shepard's indifference to his audience, albeit an obtuse one, was symptomatic of the failure of the avant-garde to shape or change American theatre. It made an asset of amateur night. Shepard wanted the audience blasted by decibels of rock 'n' roll. He distrusted technique and assumed that to communicate clearly to an audience meant to cater to it. As time went on, he got stroppy. He'd sneak beers into the auditorium under his shirt, and refused to rewrite murky passages or to cut wordy dialogue. For all his terrific talent, he clung to the romantic notion that somehow the ragged edges of his play were authentic, when they were just sloppy.

On both sides of the footlights, Lincoln Center had seen nothing like it. The authentic Indians on stage revolted when their dance had to be cut. "I'm a real Indian," shouted one. "Not one of those painted, wooden imitations. I'm real. I'm real!"

After the last preview, the head of the theatre, Jules Irving, pulled me into the white light of an empty dressing room to read the fifty audience comment cards, only two of which were favorable: "Terrible, terrible, terrible"; "Infantile"; "The artistic director and anyone connected with it should be fired."

The show lost the theatre thousands of subscribers; but as the playwright Jack Gelber, whose *The Connection* (1959) started the American new wave, said, "It was the best play ever done at Lincoln Center." Yet Shepard eschewed the play and the production. I saw him a month later at the Off-Broadway opening of *Forensic and the Navigators* (1967). Cigarette dangling from his lips, Shepard was playing drums in the lobby. He was happy among his people, and in fat city.

*

"People want a street angel. They want a saint with a cowboy mouth." Shepard's shrewd line shows how well he understands the society's hunger for hip legends. In his plays and in his life, Shepard pays close attention to American myths. Born in Fort Sheridan, Illinois, in 1943, Shepard is a protean figure. The weird, dreamlike terrains of his plays sparkle with the insights of a man who has been musician, actor, drug addict, horse breeder, screenwriter, waiter, and even, in his latest incarnation beginning with Terence Malick's *Days of Heaven,* movie star.

As a writer, Shepard has managed to make his own continuity in the no-man's-land of American drama. In the grand tradition of American letters, he has nurtured a small cult of personality. (This cult reached its apotheosis in 1978 when *Curse of the Starving Class* won the *Village Voice* "Obie" award for best play before it was even produced!) The Dark Lady of rock 'n' roll, Patti Smith (with whom Shepard has written plays and songs), wrote this typical piece of tall talk, "Sam Shepard: Nine Random Years":

> . . . he slipstreamed Salinas
> he plunged off a cliff
> the people all gathered
> and pointed to him
> they said there goes a bad boy . . .

Action and movement are part of the American experience that Shepard describes in his plays, and that Patti Smith uses to evoke him. In her paean to Shepard, she speaks of the "poetry of speed," and her last line invests Shepard with legendary swiftness: "speeding like a demon." But speed attenuates life, and some of Shepard's work is written too fast to go deep into the heart of things.

Being a lethal legend is what Shepard's best play, *Tooth of Crime* (1972), is about. The authentic hero is "a true killer. . . . True to his heart. True to his voice. . . . Lives by a code. His own code. Knows something timeless. No hesitation. Trust in himself. Plunged into fear and came out the other side. Died a million deaths. . . ." Shepard understands legendary fame, and *Tooth of Crime* probes the isolation and insecurity of the American state of grace called celebrity. In it, the king of rock 'n' roll, Hoss, is challenged by Crow, a low-rider whose language reaches heights of inspired theatricality. They battle in prose riffs that have no equal in contemporary American theatre:

> CROW: So ya' wanna be a rocker. Study the moves. Jerry Lee Lewis. Buy some blue suede shoes. Move yer head like Rod Stewart. Put yer ass in grind. Talkin' sock it to it, get the image in line. Get the image in line boy. The fantasy rhyme. It's all over the street and you can't buy the time. . . . You can't buy the slide. Got the fantasy blues and no place to hide.

The play ends with Crow victorious, singing: "Keep me in my state of grace."

Shepard left New York in the early 1970s to live for a while in London, where he raised his son, Mojo, wrote plays (including the charming *Little Ocean*, 1974, about O-Lan's pregnancy and being a parent), and raced dogs. Back in America, he didn't follow the route of his peers to Broadway or Hollywood, but continued on his own solitary adventure. He settled in Northern California, where he could drive his pick-up, raise horses, and write.

In 1979 he won the Pulitzer Prize for the accessible *Buried Child*, an award that continued the Pulitzer tradition of honoring the right playwright for the wrong play. In returning to California, Shepard was returning to his roots. (Much of his early life was spent there and *Who's Who in Theatre* quotes him as having been "horseshit remover and hot walker at Santa Anita racetrack.") In *Operation Sidewinder*, set in the West, Shepard was surveying America and losing his bearings:

> And this is the place I was born, bred and raised
> And it doesn't seem like I was ever here.

His most recent plays digest the West's spiritual wasteland. In *Geography of a Horse Dreamer* (1975), the visionary Cody, rescued from captors who want to exploit his magic, says: "Even after the smoke cleared I couldn't see my home." In *Angel City* (1976), Shepard's sometimes inspired satire on Hollywood, the characters are lost to themselves and the world around them. Says one movie fan, explaining the enchantment and alienation film-colony glamour inspires, "I look at the movie and I am the star. I hate my life not being a movie. I hate my life not being a star . . . I hate . . . having to live in this body which isn't a star's body and all the time knowing that stars exist."

The wasteland claims more victims in *True West* (1980). Two brothers—one a successful screenwriter, the other a desert drifter and petty thief—swap roles, and end up destroying their mother's house. "This is worse than being homeless," the Mother says, surveying the wreckage and deciding to leave. "I don't recognize it at all." Shepard is dramatizing the confusion of the West, neither pioneer experience nor earthly paradise.

The vagueness in the land is what punishes the brothers. They are infected by the twin emotions of the West: primitive self-sufficiency and modern luxury. The screenwriter wants to get back to the desert to make contact with something he thinks is authentic. His business is making myths out of a place whose spiritual impoverishment belies the romance about it. His drifter-brother, brutalized by the land, promises to show the writer the authentic West after he's tasted the sweet life of success. They collaborate on a western, which the drifter sells to the writer's producer.

When the drifter gives up on the "dumb story" and reneges on his promise to go back to the desert ("I'm tired out eatin' with my hands, ye know. It's not civilized"), the writer tries to strangle him. At the finale, they face each other as the lights fade to moonlight: "The figures of the brothers now appear to be caught in a vast desert-like landscape."

The stand-off is between two mythic psychopathic styles of American individualism: the killer instincts of success and crime. The division between the brothers reflects the split in Shepard between renegade and literary success. Shepard, the bad boy, is still contending with Shepard, the artist, to find a home in America.

4

Leiber & Stoller

A Sunday, 1957. Over the last five years, it has become the center of the household. All the furniture in the bedroom faces it. Dad watches it from his desk; Mom from the bed; Sis from the floor. I'm usually on the sofa. Sunday is reserved not for Church, but for Television. Ed Sullivan grins stiffly, promises "a really great *shew*," and, courtesy of Lincoln-Mercury dealers, provides our communion with the rest of America. Athletes, singers, politicians, comedians parade across his stage—all part of our diet of distraction, their well-scrubbed, successful smiles reassuring us that we are part of the club.

Tonight is special. There's a notorious singer on TV, and danger is in the air. CBS has already decreed that he may be televised only from the waist up. What is there below the belt of this country boy with the unforgettable name of Elvis Presley that can't be shown to us city folk? I mean, we've seen murder on *Dragnet,* we've seen Senator McCarthy on the Six O'Clock News waving an envelope with the names of card-carrying Communists, we've seen Uncle Miltie in panties and bra, and we've ogled Marilyn Monroe's cleavage.

In the suspenseful moments before his appearance, Mom

studies the Presley LP we made her buy. Dad just shakes his head. He's watched Sis and me dance to Elvis after dinner, and he's listened in disbelief. 'What's happened to show-business standards?" he says. "Jerry Vale. Now, there's a voice. You kids want to hear a performer? Get out the Billy Daniels records."

Suddenly Elvis is in front of us. He's been cleaned up for the TV audience. He's exchanged black leather for silver lamé. He stands there sparkling, with his guitar slung across his stomach like a machine gun as the squeals from the audience subside. His lips are poised between a seductive pout and an insolent smirk. He nods to the sidemen, steps up to the microphone, and unleashes a sound that pierces our viscera like a shot of Vitamin B.

> You ain't nothin' but a hound dog,
> Cryin' all the time.
> You ain't nothin' but a hound dog,
> Cryin' all the time.
> You ain't never caught a rabbit
> And you ain't no friend of mine

A black curl lashes his forehead as he starts his censored wiggle. This is where I lose control—knocked out of my seat by his kinetic outrageousness. Sprawled on the floor, I can't believe my eyes. Even Dad is having a ball.

On the way to bed, I pick up the Presley LP. There, in small type, in a parenthesis beside "Hound Dog," are the names J. Leiber/M. Stoller. I'd never heard of them. A few years later, Dad would hand me a *Variety* clipping about them: at twenty-six, they were pop music's *Wunderkinder.* They'd been writing for less than a decade and their songs had already been on more than 40 million records, which was more than Jerome Kern's lifetime output.

"You kids were right about 'Hound Dog,'" Dad said. It may have taken Dad a few years to come around, but I knew the minute I saw Elvis on Ed Sullivan that rock 'n' roll was here to stay.

Rock 'n' roll was rogue energy: it yanked us on our feet and made us move, stomping the floor to its strong backbeat. Leiber

& Stoller's songs were potent because they teased our longing with such sly precision. Heavily sedated with a stiff dose of fifties conformity, we were nice kids studying hard to succeed, and they —*they* were making fables about renegades. Presley was the original bad guy, the kind of "greaser" our parents told us not to talk to and whom we'd cross the street to avoid. His black leather pants were a little snugger than our Brooks Brothers' charcoal grays. It was even rumored that he didn't wear underwear when he sang.

Leiber & Stoller, who weren't all that much older than we, wrote songs that mined our deepest vein of fantasy. Timid though we were, we could sing along, buoyed up by Elvis's sheer bravado.

> You lookin' for trouble?
> You come to the right place.
> You lookin' for trouble?
> Just look right in my face.
> I was born standin' up and talkin' back
> My daddy was a green-eyed mountain Jack
> And I'm evil
> Evil as can be.
> You know I'm evil
> So don't you mess around with me

"Trouble" was not exactly the kind of song they played at dancing school.

Leiber & Stoller took us out of our routine world into a world where sound buzzed through our bodies and words flashed strange pictures of people and places we would never have thought worthy of song: a jailhouse—"Jailhouse Rock," a stripper and her show—"Little Egypt," a motorcycle rebel—"Black Denim Trousers and Motorcycle Boots," wherein they perpetuated a myth as offensive to adults as it was exciting to adolescents.

> Well, he never washed his face
> And he never combed his hair
> He had axle grease imbedded underneath his fingernails
> On the muscle of his arm was a red tattoo,

A picture of a heart
Sayin', "Mother I Love You."

Did Leiber & Stoller imagine us listening to the radio with lights out, playing pocket pool on our beds, rehearsing how to jimmy a Maidenform bra with thumb and forefinger? Our hunger was too deep for words. Rock 'n' roll alone spoke kindly to our appetites and answered our craving for sensation. Voices (a kind of voodoo?) whispered to us in the darkness: "Shoodooten Shoo-be-dah." And we answered back.

The movies overloaded our circuits with virginal ponytails: Sandra Dee, Debbie Reynolds, Annette Funicello. Cole Porter had told us breezily that love was "de-lovely" and the Gershwins told us, equally elegantly, that passion was " 'Swonderful." Theirs was clean, unphysical sex. But rock 'n' roll was hot and horny. That saxophone was downright low-down; it made connections with the body. When Elvis crooned Leiber & Stoller's "Don't" and "Love Me," he wasn't issuing an invitation to the waltz. Leiber & Stoller knew that what we wanted was sex. Little Egypt's "Ying-Yang Ying-Yang" spoke to us in the language of our private dreams of sexual glory. Her kind of woman never got into a Patti Page song!

> I went and bought myself a ticket and I sat down in the
> very first row-oh-oh
> They pulled the curtain up and when they turned the
> spotlight way down low-oh-oh
> Little Egypt came out struttin', wearin' nuttin' but a
> button and a bow-oh-oh
> Singin', "Ying-yang, ying-yang . . ."

It was flesh we craved. We would risk anything, even contamination, for a touch and tickle. In "Poison Ivy," Leiber & Stoller isolated that itch and our yearning to scratch it. They created a woman who could make us suffer for our dirty little dreams (and we loved it):

> She comes on like a rose
> But everybody knows

She'll get you in dutch
You can look but you better not touch

Poison Ivy, Poison Ivy
Late at night while you're sleepin'
Poison Ivy comes a-creepin' around

Our sexual anticipation was as outrageous and hilarious as the song's remedy for it:

You're gonna need an ocean
Of Calamine lotion

Conquest was our only concern. Even before we'd heard of erogenous zones, we talked endlessly about aphrodisiacs. Mushrooms and asparagus tips were rumored to loosen up the libido, and Spanish Fly to drive girls into an uncontrollable frenzy. We wouldn't have to pitch them; we wouldn't even have to feel guilty afterward since they wouldn't remember a thing. In fact, we would be doing them a favor by putting them out of their sexual misery—better us than the stick shift of the Chevrolet. We wanted sexual success and no stigma—in other words, magic. "Love Potion Number 9" gently mocked that daydream. What the singer confessed to the Gypsy with the gold-capped tooth, we would never have admitted to ourselves:

I told her that I was a flop with chicks
"I been this way since nineteen fifty-six"
She looked at my palm and she made a magic sign
She said, "What you need is—Love Potion Number 9"

"Love Potion Number 9" didn't take our embarrassment as seriously as we couldn't help taking it. We could be singing to ourselves and suddenly find tears in our eyes. "Kansas City," for instance, promised us everything we ever wanted: movement, sex, and satisfaction.

I'm goin' to Kansas City
Kansas City, here I come . . .
They got a crazy way of lovin' there
And I'm gonna get me some

Whether we were cruising for poon in Dad's car with the radio blaring, dancing silently in front of a mirror, or walking home alone after a date, "Kansas City" was in our ears, filling us with hope. We spent the fifties wishing—for school to end, for women, for life with a capital L to begin. The world was out there. Any day now, we would be able to reach out and actually taste it. Suddenly there would be nothing to stop us.

> Well I might take a train
> I might take a plane
> But if I have to walk
> I'm goin' just the same

Rock 'n' roll was usually long on good times and short on humor. Laughter admitted failure, which killed passion—and what adolescent could stand that? Most of the songs we listened to were in dumb earnest, a few repeated phrases interrupted by a wailing saxophone and an occasional rim shot on the drums. But Leiber & Stoller's songs played with us; many of them were tales in verse, with a surprising antic quality to them. The Coasters made these routines into standards. Leiber has described the Coasters as "a group of vaudevillians, all of them comedians." So were Leiber & Stoller: they could make us laugh at our loneliness ("Searchin' "), at our sexual frustration ("Love Potion Number 9"), at our rebellious goofing off ("Charlie Brown"), at our bossy parents ("Yakety Yak"). These songs were dramatic events in which a character and a problem were established and then comically elaborated on, as when the boy who had gone looking for the love potion described swallowing it:

> It smelled like turpentine and looked like India ink
> I held my nose, I closed my eyes, I took a drink . . .

The scene began realistically, then exploded into slapstick:

> I didn't know if it was day or night
> I started kissin' everything in sight
> But when I kissed the cop down at Thirty-fourth and Vine
> He broke my little bottle of Love Potion Number 9

With plot and dialogue, "Yakety Yak" lured the listener into the middle of family drama: nagging parents vs. captive children whose protest could be expressed only in code ("Yakety yak"). Each role in the song amounted to a neat verbal impersonation:

> You just put on your coat and hat
> And walk yourself to the laundromat
> And when you finish doin' that
> Bring in the dog and put out the cat.
> Yakety yak!
> "Don't talk back."

The characters who strutted through Leiber & Stoller's comic songs were flamboyant poseurs, making spectacles of themselves and straight-arming the adult world.

> Who walks in the classroom cool and slow?
> Who calls the English teacher "Daddy-O"?
> Charlie Brown
> Charlie Brown
> He's a clown
> That Charlie Brown . . .

We kids were just as theatrical as Charlie Brown, if not as bold. With grown-ups, we could try on mock outrage. Like Charlie, we chanted: "Why is everybody always pickin' on me?" We always knew what we'd done wrong—making prank phone calls, snowballing buses, dropping water bombs, sneaking copies of *Playboy* off the newsstand when mischief raced our engine. But too often we were timid; and how we hated ourselves for acting the innocent child when the finger was pointed at us.

> Who's always writin' on the walls?
> Who's always goofin' in the halls?
> Who's always throwin' spitballs?
> Guess who?
> "Who me?"
> Yeah, you

We worried about being "cool" and looking lethal. We logged hours in front of the mirror testing our smiles, our smirks, our hair, our walk. Our world was divided into Tweeds and Greasers, both wanting to be "tough" and irresistible. The Tweeds were would-be Ivy Leaguers who bought Hollywood's Tab Hunter/Robert Wagner hard sell: white bucks, khaki pants, button-down shirt, red-striped tie. We were shiny, formal, and eager. We trusted our facade to work for us as successfully as it had worked for our film heroes. They wore makeup; we had Clearasil. We wanted to be perfect. The Greasers swallowed James Dean and Marlon Brando whole. They were big on silence and scruffiness. They were losers in life, and, what's more, they didn't care; they gloried in it. That's why they were dangerous—they had nothing to lose. With their leather jackets, DA's, T-shirts with cigarette packs rolled in the turned-up sleeves, they wanted to be left alone. We wanted to be accepted.

The movies suited us perfectly. Nothing else was big enough or pure enough. "Searchin' " went to the core of this mystique. Behind our show of style and whispered words of passion was a movie paradigm. Our images of ourselves were all borrowed:

> Well, Sherlock Holmes, Sam Spade, got nothin',
>   child, on me
> Sergeant Friday, Charlie Chan, and Boston Blackie
> No matter where she's hidin' she's gonna hear me
>   comin'
> I'm gonna walk right down that street like Bulldog
>   Drummon'
> 'Cause I've been searchin'
> Searchin'—oh, yeah
> Searchin' every which a-way
> But I'm like that Northwest Mountie
> You know I'll bring her in some day

Leiber & Stoller turned the detritus of our life and language into an event. They took our confusion and gave it back to us as joy. They told our story to the world with a wit that made it listen. "Yakety Yak," "Poison Ivy," "Charlie Brown," "Kansas City," "Ruby Baby," "Hound Dog," "On Broadway," and so many others were more than art—they were life. Dancing and laughing, we came of age to their songs.

5

Dame Edna Everage

Barry Humphries likes to go out and make a noise on stage
before any of the paying customers for *A Night with Dame Edna*
take their seats. "I like to acquaint myself with the empty auditorium. Do a bit of vocal bouncing. Funny noises rather like whales
or dolphins do. I don't use a microphone. I think it distances an
audience. If you're in a theatre where it's too big for you to be
heard, you're being greedy. If you can't be heard, you're in the
wrong profession."

The sound of an audience just outside the doors and the sight
of those 1,200 folded maroon seats in London's Piccadilly
Theatre facing him are reassuring. Humphries goes down into
the back of the stalls for a quick chat with the ushers. "Were there
any complaints last night?" "Could everyone hear?" "Do you
understand how latecomers are to be seated?"

Comedy is a game that's best when tense, and Dame Edna is
a stickler for the rules. "I get them to show latecomers to their
seats the very long way, right round the front, which we call 'the
scenic route.' So that people who arrive late are discomforted by
being seen by the largest number of people." This evening Ian
and Deena are late. "I'll pass your name on to my friend Dame

Edna Everage," says Les Patterson, Humphries's sodden Australian cultural attaché, getting them to identify themselves at the outset as they grope for what they think is the safe harbor of their seats. "I think she'll make sure this is a night you won't forget." And she will.

"Nice house that. Nice and boisterous," Humphries says. He's back after the first act and sitting in front of his makeup table getting ready to become Dame Edna. "I like some from the older generation in the front rows." All the cameos in the first act—from the slobbering grossness of Les Patterson to the bourgeois oafishness of Sandy Stone prattling from beyond the grave—have gone over well. They are witty caricatures, but Edna is a tour de force of character. Humphries sees her as "a clown in the form of an Australian housewife." He's been impersonating her sporadically since 1956. He sees it as character acting: a man playing a woman and making points about life. But Edna is thankfully larger than life.

As one would expect of a comedian who treads so gracefully between insight and outrage, Humphries is a man of intelligence and taste. He understands that style both masks and reveals, which is why his characters—especially Edna—are at once so shrewd and so lewd. "The audiences have accepted that Edna increasingly feels at liberty to speak on any subject whatsoever— liberated by total ignorance." In this mischievous persona of the eternal provincial who has elevated herself to superstardom, Humphries has created one of the authentic antic spirits in contemporary show business.

"There are some subjects that the English get anxious about, for instance when Edna starts talking about the Royal Family, whom she loves," he remarks, sitting shirtless and in a pair of Edna's frilly knickers. "There was quite a lot of criticism because Edna discussed the confidences of Princess Margaret. Swore them to secrecy, you see. There's something very strange when someone on the stage says, 'This must go no farther.' It's part of the process of infantilizing an audience. That's what you do when you throw a party, isn't it? You somehow invoke the Bacchic spirit. Whether through alcohol or the drug of humor, you unify them into a convivial conglomerate. They came in as adults, individuals; and then you reduce them to the level of childish obedience. So, in the end, they will do the most infantile things. Preferably you save your weakest jokes till then."

(In 1977, Barry Humphries brought Dame Edna to New York's Theatre 4, as close as the housewife superstar has been to Broadway. "I carefully adapted my London and Australian material, formerly addressed to a middle-class, Anglo-Saxon audience, and soon to be exposed to an English-speaking public with an alien cultural background, Jewish Puerto Ricans, Danish Eskimos, Negroid Corsicans, et cetera. Sir Les Patterson, the Australian diplomat, opened the show by explaining to the audience where Australia was and how it had won World War II in the Pacific, thus reducing the number of Japanese restaurants in New York. Australia, it was explained, was the new America, a continent so sophisticated and fast-moving that its inhabitants loved coming to New York for peace and quiet. The show exploited this simple inversion very effectively since most comedians visiting America make jokes about its dehumanized urban life, its noise, and its muggings. I, on the contrary, described New York as a peaceful haven compared with Australia.

"Les introduced Edna, in her denim outfit, who patronized the audience and had long extempore conversations with adoring fans and look-alikes from Brooklyn Heights. It occurred to me at the time that Edna looked quite Jewish and this seemed to work in her favor. What seemed semantically foreign was genetically familiar. 'A lot of people think I'm a Red Sea pedestrian,' she confided proudly to the audience. The previews were a sensational success, and it seemed we were in for a hit. The novelty of the entertainment appealed to all who saw it, and the major problem of 'man dressed up as woman' in a tradition alien to the American theatre didn't worry anyone because most thought Edna *was* a woman." But, not for the first time, an obtuse *New York Times* review closed a fine show within a fortnight, and Humphries had to pack Dame Edna and her provocative high jinks back to London, covered in "shame and ignominy.")

Humphries studies his face as Edna starts to emerge with each stroke of makeup. "Before I ever knew I'd be in this eccentric profession, I used to do little giveaway shows to introduce an element of fantasy into what seemed very prosaic rituals. For instance, accomplices of mine would serve me dinner on a suburban train at rush hour. They would appear with courses. I would then eat them. This puzzled people. It was just a way of jolting the commuters. Mystifying them."

Humphries holds up his lipstick and gives Edna's mouth its familiar gash of red. " 'Lippy,' Edna calls it." His act is full of such hilarious Aussie sludge. "I once heard a woman describing her hysterectomy. She said she'd had a 'hizzie' at the 'hozzie.' "

Adjusting Edna's "ethnic" wig, he stands before the mirror, resplendent in Edna's squash court regalia. Somebody shouts: "One minute."

"I'm ready. Ready. Ready," Humphries yells back, taking a long slug of honey.

"Your nail varnish, Barry," the dresser says.

Thirty seconds later, with Cutex Ruby Red still wet on his fingers, Humphries heads for the wings. It's show time.

In the backstage gloom, Humphries revs up Dame Edna's falsetto. The noise of him clearing his throat is drowned out by the whoops of laughter from bogus newspaper headlines being flashed on stage: AUSSIE TV BEST IN WORLD SAYS MADMAN; NIGGER TOOLS LONGER—EYSENCK.

"There's very little danger of Edna going out of character unless I lose the falsetto," he says, flourishing Edna's squash racket. "I've given a couple of baritone performances. There was a sort of awed silence. Then you have to play Edna very hard with the eyes." Behind him, set out as neatly as a surgeon's operating equipment, are the tools of Edna's trade: bouquets of gladioli that later she'll have the audience waving at her command of "Stand and Tremble!" As a voice-over begins the introduction—"Now in concert with herself . . ."—Humphries is jumping around like a skittish racehorse straining at the gate. A stagehand bashes a cymbal at the sound of Edna Everage's name, and Dame Edna bolts from the wings into the white glare of center-stage.

Edna works the room masterfully. Deena to the right: "It's a lovely name. It just sounds ridiculous." And "Gobbler" to the left, who has made the mistake of eating sweets while Edna works: "What an interesting person you probably are." In the box, Carol of Sidcup answers Edna's request for someone to pronounce the name of her Adidas sneakers, only to have Edna reply: "What a cunning little linguist you are." Even the gallery gets a big hello: "It's not the upper circle. It's more like a wall of death."

The audience howls, and Edna turns on it with matronly fury: "Have your manners deserted you? You're tired and overexcited. There'll be tears before bedtime." But the tears are tears of laughter. "What are you doing with that handkerchief?" Edna says to a woman weeping with delight. "Got a little discharge, have you?" By playing interlocutor with the audience, Dame Edna creates a sense of danger on stage that makes the release of laughter that much greater.

The spectacle of Edna scoring so often and so well is thrilling. On the subject of pierced ears, she confides: "I could have had it done at a private clinic. I was a fool. I was a fool to have myself done at Selfridge's." She cuts off the laugh to ask Carol of Sidcup where she was done. "The usual place," Carol replies sharpish. In this battle of wits, the audience is usually unarmed. But Humphries's craft, his obvious joy in his invention, never turns the game of slap and tickle into a punch-up.

Edna relishes painting word pictures as much as she does her face. Both have a startling effect. Evoking her bridesmaid Madge Alsop's pitted skin, Edna says: "She panic-buys Nivea. She tips it into herself until she looks like a brandy snap." And when she talks about how her husband, Norm, has been taught to knit with his mouth since his hands have been strapped to his hospital bed, she adds: "He's into oral socks."

But when Edna does her party piece, describing her hated daughter-in-law's trendy house in Clapham, the material takes on the delicious precision of the best social satire. Bemoaning how everything in Joylene's kitchen is referred to as a "working surface," Edna describes her "sour little yard where there's a table for the birds. She calls it a birds' working surface." Edna's version of the kitchen, the fridge, the loo, and finally her search-and-destroy mission of the bathroom's contents are side-splitting. When she finds the cap to the footpowder on the toothpaste, Edna's disgust is uncontainable. "My son could get athlete's teeth!"

At the finale, pandemonium reigns. "There's nothing I like more than the whistle and smack of a gladi," Dame Edna says, fiercely heaving bunches of the Australian national flower into the audience. (In the upper circle, ushers throw them to the audience.) It's wonderful mayhem, with Edna getting everyone to his feet as she sings: "There's nothing more holy/Than massed gladioli . . ." But Edna's benevolence is mischievously double-edged. The clown wants to goose an audience, and the sea of swaying phallic gladioli leaves no doubt about Edna's real intention. As if to drive the point home, Edna—now in a Zandra Rhodes original—sings about the evening in a parody of the *chanteuse*'s club-turn finale. She's felt:

> A strong vibration
> Like a supernatural force.
> Would I sound foolish if I said
> We'd had a form of intercourse . . .

"Isn't this a sophisticated show?" says Dame Edna toward the finale, kicking a giant plastic Malteser into the audience. And, of course, it is. London rarely sees clowning as daring or as generous as Humphries's Dame Edna. She's a hostile sharpshooter loudly proclaiming her innocence. In her, every bourgeois value, most insidiously our notion of stardom, is mocked. Her act is superb, and still improving.

In time, perhaps, Edna will use more of her set than just one sublime surreal sight-gag when a table turns into a cannon at the finale and she tries to shoot gladis into the balcony. Her theatre is kinetic, not didactic. She corrupts an audience with pleasure. Edna will continue to astonish and knock them dead for a long time. Why? Because she's so nice; and as every mother's child knows, that niceness is a license to kill.

6

Eugene O'Neill

When Eugene O'Neill's first play was produced, the twentieth century was sixteen years old. Before O'Neill, America had entertainment; after him, it had drama. In O'Neill's plays the crude power and terrible isolation of the new age coalesced.

O'Neill (who lived from 1888 to 1953) was twenty-four when he began writing plays after a bout of TB. And by then, as the second son of the rich and celebrated James O'Neill, one of America's leading romantic actors, he had lived through both the blessings and the punishment of the American Dream: "One-night stands, cheap hotels, dirty trains, never having a home." In his autobiographical masterpiece *Long Day's Journey into Night* (written in 1941, produced in 1956), O'Neill lets his mother articulate the accumulated sense of loss that was the inheritance of James O'Neill's success. The doom and disjointedness that haunt O'Neill's plays have their origin in the restless cupidity and driving ambition of his theatrical family's early years.

As a child, O'Neill was no stranger to luxury. But as a merchant seaman, derelict, and barfly in the rebellion of his early twenties, he also experienced the other side of America's obsession with achievement: exhaustion. "Be drunken continually," says O'Neill's spokesman, Edmund Tyrone, in *Long Day's Journey into Night*, quoting Baudelaire. "With wine, with virtue, as you will. But be drunken." At first, O'Neill tried to find oblivion in a bottle; later, he found it in work. Both excesses were his way of killing time and pain, his means of rebuking himself and the world for not living up to expectations.

O'Neill's plays made his wound a public event. In revolt against the old orthodoxies, O'Neill bought and finally sold the newest romantic delirium: art. A lapsed Catholic, O'Neill made a myth of his faith in art and its power to renovate life. He began his adulthood trying to wreck himself and ended up glorifying the wreckage. Caught between the century's false gods of art and ego, O'Neill was stamped early in his career as definitively modern.

O'Neill spoke of "the ache in the heart for the things we can't forget." Foremost in the sum of agonies was his family. O'Neill's mother and father were, for different reasons, essentially absentee parents. Ella Quinlan O'Neill became addicted to morphine soon after Eugene's birth and never completely focused on her boy, or forgave him. James O'Neill, touring the country in *The Count of Monte Cristo*, the money-spinner to which he sacrificed his considerable talent, hived his son away in boarding school from the age of seven. And O'Neill's older brother, James Jr., was a failed actor and debauched drunk. The family history of betrayal and neglect left the young O'Neill isolated, depressed, and nervous. O'Neill brooded over his childhood and the apparent curse that hung over the O'Neill clan. He even charted the childhood traumas that led to such a remorselessly bleak view of life that he could look kindly on the atom bomb as "a wonderful invention because it might annihilate the whole human race."

O'Neill's "nervousness" was a family talking point before it became public legend. Writing to Eugene after the birth of his second son in 1919, Ella O'Neill said: "I have such a wonderful grandson but no more wonderful than you were when you were born and weighed *eleven pounds* and no *nerves* at that time" (her italics). She signed off with love to "the biggest baby of all the three, *You.*" In *Long Day's Journey into Night*, Edmund's mother

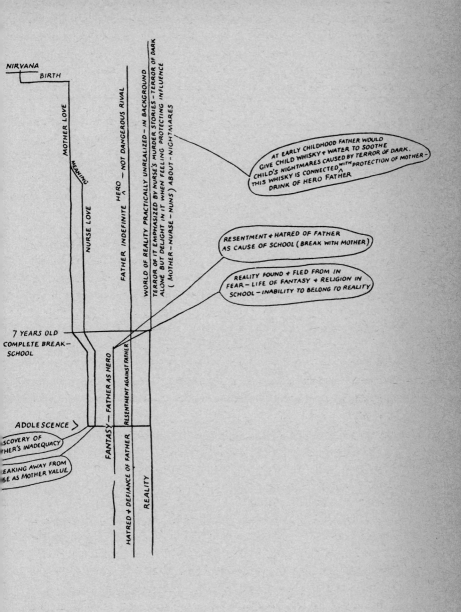

NIRVANA

BIRTH

MOTHER LOVE

MEANING

NURSE LOVE

FATHER INDEFINITE HERO — NOT DANGEROUS RIVAL

WORLD OF REALITY PRACTICALLY UNREALIZED — IN BACKGROUND
TERROR OF IT EMPHASIZED BY NURSE'S MURDER STORIES — TERROR OF DARK
ALONE BUT DELIGHT IN IT WHEN FEELING PROTECTING INFLUENCE
(MOTHER — NURSE — NUNS) ABOUT — NIGHTMARES

AT EARLY CHILDHOOD FATHER WOULD
GIVE CHILD WHISKY + WATER TO SOOTHE
CHILD'S NIGHTMARES CAUSED BY TERROR OF DARK.
THIS WHISKY IS CONNECTED WITH PROTECTION OF MOTHER —
DRINK OF HERO FATHER

RESENTMENT + HATRED OF FATHER
AS CAUSE OF SCHOOL (BREAK WITH MOTHER)

REALITY FOUND + FLED FROM IN
FEAR — LIFE OF FANTASY + RELIGION IN
SCHOOL — INABILITY TO BELONG TO REALITY

7 YEARS OLD
COMPLETE BREAK —
SCHOOL

FANTASY — FATHER AS HERO

RESENTMENT AGAINST FATHER

ADOLESCENCE >

DISCOVERY OF
FATHER'S INADEQUACY

BREAKING AWAY FROM
NURSE AS MOTHER VALUE

HATRED + DEFIANCE OF FATHER

REALITY

frequently refers to him as a big baby; and there was some truth as well as hostility in Ella O'Neill's attempt at a joke.

The need for total attention (an indulgence his compulsively long plays insist on) was apparent in O'Neill's relationship to the two wives who shared his adult writing life: the writer Agnes Boulton and the actress Carlotta Monterey. "You are the only one who can make me sure of myself," O'Neill wrote to Boulton in 1917. "I want it to be not you and me, but *us* . . . I want you alone—in an aloneness broken by nothing. Not even children. I don't understand children. They make me uneasy, and I don't know how to act with them." Boulton sent away her child by a previous marriage to live with grandparents and kept the proximity of her relatives to their Rhode Island home a secret from O'Neill. No wonder O'Neill was threatened by children: he wanted to be the child. Once Boulton had borne him two children, Shane and Oona, he soon became discontented and abandoned them all in 1928 for Carlotta Monterey.

As Carlotta remembers O'Neill's first avowal of passion, it was his needs as a son, not as a lover, that drew him to her. "He never said to me, 'I love you, I think you're wonderful.' He kept saying, 'I need you. I need you.' And he did need me, I discovered. He was never in good health. He talked about his early life—that he had no real home, no mother in the real sense, or father, no one to treat him as a child should be treated—and his face became sadder and sadder." Treating O'Neill as a genius and a child, Carlotta protected him and organized his life, even to the extent of corresponding with his children for him. At the end of his life, bedridden in a Boston hotel with Parkinson's disease, which made it impossible even to hold a pen, O'Neill said to Carlotta: "You're my Mama now."

O'Neill's plays make a myth of the sense of service his genius conventionally demanded. In *A Touch of the Poet* (written in 1940, produced in 1958), Nora Melody, who is much abused by her vain and high-falutin' husband, Con, won't let his pretensions dampen her love. The pride of Nora's devotion is somehow rewarded at the finale when Con Melody abandons his patrician airs and shows her some husbandly affection. Nora explains her all-embracing love to her daughter:

> . . . It's when you don't give a thought for all the if's and want-to's in the world! It's when, if all the fires of hell was between you, you'd walk in them gladly to be with him, and sing with joy at your own burnin', if only his kiss was on your mouth! That's love, and I'm proud I've known the great sorrow and joy of it!

But the injustice in such unswerving and one-sided loyalty takes its toll in bitterness, which O'Neill's life, if not the wish fulfill-ments of his plays, dramatized. O'Neill inscribed the manuscript of *Mourning Becomes Electra* (1931) to Carlotta; his fine words cannot make his tyrannical will or her living hell more acceptable:

> In memory of the interminable days of rain in which you bravely suffered in silence that this trilogy might be born. Days when I had my work and you had nothing . . . when you had self-forgetting love to greet me at lunchtime, depressing such preoc-cupations with a courageous, charming banter on days which for you were bitterly lonely, when I seemed far away and lost in a grim savage gloomy country of my own, days which were for you like hateful, boring inseparable enemies. . . .

During their stormy relationship, O'Neill and Carlotta sepa-rated twice, in 1948 and 1951. On the second occasion, Carlotta charged O'Neill with "cruel and abusive treatment" on "diverse occasions." And O'Neill, for his part, contended that Carlotta was "incapable of taking care of herself" and threatened to dis-patch her to a mental home. Finally, however, the couple re-united, both falling back on the ruling credos of their lives. For Carlotta, it was service. She told the press O'Neill "needed her more than anything else." And O'Neill, always prepared to assign to fate what he would not concede to self-awareness, said: "It's my destiny to go back."

Because of the maternal deprivation in his own life, O'Neill's attitude toward women was as strident and ambivalent as Anna Christie's (1921) toward men. "Men, I hate 'em—all of 'em," says Anna, a whore and, like O'Neill, an abandoned child. Despite the

brooding lean good looks that made him catnip to women,
O'Neill frequently referred to women as "pigs." Anna is one of
the early versions of the whore/mother figure that is O'Neill's
theatrical erotic ideal. Anna is purified by life on the sea. "Being
on the sea has changed me and made me feel differently about
things," she tells the once-spurned Burke, who is hurt and bewil-
dered by her confession of her "bad past." Before they finally
agree to marry, Burke makes Anna take an oath of loyalty and
purity. She gladly accedes, saying: "May the blackest curse of
God strike me dead if I'm lying." The obsession never left
O'Neill. The virgin whore is personified in Josie Hogan in *A Moon
for the Misbegotten* (1947), a character conceived from the first
stage direction as an archetypal earth mother. *"She is so oversized
for a woman that she is almost a freak—five feet eleven in her stocking feet
and weighs around a hundred and eighty."* Josie broadcasts her slut-
tishness, but she is really a virgin. She's in love with James Tyrone
—O'Neill's stage embodiment of his wayward brother—and
schemes to seduce him. When Tyrone comes around for a night
of love, what he wants is not a chippie but a mother:

> JOSIE (*Watches him for a second, fighting the love that, in spite of her,
> responds to his appeal—then she springs up and runs to him—with a
> fierce, possessive, maternal tenderness*): Come here to me, you
> great fool, and stop your silly blather. There's nothing to hate
> you for. There's nothing to forgive. Sure I was only trying to
> give you happiness, because I love you. I'm sorry I was so
> stupid and didn't see— But I see now, and you'll find I have
> all the love you need. (*She gives him a hug and kisses him. There
> is passion in her kiss but it is a tender, protective maternal passion,
> which he responds to with an instant grateful yielding.*)

All-embracing, all-forgiving, all-constant, Josie brings succor
to the drunken and tormented James. He sleeps like a baby with
his head in Josie's lap, a consummation in friendship, not lust. In
O'Neill's bittersweet daydream, mother love brings a momentary
peace. Josie's last elegiac words invoke peace as she speaks of
James from the porch of the farm that is destined to be her lonely
home. "May you have your wish and die in your sleep soon, Jim

darling," she says, generous to the end. "May you rest forever in forgiveness and peace."

Forgiveness and peace were two things O'Neill never managed in life. His plays brood over the power of the female to bestow this security or destroy it. To O'Neill, women are figures to be at once prized and hated for their power. The duality in O'Neill's temperament is brilliantly captured in the mother-haunted Cabot farm in *Desire Under the Elms* (1924) whose trees, the stage directions read, *"are like exhausted women resting their sagging breasts and hands and hair on its roof . . . a sinister maternity in their aspect."*

The wife that old Ephraim Cabot brings home to his farm is a young widow with all the calculating, sexual rapacity of a whore. She had married Cabot for his property and finds herself soon coveting his son, Eben. "I got t' fight fur what's due me out o' life, if I ever 'spect t' git it," Abbie tells Eben, holding out her hand in a seductive gesture of friendship. But at first Eben doesn't want to be friends. His hostility stems from both reverence for his dead mother and fear of his own sexual longing for his stepmother. "Nature'll beat ye, Eben," Abbie shrewdly tells him. And it does. He mourns his mother, "She was soft an' easy. He couldn't 'preciate her. . . . He murdered her with his hardness," and finally sobs: "She died. Sometimes she used to sing fur me." In this moment, O'Neill brings the longing for mother love into violent and losing battle with adult passion, a contest that leads Eben and Abbie into tragedy and ruination. Abbie, "her arms around him with wild passion," says: "I'll sing for you." The whore mother incarnate, Abbie is irresistible as a source of solace and sexual temptation. *"In spite of her overwhelming desire for him,"* reads the stage direction, *"there is a sincere maternal love in her manner and voice—a horribly frank mixture of lust and mother love."* Abbie continues:

> Don't cry, Eben! I'll take yer Maw's place! I'll be everythin' she was t' ye! Let me kiss ye, Eben . . . same's if I was a Maw t' ye—an' ye kin kiss me back 's if yew was my son—my boy —sayin' good-night t' me! Kiss me, Eben.

(They kiss in restrained fashion. Then suddenly wild passion overcomes her. She kisses him lustfully again and again and he flings his arms around her and returns her kisses. Suddenly, as in the bedroom, he frees himself from her violently and springs to his feet. He is trembling all over, in a strange state of terror . . .)
Don't ye leave me, Eben! Can't ye see it hain't enuf—lovin' ye like a Maw—can't ye see it's got t' be that an' more—much more—a hundred times more—fur me t' be happy—fur yew t' be happy?

Caught between the forces of life and death, Abbie and Eben exist in a perpetual restless intensity that typifies O'Neill's alienation. In his plays there is great show of passion but little romance. O'Neill saves romance not for love, but for death. He makes this romantic agony clear in *Long Day's Journey into Night.* "I will always be a stranger who never feels at home, who does not really want and is not really wanted, who can never belong," Edmund Tyrone says. "Who must always be a little in love with death."

O'Neill's courtship of oblivion began early. Kicked out of Princeton after his freshman year, and at twenty-one the father of a child in a short, hapless first marriage, O'Neill turned these small failures into a destiny of self-destruction. He wandered the globe searching for meanings in the romantic isolation he cultivated. The young man prospected for gold in Spanish Honduras, shipped out to sea, bummed around the waterfront dives of Buenos Aires and New York, where, at the age of twenty-three, he attempted suicide with an overdose of Veronal. In later years, O'Neill came to understand his self-destructive guilt. In *The Iceman Cometh* (written in 1939 and produced in 1946), Hickey explains that Parritt "has to be pardoned so he can forgive himself." O'Neill finally sought this forgiveness in the absolution of Art.

"Romantic imagination," says a character in *Strange Interlude* (1928). "It has ruined more lives than all diseases. A form of insanity." O'Neill had been infected early by romanticism. Instead of practicing self-destruction in his flophouse benders, he turned in adulthood to idealizing it. In one of his early plays, *Fog* (1916), a character speaks of being so sick of disappointment and

weary of life "that death seems the only way out." Fog itself is a
crucial symbol for O'Neill's romance of death—the twilight zone
that typifies his separation from life. "The fog is where I wanted
to be," says Edmund Tyrone in *Long Day's Journey into Night*. "I
was a ghost belonging to the fog, and the fog was the ghost of
the sea." Besides exemplifying O'Neill's hauntedness, the fog is
also a refuge: the impermeable haze behind which he could
dream his romantic dreams.

In the poem "Submarine" (1917), he already had begun to
turn his subterranean life into a heroic project:

> My soul is a submarine.
> My aspirations are torpedoes.
> I will hide unseen
> Beneath the surface of life
> Watching for ships . . .
>
> I will destroy them
> Because the sea is beautiful.
>
> That is why I lurk
> Menacingly
> In green depths.

Through writing, O'Neill found an anodyne for his anxiety.
Writing became a defense. "Keep writing, no matter what!" he
told a discouraged author. "As long as you have a job on hand that
absorbs all your mental energy, you haven't much worry to spare
over other things. It serves as a suit of armor." Art engineered and
excused O'Neill's detachment from life. In his notebooks, he
copied out Nietzsche's dictum: "Do I strive after happiness? I
strive after my own work." Both victim and perpetrator of the
romance of Art, O'Neill gave everything to his work and little to
the real life around him. "When I am writing, I am alive," he said.
"Writing is a vacation from living."

O'Neill glorified his despair. "My vultures are screaming," he
wrote to a friend. His self-dramatizing anguish was part of his
personality as well as his plays. Like Con Melody in *A Touch of the
Poet*, O'Neill enjoyed declaiming gloomy portions of Byron's

Childe Harold. "He quoted it with a touch of irony," Agnes Boulton recalled, "while at the same time it was also clear that he accepted it on its face value." O'Neill treated himself as the answer to his own prayers. As Boulton remembers, O'Neill's apocalyptic pronouncements were made, where possible, near a mirror. "If there had been a mirror Gene would have been observing himself in it as he talked," she says in her account of their courtship and early marriage, *Part of a Long Story*, "as he always did where there was a mirror around." O'Neill, who wrote of wanting "to give pain a voice," needed his "vultures" and encouraged them. He thought they kept him "pure." The "vultures," he said, came from the "great dark behind and inside and not from the bright lights without"; without them, he told the press, he would be "at a complete loss." To heal his life might jeopardize his art. And therefore desolation became a self-fulfilling romantic prophecy. "He saw life as a tragedy and had neither the desire nor the curiosity to go beyond the limits of his own vision," Boulton explained, implying O'Neill's secondary gain in keeping his wound open. "He loved his tragic conception of the world and would not have given it up for the world." In typical romantic fashion, O'Neill saw anguish as the only valid credential for truth. "Before the soul can fly," he wrote on his studio wall, "it must be washed in the blood of the heart." O'Neill put himself in the avant-garde of suffering and quickly set about making a future of regrets.

O'Neill did for pessimism what the American musical did for "pep": made it sensational. One pundit counted twelve murders, eight suicides, and seven cases of insanity in his plays.

> Oh, I have tried to scream!
> Give pain a voice!
> Make it a street singer
> Acting a pantomime of tragic song,
> To beg the common copper
> Of response:
> An ear
> To hear.
>
> ("Fragments")

With all the optimism of the plague-stricken, O'Neill contended that in his tragedies, "we should feel exalted to think that there is something—some vital, unquenchable flame which makes him [man] triumph over his miseries. Dying, he is still victorious." In life as in his theatre, O'Neill held fast to the idea of psychological fate. The "O'Neill curse," like the curse on the lives of so many of his characters (Mary Tyrone, Nina Leeds, Lavinia Mannon), is at once awful and comforting. Fate takes the issue of responsibility out of one's hands. However terrible, fate still provides a motive, a symmetry to the chaos the characters find and create about them. O'Neill needed to believe in fate. Like his bar-room daydreamers in *The Iceman Cometh*, it was the saving lie that kept the playwright from facing the brutalities of his own life.

"One's outer life," O'Neill said, "passes in a solitude haunted by the ghosts of others. One's inner life passes in a solitude haunted by the masks of oneself." In *Long Day's Journey into Night*, O'Neill describes himself as a ghost, and shows the sins of the past haunting the present. The ghosts of murdered selves abound in O'Neill's plays. *Strange Interlude* is lover- and child-haunted, as is *Mourning Becomes Electra*. *Emperor Jones* (1920) fires gunshots at the ghosts that oppress him; in *Hughie* (completed in 1942, produced in 1958), the small-time hustler yammering to the night clerk is friend-haunted, his name, "Erie" Smith, implying his ghostly, threadbare life. And in *Long Day's Journey into Night*, Mary Tyrone's appearance at the finale, "paler than ever" and "in her sky blue wedding dress," is preceded by the ghostly effect of lights going out and strange, unexplained music coming from another room. In this moment, Mary Tyrone is the ghost of her marriage and her early hope. "I fell in love with James Tyrone and was so happy for a time," she says vaguely in the play's final beat.

These hauntings are manifestations of O'Neill's guilt, a guilt, as Harold Clurman observes in *Lies Like Truth*, "in relation to love." Clurman goes on:

> From this sense of guilt—all his characters suffer it in one form or another . . . comes a constant alteration of mood. Every character speaks in two voices, two moods—one of rage, the other of

apology. This produces a kind of moral schizophrenia which in some of O'Neill's other plays has necessitated an interior monologue and a speech for social use (*Strange Interlude*) or, as in *The Great God Brown* (1926) and *Days Without End* (1934), two sets of masks. In this everlasting duality, with its equal pressures in several directions, lies the brooding power, the emotional grip of O'Neill's work.

In art, O'Neill tried to admit the pain he would continue to inflict on his own family:

> So am I isolate,
> Inviolate
> Untouchable,
> Bitterest of all, ungiveable,
> Unable to bestow,
> Break from my solitude
> A lonely gift,
> Myself.

Having been punished by abandonment as a child, he abandoned his own children, with equally disastrous results. O'Neill's first son, Eugene Jr. (who'd never seen or known his real father until the age of twelve), committed suicide at forty. Shane O'Neill became a drug addict. And Oona O'Neill at seventeen broke off all communication with her father to marry the puckish, flamboyant comic genius of the twentieth century, the poet of grace, not gravity, whose influence on theatre was greater than her father's: Charlie Chaplin. O'Neill's tragedy was that he could not give to life the dedication and concentration he gave to his work. His predicament, like his plays, was emblematic of his era. Mourning the death of God, O'Neill made a god of the self. Unable to sacrifice himself to God, he ended up sacrificing others to himself.

I I

O'Neill means "champion" in Gaelic. From the outset of his playwrighting career, O'Neill was hellbent on greatness. "It's because

I want to be an artist or nothing," he said, applying to George Pierce Baker's famous Harvard course in playwrighting in 1914, "that I am writing to you." Having worked hard at destroying himself, he turned to building an oeuvre of serious drama with a passionate, big-hearted, obsessive energy. "At first," Lionel Trilling said, "it was the mere technical inventiveness of Eugene O'Neill, his daring subjects and language which caught the public imagination." A pathfinder, O'Neill, with fierce single-mindedness, blazed the theatrical trail generations of playwrights would follow. He was the first to stage the life and vernacular of the American lower classes; the first to put the American black man on stage as a figure of substance and complexity; the first to face the soullessness of America's material progress; and the first to adapt the innovations of European drama to the American experience. A man of industry and output, O'Neill was manifest destiny with pen and paper. "Instantly, or so it seemed, the stage began to breathe again," George Jean Nathan wrote of O'Neill's emergence on the theatre scene. O'Neill also assumed his stature, and nurtured it. "Life is growth or a joke one plays on oneself," he said. "One has to choose." O'Neill chose growth—going so far as to withdraw from Broadway and cease the production of his plays from 1933 to 1946 so he could concentrate on his writing. O'Neill disdained Broadway as a "show shop," and with the example of his father, who had compromised his talent to popular success, O'Neill swore "that they would never get me. I determined I would never sell out."

From his earliest production (*Bound East for Cardiff*, 1916, mounted by the Provincetown Players on a Cape Cod wharf with fog in the harbor and the sound of the sea under the floorboards), O'Neill aimed for bold narrative experiment. Although many of these early sea plays now seem creaky, then, in 1916, life at sea had never been shown with such compassion and command of the vernacular. O'Neill's sea tales were autobiographical, and in rebellion against the old, ranting, artificial "romantic stuff" he associated with his father's performing and that then dominated the American stage. By 1920, with the Broadway production of *Beyond the Horizon*—a bad play that won him the first of his four Pulitzer prizes—O'Neill was the darling of the Smart Set, and the Roaring Twenties had found its Jeremiah.

Ravished at once by a revolt against the old and the ideas of new "big work," O'Neill whipped himself up for bigger and more onerous theatrical challenges. "It seems to me most emphatically a case of shooting àt a star or being a dud," he wrote to his cohort Kenneth Macgowan, who spoke O'Neill's language of aspiration and said that O'Neill got to the "big emotional heart of things." "I want to howl: Imagination, Beauty, Daring, or bust." O'Neill didn't shy from bold, risky effects: the masks in *The Great God Brown*, the asides in *Strange Interlude*, the gorilla cage in *The Hairy Ape* (1922). The habit of thinking big never left him. Even when he considered writing a comedy, as he did in 1939, projecting *The Iceman Cometh*, it was to be "a big kind of comedy that doesn't stay funny for very long." O'Neill was both a hero and a victim of the society's overreaching sense of monumentality. While he didn't fall prey to Broadway, he was trapped early by America's High Culture vultures. O'Neill grumbled that there were no "Big Men" in experimental theatre, and that "big work" had to face up to the hard facts of the new century. And what were they?

> . . . the death of an old God and the failures of science and materialism to give any satisfying new one for the surviving primitive religious instinct to find meaning for life in, and to comfort its fears of death with. It seems to me anyone trying to do big work nowadays must have this subject behind all the little subjects of his plays or novels.

The only play in which O'Neill tackled this theme directly was *Dynamo* (1929), a disaster by any standard. But treated early by the public as a colossus, O'Neill was eager to test his power. "A man wills his own defeat when he pursues the unattainable. But the *struggle* is his success," he said. "Such a figure is necessarily tragic. But to me he is not depressing, he is exhilarating." Often both O'Neill's plays and his pronouncements about them teetered under the weight of the meanings he tried to shoulder. In 1925, like a champion announcing the next contender, O'Neill explained in a letter to Thomas Hobson Quinn that he was about to take on classical tragedy:

> . . . the one eternal tragedy of Man in his glorious, self-destruc-
> tive struggle *to make the Force express him instead of being, as an animal
> is, an infinitesimal incident in its expression.* And my profound convic-
> tion is that this is the only subject worth writing about and that
> it is possible—or can be—to develop a tragic expression in terms
> of transfigured modern values and symbols in the theater which
> may to some degree bring home to members of a modern audi-
> ence their ennobling identity with the tragic figures on the stage.
> Of course, this is very much of a dream, but where theater is
> concerned, one must have a dream and the Greek dream in
> tragedy is the noblest ever!

Out of O'Neill's dream of himself as a poet on a grand scale came some second-rate experiments with tragic form (*The Great God Brown; Lazarus Laughed,* 1927) and a couple of windy High Art "victories" in the five-hour *Strange Interlude* and the six-hour trilogy *Mourning Becomes Electra,* which don't so much strip life down as wear it down. They excite pity without admiration, and therefore without terror. O'Neill, as Eric Bentley has said, "had tragedy in the head . . . the more he attempts, the less he achieves."

When O'Neill forgoes his big bow-wow ideas, as he does in *Desire Under the Elms,* he can be riveting. In this peasant tragedy, the themes of greed, rootlessness, and psychological fate combine in an obsessive personal way that transcends the play's schematic structure. In Ephraim Cabot's ruthless control of his farm, critics have seen the low peasant cunning of O'Neill's father. But more than his father, O'Neill is writing about his obsession with his own creation. The stone wall in the foreground of the Cabot house is the visual reminder of Cabot's labor, which has turned the unpromising land into profit. Built stone by stone, the wall is a metaphor of the life's work which keeps Cabot tied to his farm in the same dogged, possessive, crazed way that kept O'Neill allied to his writing and not to life. O'Neill finds something of himself in Cabot and his writing takes on a special passion. The old man's myopic egotism eerily foreshadows O'Neill's own story. In the same way, *Mourning Becomes Electra*, which lays an ambush for the imagination by invoking the high shadows of classical associations, actually produces moments of genuine power when the story coalesces with O'Neill's private terror: " . . . there's no one left to punish me. I'm the last Mannon. I've got to punish myself!" says Lavinia at the finale. "Living alone here with the dead is a worse act of justice than death or prison!" When the shutters close "with a decisive bang" and Lavinia turns to immure herself in the family home, both her isolation and O'Neill's combine in a chilling, concise stage picture.

After 1933, O'Neill intentionally cut himself off from public life to get on with a projected historical cycle of nine plays with the general title *A Tale of Possessors, Self-Dispossessed*. *A Touch of the Poet* and *More Stately Mansions* (completed in 1939, produced in 1958) were the only plays to emerge from the project, an undertaking as pretentious and impossible as the general title itself. But in isolating himself from society, O'Neill also set himself apart from the currency of American speech. This deficiency is alibied in his historical plays by the skillful use of Irish dialect, which makes up in rhythm for the freshness he could no longer convey in the American vernacular. "Musha, but it's you have the blarneyin' tongue. God forgive you," says Sara Melody, teasing her father's genteel pretensions with her brogue. The issue of dialect is part of the immigrant dilemma O'Neill is dramatizing in *A Touch of the Poet*, and Con Melody sheds his role of aristocrat at the finale, only to adopt the "begorah" and "bejaysus" locutions of the shanty Irish bar-keep.

In the final, ambitious burst of energy that created *The Iceman Cometh* and *Long Day's Journey into Night* (O'Neill is the only American playwright to improve with age), the stiltedness of O'Neill's language is hidden by the plays' being set just far enough in the past (1912) to make his idiom seem accurate rather than antique. But for a major playwright (he won the Nobel Prize for Literature in 1936), O'Neill always exhibited a tin ear for the spoken word. He was, as George Steiner bitchily observes, "committed in a somber, rather moving way, to bad writing." In *Welded* (1924), an extraordinarily inept account of his second marriage, the play-wright hero returns home with a finished manuscript to show his wife: "It's *real,* Nelly! You'll see when I read you—the whole play has power and truth. I know it." When O'Neill writes conven-tional American speech, there is no pulse behind the words. Early in his career O'Neill had complained: "Oh for a language to write in—I'm so strait-jacketed in terms of talk."

This creative pressure led him to many evocative aural discov-eries (the Creole lament in *The Moon of the Caribbees* (1918); the tom-tom in *Emperor Jones;* the generator in *Dynamo*) and the idi-omatic sludge of lower-class talk, which he made poetic. "Where I feel myself most neglected is just where I set most store by myself—as a bit of a poet, who had labored with the spoken word to evolve original rhythms of beauty where beauty apparently isn't—*Jones, Ape, God's Chillun, Desire.*" But in his late plays, the poetry in O'Neill's slang is strained rather than achieved. In *Hughie,* an anecdote that has been ballyhooed by critics into a minor O'Neill classic, "Erie" Smith explains the gambling he used to do with the night clerk to pass the early-morning hours. "I'd always take him to the cleaners in the end. But he never suspicioned nothing . . ." The archness of the poetic turn of phrase in *Hughie* is as heavy-handed as O'Neill straining for verisimilitude in the bar-room badinage of *The Iceman Cometh.* At one point, after a fight, the bartender Rocky says: "Aw right, you. Leggo dat shiv and I'll put dis gat away." In giving "pain a voice," O'Neill privately admitted as late as 1942 that his problem was in language:

> But something was born wrong.
> The voice
> Strains towards a sob.
> Begins and ends in silence.

Stammering—what O'Neill called "the native eloquence of us fog people"—was a term he frequently used to describe his at-tempts to make American speech bend to his dramatic needs. Having explored realistic vernacular in his early period, he turned to eloquence in his middle period. The stop-start staging of *Strange Interlude* is a kind of stammering in action. Both the style of the language and its delivery proclaim its Significance. Theatre, O'Neill said, "should give us what the church no longer gives us—a meaning. In brief, we should return to the spirit of Greek grandeur. And if we have no Gods, or heroes to portray, we have the subconscious, the mother of all gods and heroes."

Strange Interlude tries to stage the subconscious; but instead of finding grandeur, it achieves merely affectation. "Little subconscious mind, says I," O'Neill said, describing the gestation of a new play, "bring home the bacon." In the case of *Strange Interlude,* the bacon is hard to swallow. "How we poor monkeys hide from ourselves behind the sounds called words," says Nina Leeds, who, haunted by the death of her lover, decides on marriage as a cure for her morbidity. Typically, searching for a language that shows this psychological evasion, O'Neill settles for an idiom that describes every feeling. Fine words spew out of the characters, words chiseled in hard work and high seriousness. "Strange interlude!" says one character. "Yes, our lives are merely strange dark interludes in the electrical display of God the Father." O'Neill uses the word "strange" more than fifty times in the play, but there is nothing strange about it. Every mystery of personality is explained. The cumulative effect of this language is inundation, not illumination. As an act of will, O'Neill's elaborate tale is "an achievement"; as a piece of writing, it verges on parody:

> NINA (*thinking*): Talking . . . his voice like a fatiguing dying tune droned on a beggar's organ . . . his words arising from the tomb of a soul in puffs of ashes . . .
> (*Torturedly*)
> Ashes! . . . oh, Gordon, my dear one! . . . oh, lips on my lips, oh, strong arms around me, oh, spirit so brave and generous and gay! . . . ashes dissolving into mud! . . . mud and ashes! . . . that's all! . . . gone! . . . and gone forever from me . . .

Strange Interlude was a huge commercial success on Broadway. The reason lies not with the success of O'Neill's language but with its failure. Having disdained his father's penchant for melodrama, O'Neill nonetheless couldn't resist it. His language inflates with melodramatic flourishes, confusing impact with thought, oratory with authentic dramatic dialogue. Drama is a game of show and tell; and O'Neill simply tells. The play shoves every emotion right up under the chin of its audience. Through speechifying, O'Neill puts passion on a plate, where it can be easily consumed.

As he seeks forms to give size and grandeur to his own sense of suffering, O'Neill's plays inflate with "cultural gas" (Eric Bentley's term for the showy articulateness of the playwright's middle period): the masks of *Lazarus Laughed,* the choric chants of *The Great God Brown,* the retelling of the history of the House of Atreus in *Mourning Becomes Electra.* In *Mourning Becomes Electra,* O'Neill corseted the Civil War characters with the Greek story and fleshed it out with sex talk, "not sex lived and embodied but sex talked. The sex talk of the subintelligentsia," according to Bentley. In this play, like so many others, concept overwhelms character, and eloquence passes for authentic dramatic language. "O'Neill commits inner vandalism by sheer inadequacy of style," George Steiner observes of the play O'Neill thought his magnum opus. "In the morass of his language, the high griefs of the House of Atreus dwindle to a case of adultery and murder in a provincial rathole." O'Neill himself had to admit that language had yet again defeated him. "It needed great language to lift it beyond itself. I haven't got that," he wrote. "By way of self-consolation . . . I don't think that great language is possible for anyone living in the discordant, broken, faithless rhythm of our time. The best one can do is be pathetically eloquent by one's moving dramatic articulations." In *Mourning Becomes Electra,* the tedium is the message.

By trying unsuccessfully to force himself into the mold of tragedian, O'Neill played down his more mundane but substantial talent as reporter. Like Theodore Dreiser in the novel and Jacob Riis in photo journalism, O'Neill called attention to his vision not by the elegance of his style, but by the weight of detail that recorded the split personality of American life. The sounds and cramped space of a ship's engine room (*The Hairy Ape*), the moonlit deck of a freighter (*The Moon of the Caribbees*), the subterranean calm of a derelict saloon (*The Iceman Cometh*), these realistic atmospheres convey the outcast's suffering more eloquently than O'Neill's words often do. O'Neill had a passion for the detritus of American life long before the public saw their own image in his pictures of waste. But striving for the big statement, O'Neill would not let his stage pictures speak for themselves. He is compelled to underline, to decorate, to pin down the mysterious truth of these atmospheres with fine words and big themes. Instead of calling attention to the reality of the experience, the talk calls attention to the playwright's literary gift of gab. Harry Hope's Saloon, for instance, a crucial landmark in O'Neill's personal geography, is explained poetically to the audience by the pessimist Larry Slade in the first moments of *The Iceman Cometh* before the poetry of the place can be made dramatic. The audience knows the experience before it has it. Says Slade:

> What is it? It's the No Chance Saloon. It's Bedrock Bar, The End of the Line Café, The Bottom of the Sea Rathskeller! Don't you notice the beautiful calm in the atmosphere? That's because it's the last harbor. No one here has to worry about where they're going next, because there is no farther they can go. It's a great comfort to them. Although even here they keep up the appearances of life with a few harmless pipe dreams about their yesterdays and tomorrows, as you'll see for yourself if you're here long.

In *The Iceman Cometh* and *Long Day's Journey into Night*, O'Neill's lifelong artistic struggle to find a significant form for his intimations about America yielded its most powerful results. "I'm going on the theory that the United States, instead of being the most successful country in the world, is the greatest failure," O'Neill told *Time* in 1946, the year *Iceman* was produced.

> It's the greatest failure because it was given everything, more than any other country. Through moving as rapidly as it has, it hasn't acquired any real roots. Its main idea is the everlasting game of trying to possess your own soul by the possession of something outside it, thereby losing your own soul and the thing

outside it, too. America is the prime example of this because it happened so quickly and with such immense resources. . . . We are the greatest example of "For what shall it profit a man, if he shall gain the whole world and lose his own soul."

The sin O'Neill saw in the land was also the sin he could not face in himself. He was projecting onto society his own personal dilemma. In trying to possess his craft, O'Neill too had lost his soul.

> . . . I,
> A quiet man,
> In love with quiet,
> Live quietly
> Among the visions of my drowned,
> Deep in my silent sea.

Cut off from community, from family, from ordinary life, he floundered. The last plays, so passionate and so nostalgic, brood over the time when his course into adulthood was being set. They are reports from his hellish interior. "I know 'em all, I've known 'em for years," O'Neill said in a press conference about *The Iceman Cometh.* "I've tried to show the inmates of Harry Hope's saloon with their dreams . . . there is always one dream left, one final dream, no matter how low you've fallen. I know because I saw it." O'Neill also witnessed the punishing scenes played out in *Long Day's Journey into Night.* In *Iceman,* O'Neill's new autobiographical backward glance is mixed with the old impulse to be definitive. O'Neill creates an epic out of the histories of seventeen daydreamers, making up in scope what he can't find in depth. For all its effective bawdy moments and fascinating cameos, the play finally fails to transmute fact into metaphor. But *Long Day's Journey into Night,* a play "of old sorrows written in tears and blood," which O'Neill never intended to be produced in his lifetime, has no aspirations to big intentions, only authenticity. Written to reveal himself to himself, *Long Day's Journey into Night* is a spiritual necessity, not a theatrical project intended to show off his thought to others. Forcing nothing, O'Neill, astonishingly, finds everything. His writing is direct, unpretentious, poetic. Through the Tyrones, the themes and symbols of his early plays are not imposed but embodied in great drama.

I I I

The Iceman Cometh, itself a tall tale, serves O'Neill in the same magical way that the tall tales serve the denizens of Harry Hope's Saloon: both as a mask and an admission "that they cannot forgive themselves for what they're not." In the case of the play's central drama, the high-rolling salesman Hickey turns out to be a maniac who has killed his "beloved" wife; and the outsider Don Parritt finally gets the death he seeks after admitting that he informed on his hated activist mother. In O'Neill's case, the play's ungainliness shows him to be not the stage poet he had ruined his life to become. *Iceman* stalls on this failure of imagination. In the play, O'Neill depicts human character as a vital lie, an exercise in heroics in which man's litany of self-revelations hides his own panic and impoverishment. Each character lives a lie to protect himself from a fear of life and of death. The point is made early in the play by Larry Slade, and then restated ad nauseam as each character factors out of O'Neill's dramatic equation. "To hell with the truth!" says Slade. "As the history of the world proves, the truth has no bearing on anything. . . . The lie of a pipe dream is what gives life to the whole misbegotten mad lot of us, drunk or sober." O'Neill can face the lie in others, but not the lie in his romance of art.

O'Neill repeats the phrase "pipe dream" fifteen times in the play, and refused to cut even one mention. But the reiteration of an idea on stage doesn't clinch it. In fact, it's proof positive that the idea has not been successfully dramatized. Besides the repetitiveness of each character's dream and the ineluctable hunger of the spellbound for his spell, O'Neill is at a loss in *Iceman* to analyze the brilliant atmosphere he describes. A dream is something you wake up from; but O'Neill believed in dreaming, and sacrificed not only his life but the lives of his family to the fantasy of literary perfection. "You can't keep a hophead off his dope," he said about his own writing, starting *Long Day's Journey into Night* soon after finishing *The Iceman Cometh.* O'Neill was too much part of the problem to offer solutions. The play's sprawling lack of focus reflects the playwright's own moral vacuum. "O'Neill's eye," writes Eric Bentley of *Iceman* in *In Search of Theater,* "was off the object and on Dramatic and Poetic Effects. . . ." O'Neill insisted on size. "You would find if I did not build up the complete picture of the group as it is in the first part," he wrote to Kenneth Macgowan, "the atmosphere of the place, the humanity and friendship and human warmth, *the deep inner contentment of the bottom,* you would find the impact of what follows a lot less profoundly disturbing." Size allows O'Neill to show off technique, which he mistakes for content, the inevitable confusion of any writer whose sense of life has been reduced to the puny goal of self-expression.

"Gene came in and talked to me all night which he frequently did when he couldn't sleep. He was thinking about this play, you see, in his youth," Carlotta O'Neill recalled about the beginnings of *Long Day's Journey into Night.* "He explained to me then that he had to write this play. He had to write it because it was a thing that haunted him and he had to forgive whatever caused this in them (in his mother and father and brother) and in himself." In his previous plays, O'Neill had cannibalized aspects of his family history and served them up piecemeal in various theatrical disguises. (His brother James is James Tyrone in *A Moon for the Misbegotten;* parts of his father are in Ephraim Cabot in *Desire Under the Elms,* Con Melody in *A Touch of the Poet,* Chris Christopherson in *Anna Christie;* and his mother's isolation and mistreatment by his father are in *Desire Under the Elms* and *A Touch of the Poet.*) *Long Day's Journey into Night* focuses on a day at the Tyrone's sea-front Connecticut house—a day in which the youngest Tyrone, Edmund, learns that he has TB and his mother, Mary Tyrone, lapses back into her morphine addiction. Within the melodrama of this painful realistic situation, the family's hopes and past grievances are played out.

In Mary Tyrone's awful isolation, an isolation first enforced by years of touring with her husband and later by the odium of her addiction, O'Neill faces the spiritual malaise which he began by decrying and by which he was finally claimed. "None of us can help the things life has done to us," she says, spelling out her fatalism. "They're done before you realize it, and once they're done they make you do other things until at last everything comes between you and what you'd like to be, and you've lost your true self for ever." As with O'Neill, Mary Tyrone has lost her soul and says so. ". . . One day long ago I found I could no longer call my soul my own." And later: "If I could only find the faith I lost, so I could pray again!" Mary Tyrone's faith and her life have been sacrificed to James Tyrone's work. Irish peasant turned immigrant actor and star, Tyrone's glory and wealth have meant his family's fall and impoverishment. His dream of mobility has condemned his family to a lifetime of restlessness.

Stardom is the heroic face the culture puts on emotional greed—a greed manifested in James Tyrone's case in his property speculation, his tight-fistedness with money, and his obsession with the box-office success of *The Count of Monte Cristo*. ". . . From thirty-five to forty thousand net profit a season! A fortune in those days," Tyrone tells his son, who would rebel against his father's hunger for money, only to be victimized by the more insidious hunger for greatness. Tyrone continues bitterly: "What the hell was it I wanted to buy, I wonder, that was worth . . . Well, no matter. . . ." The characters see their dilemma but, in their fatalism, won't risk change. The heart-rending poignance of their lives—and O'Neill's—is the moral myopia that prevents them from forestalling the inevitable clash between ego and personal salvation. The tears O'Neill shed in writing *Long Day's Journey into Night* were not only for his past, but for his present.

In the riveting tension of the play, O'Neill's familiar metaphors emerge not as symbols but as active characters in the drama. The fog that sweeps in from the sea surrounds and isolates the Tyrone house. Out of the pain and confusion in the Tyrone family relationships, the fog assumes the impenetrability and protection of the past itself. "It hides you from the world and the world from you," says Mary Tyrone, welcoming it. "You feel that everything has changed and nothing is what it seemed. No one can find or touch you any more." And Edmund, too, admits his craving for the invisibility of fog. "The fog was where I wanted to be. Halfway down the path you can't see this house. You'd never know it was here . . . I couldn't see but a few feet ahead," he says, his words unwittingly heavy with deeper insinuations. "I didn't meet a soul. . . ."

The doom of the foghorn compounds the soulless, lost world the Tyrones inhabit. The fog is a fact of the stage world before the play's passion elevates it, by degrees, to symbol. Likewise, the hauntedness O'Neill so frequently speechified about is here incarnated in Mary Tyrone's punishing spectral presence. As the morphine takes hold, Mary Tyrone starts to withdraw from the life around her, and her "detached affection" becomes apparent to both the audience and her family. "You can't talk to her now," Jamie tells Edmund. "She'll listen but she won't listen. She'll be here and she won't be here." In *Long Day's Journey into Night,* O'Neill produces the ghost-in-life his other plays merely talk about. "You'll be like a mad ghost before the night's over," James Tyrone sadly warns his wife. And by the end of the play, she is. Haunted and haunting them, she moves dreamily amid her men, recalling an innocence forever lost. And the other Tyrones, who watch this ghostly performance, know that they, too, are among the living dead. James Tyrone's life is a tortured half-life, his accomplishments denied by the destruction they have wreaked on his family. Edmund confesses to "living as a ghost." And Jamie, the most self-destructive of the men, admits the dead heart that all can see. "The dead part of me hopes you won't get well," he tells Edmund, articulating the revenge that eats away at him. "Maybe he's even glad the game has got Mama again! He wants company, he doesn't want to be the only corpse in the house!"

Beneath the scars of their family life, the story of the O'Neills contains the deeper brutalizing national themes of immigration and assimilation, mobility and identity, success and failure, well-being and salvation. The Tyrones' house is never a home. The material dream come true does not open the Tyrones up to life, but cuts them off from it. Isolation dominates their life just as it dominates the land. O'Neill's masterpiece puts into dramatic terms a paradox of democracy de Tocqueville had observed as early as 1835: "Not only does democracy make every man forget his ancestors; but it hides his descendants and separates his contemporaries from him: it throws him back forever upon himself alone and threatens in the end to confine him entirely within the solitude of his own heart."

Within O'Neill's spectacular solitude, *Long Day's Journey into Night* emerges almost as a freak of his imagination. It is not merely O'Neill's best story; it is, really, his *only* story. The intensely personal mission of the play divests it of O'Neill's familiar artistic swagger. Pursuing the truth of his past with ruthless candor, he confesses his own theatrical limitations. When James Tyrone tells Edmund he has the makings of a poet, Edmund counters: "The *makings* of a poet. No, I'm afraid I'm like the guy who is always panhandling for a smoke. He hasn't even got the makings. He's only got the habit. I couldn't touch what I tried to tell you just now. I just stammered. That's the best I'll ever do. . . ." *Long Day's Journey into Night* was, indeed, the best O'Neill ever did, where his voice found words to elevate his vision beyond a stammer.

"There is something moving, even great, in the impulse of the play," Harold Clurman said of *Long Day's Journey into Night*. "And no one can witness it without reverence for the *selflessness* of this extremely personal act." But there is nothing selfless about the play. It is O'Neill's attempt to redeem the sins of the present by confessing the sins of the past. As a literary gesture, it is bold and big-hearted. Yet the real act of bravery would have been to break the O'Neill neurotic pattern for the living, not chronicle its self-destruction in the dead. O'Neill could make peace with his past but not his present. At the end of his life, he disinherited his children, quarreled miserably with his wife, and retreated into the kind of barbarous isolation his plays dramatized. Art, O'Neill and his family discovered too late, is no substitute for life.

7

Woody Allen

Who should I look like? I'm your death.
Death Knocks

As schlepper triumphant, Woody Allen is living refutation of every Jewish mother's nightmare: a sixty-pound weakling who has parlayed his inheritance of fear, self-hate, and love of finger foods into a fortune big enough to buy up all the chopped liver on New York's Upper West Side.

As America has become more educated and self-conscious, its humor has become more verbal and less physical. Allen is the bellwether of this change. The great American clowns of the early twentieth century were kinetic. Their antics epitomized both the panic and purposefulness of the industrial boom. Wrote Henry Adams of this dynamic era in his *Autobiography* (1905): "Prosperity never before imagined, power never reached by anything but a meteor had made the world irritable, nervous, querulous, unreasonable and afraid." The new rhythm brought a new kind of laughter, which admitted the agitation and the credulity of a people that had always been restless in the midst of abundance. "I was alien to the slick tempo," Chaplin recalled about his first visit to New York from London in 1910. "Even the owner of the smallest enterprise acts with alacrity. The shoe black flips his polishing rag with alacrity, the bartender serves a beer with alacrity, sliding it up to you along the polished surface of the bar. The soda jerk, when serving an egg malted milk, performs like a hopped up juggler." The old clowns fed a young generation's will to run wild. The clown's pratfall was the emblem of the society's resilient hopefulness.

Where the old-timers reflected myths of hope, Allen reflects a myth of defeat. A sense of elegant dread has replaced hilarious excess. ("It's impossible to experience one's own death, and still carry a tune," Allen writes in *Getting Even.*) His humor is about emotional paralysis. It was the right subject for uneasy times when Allen first came on the scene in the mid-sixties. A conventional society wanted the titillation of the unconventional. Lenny Bruce found vulgarity; Mort Sahl found politics; and Allen—best exemplifying his narcissistic era—found himself. Allen's losing battles with his psyche substitute the shrug for the pratfall. "How is it possible," he asks, "to find meaning in a finite world given my waist and shirt size?"

"Early in life I was visited by the bluebird of anxiety." Allen is a veteran of more than two decades of psychoanalysis, his introspection reflects a society that now looks on behavior not as a mystery but as a system of motives and explanations. The old-timers were not in the habit of analysis: they concentrated on mayhem and left the meanings to others. "I never realized that I was doing anything but trying to make people laugh when I threw my custard pies and took my pratfalls," said Buster Keaton. The old-guard clowns promoted their fear as playfulness; Allen promotes it as exposition. Both are obsessed, the old-timers with their product and Allen with the added burden of his problems. The difference reflects a change in the society that made the clown and the audience that applauds him. The charm of action has been replaced by the charm of agony.

First-generation Americans, oppressed by their illiteracy, the old-timers used action to decoy ignorance. But their illiteracy also served their low comedy, making its predicaments and its passions convincing. The malaprop now has been replaced by wit; the cavorting racial caricature by the sophisticated stand-up comic. The body is played down, and the talking head holds sway on stage and screen. Allen's mind is his burden and his blessing. His literate range of references adds a veneer of learning to his jokes, at once teasing and flattering a middle-class audience about its hard-won sophistication. In his short story "The Whore of Mensa," a detective pastiche about whores who turn intellectual tricks, the conversation-starved "Woody" narrator asks, dickering: "Suppose I wanted Noam Chomsky explained to me by two girls?"

Allen shares the old clowns' anxiety about physical attractiveness. W. C. Fields juggled in white gloves so his skin condition couldn't be seen; Bert Lahr confided that he'd become a clown "because I wanted to put my arms around a girl." All comedians seek vindictive triumph for their looks on stage, but Allen has developed a unique line in self-abuse. "Art and masturbation. Two areas where I'm an absolute expert," says Allen's spokesman Sandy (Master?) Bates in *Stardust Memories* (1981).

While the old-timers tried to live up to the American ideal of beauty which oppressed them, Allen uses his puny physique to satirize its preposterousness. Allen's posture as victim is a radical reversal of the traditional clown role of activator who gets even for any injustice. Allen's early stand-up gambits put the psychoanalytic model on the stage: "I think I will review some of the outstanding features of my private life and put them in perspective. Then we'll have a brief question and answer period and evaluate them." His mock confessions were a litany of failure made all the more believable by his timid, stammering, nonaggressive delivery—a delivery that Richard Schickel aptly said "parodied the conventions of his art." His neighborhood was so tough the kids stole hubcaps from passing cars; he was so poor that instead of a dog, he had an ant named Spot; when he was sent to an interdenominational camp, he was sadistically beaten by boys of every race, creed, and color. The old clowns were rapacious and aggressive; "Woody" is rapacious and passive.

Chaplin is Allen's favorite early screen clown ("As soon as Chaplin comes down the street I start to laugh—his really primitive unmotivated hostility"). Chaplin's "Charlie" is an anarchist whose high jinks range across classes and call them all into question. Allen's "Woody" is, at best, a middle-class ironist, too refined, too successful, and too isolated to have an instinct for "primitive . . . hostility." Charlie is always on the attack; Woody is always in retreat. Chaplin's comedies are a romance of life, where Allen's, typical of a society full of lucid doubts, are a romance of dread. "Dostoievski, Camus, Kierkegaard, Berdayev —the minds I like—I consider romantic," Allen says. "I guess I equate 'dread' with romance, which is why I'm not invited to more parties." Allen likes to remind reporters that *Annie Hall* (1977) was originally entitled *Anhedonia*—the inability to experience pleasure. Frailty, dilapidation, terror, and disgust poison all "Woody's," pleasures and make regret sensational. "Sex and death," Allen observes as Miles Monroe at the finale of *Sleeper* (1973). "Two things that happen to me only once in my life. Only, after death you're not nauseous."

Allen's conservative self-absorption is typical of his times. Whereas the early clowns took the dead world around them—the classroom, the courtroom, the boring job, the abusive authority figure—and gave it life, Allen's specialty is taking life and giving it a sense of death. Of *Love and Death* (1976), he commented: ". . . a comedy about death and one's existence in a godless universe. The commercial possibilities were immediately apparent to me. Sight gags and slapstick sequences about despair and emptiness. Dialogue jokes about anguish and dread. Finality, mortality, human suffering, anxiety. In short the standard ploys of the professional funnyman." Allen's jokes turn death into a commercial proposition. The gags about evading terror are themselves evasions. They raise serious issues but refuse any serious conclusions:

—The key here, I think, is to not think of death as an end but to think of it more as a very effective way to cut down on your expenses.

—I don't believe in an afterlife although I'm bringing a change of underwear.

—I don't want to achieve immortality through my work, I want to achieve it through not dying.

These funny lines have the shape of ideas, but are without insight. What they achieve is a mood of decline.

For the old guard, parody was just part of their comic arsenal;
for Allen, it's his statement about life. Parody is skepticism acted
out. When Groucho sent up the soliloquies in Eugene O'Neill's
Strange Interlude or Bert Lahr's "Song of the Woodsman" skew-
ered the vibrato of Chaliapin, they were mocking pretension. But
Allen uses parody to show off his mastery of styles while trivializing the content:

> BORIS: He must have been *Possessed*.
> FATHER: Well, he was *A Raw Youth*.
> BORIS: *Raw Youth!* He was an *Idiot* . . . I hear he was a *Gambler*.
> FATHER: You know, he could be your *Double*.
> BORIS: Really. How novel.
>
> (*Love and Death*)

Allen's compulsion to parody is the reflection of an imagina-
tion submerged more in art than in life. It signals an absence of
curiosity and of will. The range of Allen's vicariousness is best
dramatized in *Manhattan* (1979), in which his spokesman Ike
Davis lists his reasons for staying alive: "I would say . . . Groucho
Marx . . . Willie Mays. . . . the second movement of the Jupiter
Symphony . . . Louis Armstrong's recording of 'Potatohead
Blues' . . . Swedish movies, naturally . . . *Sentimental Education* by
Flaubert. . . ." Unlike the proletarian funny men of the first half
century, who read little and late (Chaplin learned a new word a
day; Lahr built his vocabulary by doing crossword puzzles), Allen
is the archetypal middle-class culture vulture for whom art is a
false god. "The word 'art' never entered my head," Chaplin
wrote of his early days as a film clown (before it did).

Allen has filled his solitude with reading and movies; his mind
percolates with references and borrowed images. In his brilliant
story "The Kugelmass Episode," the beleaguered Professor
Kugelmass seeks emotional rebirth in some passionate relationship with no strings and finally goes to a magician, who puts him
in a time machine with his favorite work of fiction. ("My God, I'm
doing it with Madame Bovary," Kugelmass exclaims, hardly be-

lieving his luck. "Me who failed freshman English!") Kugelmass not only walks into the book but into everybody else's copy. When they see Madame Bovary, they see him. In his plays and movies, Allen has been doing the same thing: living in his favorite fictions.

This promiscuity with art forms is an affair from which Allen seems fated never to escape. "When I get an idea for a play," he told a biographer, "I think to myself 'What play does this most closely resemble that was successful?' " *Don't Drink the Water* (1966) is built on the premise of George S. Kaufman's *You Can't Take It With You* and the structure of John Patrick's *Teahouse of the August Moon. Play It Again Sam* (1972) amalgamates Bogart pastiche from *Casablanca* structured in imitation of George Axelrod's *The Seven Year Itch* in a story about a writer (as the stage direction reads) *"who daydreams of someday doing something important in either literature or film." God* (1975) is Allen's *Waiting for Godot*, except that God appears, strangled, toward the finale. Allen parodies great films in his attempt to be a significant filmmaker; as a result, his films end up being as much about film as life. *A Midsummer Night's Sex Comedy* (1982) is his vain attempt to marry Bergman's *Smiles of a Summer Night* with the farce in Renoir's *Rules of the Game; Stardust Memories* attempts Fellini's self-probing in *8½; Interiors* (1978) is Allen being Bergman via Chekhov's *The Three Sisters; Love and Death*, his parody of Russian literature, combines Bergman's *The Seventh Seal* with pastiches of Eisenstein and Chaplin. In all these films, Allen uses the camera as Kugelmass uses the time machine—to get himself into the classics. *Zelig* (1983) is the acme of this ambition, a cinematic conjuring trick that allows Allen to put himself among the fantasy figures of his past and present. Zelig's protean personality is parody incarnate. He can't help becoming like the people he's around. Susan Sontag, Bruno Bettelheim, Saul Bellow, Irving Howe, John Morton Blum are interviewed in this mock documentary as they discuss Zelig's trickster persona. By this sleight of hand, Allen brings the real world into his fantasy and alters the past to include him. Leonard Zelig (played by Allen) is seen with Babe Ruth, Chaplin, Hitler. Allen has nothing to say about them but the extended joke gives his penchant for parody not only a new look but the patina of intellectual respectability. Zelig, Allen endlessly repeats, is just looking for love. Allen's admission is a way of dodging the issue.

The problem with parody is that it takes its energy from other sources. This works fine for Allen in his early films, where he wants a plot on which to hang his jokes. But in his "serious" films, parody shows up his deficiencies. Allen doesn't have within himself the emotional resources to re-create in his own terms the narrative ideas and styles he admires. Allen, who as Alvy Singer in *Annie Hall* admits, doesn't "respond well to mellow," has no instinct for the holiday humor of Renoir or Bergman's lusty version of the pastoral. Small wonder, then, that *A Midsummer Night's Sex Comedy* should seem so anemic and strained. Similarly, *Sleeper*'s botched attempt at sci-fi slapstick only shows off the absence of poetry in Allen's clumsy body. Allen has no gift as a mimic—he doesn't observe individuals as carefully as ideas. "I don't get an enormous input from the rest of the world," he has said. "I wish I could, but I can't." His early films, as Vincent Canby said of *Take the Money and Run* (1969), are "visual monologues" that play fast and loose with his standoffish wit. "I gave Diane [Keaton] a certain amount of character in *Sleeper,* but it was an afterthought," Allen says. In *Annie Hall* and *Manhattan,* he partially succeeded in giving character to his leading ladies, but these characters were based largely on his relationship with Diane Keaton, who played them. Allen's inability to write from the inside of other people's predicaments reaches its apex in *Interiors,* which would have been more aptly titled *Exteriors.* This deadpan chronicle of a wife's vain attempt to win back her husband, and the impact of her anguish on her three daughters, attempts the profounder ironies of a philosophical overview. But mistaking gravity for seriousness, Allen weighs his stick-figure characters down with meanings.

"We love your work . . . especially the early funny ones," two movie buffs say to Sandy Bates, a cult director of film comedy, in *Stardust Memories.* Although Allen tries to disarm criticism by anticipating it, there's no doubt that his early work has an unpretentious, fresh, vulgar directness that makes those movies—

What's Up Tiger Lily? (1967), *Take the Money and Run, Bananas* (1971), *Everything You Always Wanted To Know About Sex* (1972)— often wildly hilarious and genuine. As joke films, they play to Allen's strength in surreal absurdities, using the wisecrack to swat away many of the harassing stupidities of American life. *Take the Money and Run* also spoofs cinéma vérité; *What's Up Tiger Lily?* adds Allen's subtitles to a Japanese send-up of Bond thrillers, and *Everything You Always Wanted To Know About Sex* manages an Antonioni parody. But these films have no pretension to depth. They go for laughs, and they get them. By Allen's own admission, these films are crude. Allen isn't particularly interested in where he puts the camera. In his subsequent collaboration with the photographer Gordon Willis, he has ensured that the later films are stylish; but whether the look is Bergman or Renoir or Fellini, the borrowed style is not organic to the material. Where the early clowns struggled to find a theatrical language that allowed them to be uniquely themselves on stage and screen, Allen in his art films is busy trying to be somebody else.

"Comedy is harder to do than serious stuff," Allen used to say; but now his tune has changed. "Comedy is impossible if you can't do it, but it's no big deal if you can." Allen wants to replay his melancholy and call it seriousness. "There's not any substance to the comedy," insists Ike Davis, quitting his TV screenwriting job in *Manhattan.* And in *Stardust Memories,* Sandy Bates, like Allen a voluptuary of decline, bleats: "I don't want to make funny movies anymore. They can't force me to . . . I don't feel funny. I look around the world and all I see is human suffering." Allen believes himself lost, he is lost, and he adds to the society's idea of being lost.

In his prose, Allen thankfully is not worried about wisdom; he gives up the pose of rabbi and adopts the role of trickster. In the story "Fabrizio's: Criticism and Response," Allen shows up the uses and abuses of education and dramatizes in three pages what *Manhattan* in an hour and a half never quite clinches, that education doesn't lead to understanding or wisdom. Using as a premise a debate about an Italian restaurant carried out in the style of the letters column of the *New York Review of Books,* Allen's cunning wit has a field day, with no abstractions and no apologies for his high spirits. Fabian Plotkin discusses the social implications of the chef's antipasto: "Was Spinelli trying to say that all life was represented here in his antipasto, with the black olives an unbearable reminder of mortality? If so where was the celery?" Plotkin has a hilarious line in lit-crit name dropping. "As Hannah Arendt told me once," he concludes, the restaurant's prices are "reasonable without being historically inevitable." Even the metaphysical shellac Allen applies to his screenplays has a more appealing, modest shine when he moves from the sound stage to the page. In "Mr. Big," his parody of hard-bitten detective fiction, Kaiser Lupowitz, a Sam Spade type, gets an assignment to find God from a Vassar philosophy student who turns out to be His killer. "When the Supreme Being gets knocked off," Lupowitz tells her, about to turn her in, "somebody's got to take the rap." The girl replies: "Oh, Kaiser, we could go away together. Just the two of us. We could forget about philosophy. Settle down and maybe get into semantics."

Allen cannot rest on his substantial achievements as a comic writer. As he tries to force his comedy to carry more weight than it can hold, his real concerns become postures. The pose of the characters in his art films is that they are searching for meaning in a godless, decadent world. In *Love and Death*, Allen dances with Death. In *Annie Hall*, the very first speech announces: "Well, that's how I feel about life. Full of loneliness and misery and suffering and unhappiness and it's all over too quickly." Alvy Singer gives two books to Annie as clues to his character: *Death and Western Thought* and *Denial of Death*. Angst can be boned up; and Allen, like his characters, has learned it well. "Maturity has borne out my childhood," he says. "I'd always thought death was the sole driving force: I mean that our effort to avoid it is the only thing that gives impetus to our existence." Wonder has been replaced by worry; and instead of letting laughter renew life, Allen is in danger of scaring his comedy to death. In *Stardust Memories*, Sandy Bates revels in disintegration. "Hey," he asks his entourage of lawyer, press agent, and doctor, "did-did anybody read on the front page of the *Times* that matter is decaying? Am

I the only one that saw that? The universe is gradually breaking down. There's not gonna be anything left . . . I'm not talking about my stupid little films here. I'm— Uh, eventually there's not gonna be any, any Beethoven or Shakespeare." Bates, who worries that his career is nothing more than a lifelong affair with his own image, flatters himself that such insights show his connection to the world.

Such confessions are a form of hiding, a means of exempting Allen and his characters from action. "Should I change my-my movie? Should I change my life?" whines Sandy Bates. But change requires sacrifice; and none of Allen's egotists is willing to risk that. "He saw reality too clearly," says Bates's analyst in a fantasy sequence of his film retrospective. "Faulty denial mechanism." In fact, Bates sees no reality at all: he merely chews the cud of his own emptiness. Bates, like Allen and all his comic spokesmen, suborns himself and others to his self-absorption. Far from wanting to shed despair, Allen and his comic surrogates relish it, savor it, wrap themselves in it, because the lacerations rationalize their sensational selfishness. Inevitably, they *must* find no meaning. They have given up everything that imparts meaning, unwilling to commit themselves to relationships, to children, to life outside their immediate work, to a community larger than their own charmed circle. Isolated variously by work, fame, money, and self-consciousness, Allen's comic spokesmen see people more as a threat than as a promise of salvation. *"The mass of people looks slightly off-kilter, almost carnivorous in their need to see and touch Sandy,"* reads a stage direction for *Stardust Memories*. The implication of this attitude as dramatized in *Stardust Memories* and epitomized in Allen's self-absorption is that other people are not worth caring about. His showy vulnerability hides the pride of his despair. He pretends to be concerned about the world; but he is temperamentally unwilling to do anything about it.

It's hard not to be fond of someone who can write a throwaway line in *Manhattan* like "I . . . uh, I finally had an orgasm but my doctor told me it was the wrong kind." As a social reporter and cosmic kvetcher ("If God is testing us, why doesn't He give us a written?"), Allen is terrific. He can juggle adroitly with the academic jargon of the day (the philosopher-monster Sandor Needleman in "Remembering Needleman" is the author of *Styles of Modes* and *Non-Existence: What To Do When It Suddenly Strikes You*). But when he gives up the wisecrack for the role of wise man, Allen runs into trouble. His art films dramatize his separation from life and make this alienation seem like maturity. Allen is an entrepreneur of his alienation; his success at exploiting his wound makes it impossible for him to heal it. Suffering itself becomes a posture. "Mr. Allen's one regret," reads the potted biography in his recent collection, *Side Effects*, "is that he is not someone else." If he were, films as badly written and uncompromising as *Interiors*, and as downright banal as *A Midsummer Night's Sex Comedy*, would never have been made.

8

The Beatles

John Lennon was shot on December 8, 1980, finally laying to rest the dream that the Beatles would rise again. Lennon's murder guaranteed the legend of the Beatles. History is kind to those who do not die in their beds. And the massive mourning surrounding Lennon's death confirmed the opinions of those who saw the Beatles not only as singers but as symbols. A generation that had come of age to their music now mourned not only a hero but a lost hope.

In 1963, when the Beatles emerged from Liverpool onto the national scene, England was in radical transition. The society was changing from being top dog to becoming America's poodle, from thirteen years of Conservative rule to a Labour government. It was the era of the miniskirt and the Twist, when the English were beginning to move to new rhythms and to adopt new styles. "I saw no reason why childhood shouldn't last forever," the fashion designer Mary Quant said. "I wanted everyone to retain the grace of a child and not to have to become stilted, confined, ugly beings. So I created clothes that worked and moved and allowed people to run, to jump, to leap, to retain their precious freedom." The Beatles, those "lads" who mixed Cardin chic with

Liverpool cheek, embodied the daydream of abundance and eternal youthfulness. Their success was as exciting as their songs. By
late 1963, even if Britannia no longer ruled the waves, the Beatles
dominated the airwaves. They were at the center of the new-boy
network of renegade energy and classless achievement. The Beatles' songs and their public high jinks gave British life the backbeat of promise.

The Beatles coincided with the renaissance in English theatre,
and they learned to "make show." The phrase "*Macht* show,
Beatles! *Macht* show!" was screamed at them by the owner of the
Hamburg club where in 1961 they were losing listeners and business to the livelier bands along the Reeperbahn. Stomping,
gyrating, shouting "Nazi!" and "*Sieg Heil!*" at the customers, the
Beatles soon figured out that a little stage anarchy went a long
way at the box office. Having named themselves in homage to
Buddy Holly and the Crickets, the Beatles also aped, in their
stage carry-on, the frenzy of Gene Vincent, Little Richard, Jerry
Lee Lewis, Elvis, and the other American rock 'n' rollers whose
pulverizing energy they loved. "We had cooked up this whole
new British thing," Paul McCartney later recollected of the Hamburg days, when they were an amalgam of American sound and
European fashion. "We had a long time to work it out and make
all the mistakes in Hamburg with almost no one watching. . . . A
lot of things had been happening with our chemistry. . . . We'd
put in a lot of work. In Hamburg we'd work eight hours a day
while most bands never worked that hard."

By 1962, the stomping and the "Beatle" hairstyle they'd carried back from Germany (it gave them the look of cuddly Teddy
Boys) had turned them from a rock-and-dole group into the most
popular scouse (that is, Liverpudlian) band. Playing lunchtime
and evening gigs, the Beatles packed the Cavern, a subterranean
rock-'n'-roll club that tapped the army of adolescents who wanted
to get high on music instead of on draft Guinness. The Cavern,
which became the Mecca of the Mersey sound after the Beatles
vaulted to superstardom, offered a venue for the proliferating
number of local bands. Rock 'n' roll, like the American kid acts
in the early part of this century, put a premium on energy, not

expertise; and places like the Cavern were a new kind of vaudeville. As with the vaudeville of yesteryear, the ill-educated, the outcasts, renegades, and dropouts with an ambition to shine but no credentials for conventional success were attracted to it. They could act out their daydreams of vindictive triumph and get paid for it. "I was always different," Lennon recalled in Jann Wenner's *Lennon Remembers: The Rolling Stone Interviews,* voicing the infantile longing behind every star's obsession. "Why didn't anybody notice me?"

Lennon especially was noticed by Brian Epstein, the twenty-seven-year-old businessman turned impresario, who had an eye for the boys as well as business. A failed actor who had trained at the Royal Academy of Dramatic Art, Epstein encouraged their offstage theatricality while he coaxed them out of smoking, swearing, and eating onstage. "We were very popular, not being goody-goodies," Lennon recalled of their success with the tough Liverpool kids. But once Epstein had finally gotten them a record contract (he purchased 10,000 copies of the debut single "Love Me Do" to ensure the Beatles made the Top 20), the act was tarted up for the mass audience. The image of stomping tearaways was tossed out with their Hamburg leathers; the Beatles now only shook their forelocks. They were "lovable mopheads" and "happy little rockers." While other English groups like the Rolling Stones and The Who followed the hot, horny message of rock 'n' roll and sold the posture of the aesthetic outlaw, the Beatles were spectacularly ordinary. They presented themselves as decent English blokes at heart. When they asked for love in their early hit songs, they said please. "Oh, please say to me and let me be your man," they pleaded, wanting only to hold hands. Their songs were more about camaraderie than conquest. "Please please me," they sang, just as they had politely bleated on their first record, "So, ple-e-e-ease, love me do."

Before the Beatles, rock-'n'-roll stars were faces and voices. The Beatles changed that. They took rock 'n' roll off the entertainment pages and put it in the headlines. "We turned everything into events," Lennon said of the group's genius for making a spectacle of itself. Between October and December 1963, the Beatles, by then boasting a fantastic list of hits including "Please Please Me," "Ask Me Why," "From Me to You," "She Loves You," were on the front page of at least one major English paper every day. Their music was fresh and fun, but hardly extraordinary. There were Lennon-McCartney songs (like "One After 909") that only showed them to be slick hit-makers who could sometimes write as shoddily as the next man:

> Move over once, move over twice
> Hey baby, don't be cold as ice.

The Beatles succeeded and survived because they were theatre. They turned a press conference into a cabaret and treated the reporters like the Hamburg audiences for whom they made show. Their ad-libs had the wit and vivacity of comic crosstalk:

RINGO: A guy at Decca turned us down.
PAUL: He must be kicking himself now.
JOHN: I 'ope he kicks himself to death.

They were not a faceless group of musicians with a new sound, but a collection of affectionate, endearing individuals whose personalities were increasingly acted out in their music. The drummer, Ringo Starr, who could barely read or write, was steady, uninspired, constant, good-humored. The lead guitarist, George Harrison, the youngest of the group, was intense and introverted. The handsome Paul McCartney, who wrote with John Lennon the songs he sang and actually had some academic and musical training, was flashy, romantic, and professionally charming. Lennon, the founder in 1957 of the Quarry Men, the skiffle band that evolved into the Beatles, was the hard man, the loner, the prankster who best embodied rock 'n' roll's rogue energy. Together, the group's humanity and high spirits were infectious. As the Beatles became more sophisticated and musically ambitious, they seized on the drama of their differences and built it into their music. Increasingly isolated by their fame, the Beatles drew finally on their past and their future as their main musical subjects. *Sgt. Pepper's Lonely Hearts Club Band* (1967), *Magical Mystery Tour* (1967), *Abbey Road*, side 2 (1969)—among their finest musical achievements—mythologize both their personalities and their problems in song. These records, after they'd stopped touring in 1966, are vaudevilles on disc—a collection of astonishments and virtuoso turns that carried messages from their own well-publicized lives to their public. *Abbey Road*, their last recording session before the group broke up over musical and business differences, turns even that disintegration into a spectacular show. Harrison's "Here Comes the Sun" holds out the promise of hope and harmony:

> Here comes the sun
> And I say, "It's all right."

The hint of harmony is picked up by McCartney's lullaby "Golden Slumbers" and turned into a bitter nightmare. "Boy," they sing of their Beatles fame,

> . . . you're gonna carry that weight
> Carry that weight a long time.

In "The End," the Lennon-McCartney partnership, recalling their rock-'n'-roll beginnings, shouts:

> Oh, yeah, ALL RIGHT
> Are you gonna be in my dreams tonight?

But instead of the usual Beatles backing, the musicians erupt into an instrumental battle, with Ringo performing his first drum solo. "The separation of the four instruments," writes Milton Okun about the instrumentation in the behemoth, two-volume *The Compleat Beatles*, which contains the arrangements of more than two hundred of their nearly three hundred songs, "can be understood as a musical separation of the group themselves." There is no musical irony in the Beatles' poignant farewell:

And in the end
The love you take
Is equal to the love you make.

They play the clown up to the very end, and the record's coda
lightly sidesteps the sadness of their curtain call to cock a snook
at royalty. "Her Majesty's a pretty nice girl," sings Paul, ending
with a throwaway laugh, not a lament. "But she doesn't have a
lot to say." The Beatles' end takes them back to their beginning.

At a Royal Command Performance given in aid of charity in
December 1963, English television viewers got their first prime-
time look at the Beatles. They saw John Lennon lean away from
his microphone and say: "Those in the cheap seats clap your
hands." Then, glancing up at the Royal Box, where the Queen
Mother and her entourage sat, he added: "The rest of you just
rattle your jewelry." The rehearsed quip made headlines. The
Royal Family and the general public were at once startled and
titillated by this brashness, the unfamiliar voice of the havenots
publicly tweaking the noblesse. The style was familiar in the
English market stall, but not on the stage. "Taste can be vulgar,
but it must never be embarrassing," lectured Noël Coward, the
king of English boulevard entertainment, after the incident. Now
the mood of England was brazen and bumptious, and taste could
be offensive as long as it had style. The Beatles had plenty of that;
and, at least at the beginning, it was earthy, funny, frank, spon-
taneous, egalitarian. Their films—*A Hard Day's Night* and *Help!*—
capitalized on their antic spirit and the public's love of seeing the
"lads" get away with everything.

Everything was exactly what they got. In 1965, the Beatles
were given the prestigious Member of the British Empire (MBE)
award—and the public thrilled at the false rumor that John had
smoked a reefer in Buckingham Palace. Their biographies were
in the *Encyclopaedia Britannica.* Even Harrods bowed to their
whims and extended a courtesy previously offered only to the
Royal Family: the emporium was opened after hours so the Beatles could shop. By 1968 the Beatles were having their latest

single, *Hey Jude,* sent in special gift boxes to the Queen, the Queen Mother, and the Prime Minister.

It was a Labour government that honored the Beatles, and Prime Minister Harold Wilson (the Beatles insisted on calling him Mr. Dobson) was quick to exploit his acquaintance with them. But he was not the only world leader who scrambled to wrap himself in the Beatles' aura. The power of song to unite the body politic in wartime had always been conceded; now the political implications of song in peacetime were suddenly and dramatically apparent with "Beatlemania." Their music and their phenomenon promoted social contentment on a massive scale.

"Songs," Plato wrote in *Laws,* "are spells for souls directed in all earnest to the production of . . . concord." "Beatlemania" was a misnomer. Beatle fans were not so much hysterical as spellbound. The Beatles' music was a form of sympathetic magic, and the Beatles were local divinities who could change the mood and the look of their times by a song, a style, a word. "We're more popular than Jesus," Lennon wisecracked; but at first the Beatles didn't understand either their healing power or their shamanistic role. "It seemed that we were just surrounded by cripples and blind people all the time," Lennon recalled. "And when we would go through the corridors, they would be touching us."

Lennon said of the public's credulity: "They gave us the freedom." In *Magical Mystery Tour,* the Beatles teased the power of their spell by dressing up as wizards with wands:

> The Magical Mystery Tour is waiting to take you away
> (Waiting to take you away) . . .

Their music exuded confidence in its enchantment. "Changing a lifestyle and the appearance of youth didn't just happen," Lennon told the *National Observer* in 1973. "We set out to do it." Song was no longer seen just as entertainment but as a force for social change. As the Beatles' power to shape consciousness became more apparent to them, their songs spoke more directly to their times. "We started putting out messages," Lennon explained. The Beatles both molded their era and were a reflection of it. The messages were compelling and simple. "Love, love, love," they sang on a TV special, "Our World," that was beamed instantaneously by satellite to 150 million people waiting for their words, "All you need is love." A whole generation of radical rebellion and protest was played out behind Lennon's slogan: "Give Peace a Chance." ("We don't have a leader," Pete Seeger said during the 1969 March on Washington, "but we have a song.") The Beatles were agents of optimism; their music didn't fan the flames of discontent, but cooled them in the name of peace. "Don't you know it's gonna be alright, alright, alright," they sang at the height of the 1960s disruption in "Revolution," a Lennon number that scolded:

> But if you want money for people with minds that hate
> All I can tell you is brother you have to wait. . . .

Despite the Vietnam War and massive urban unrest, life was celebrated as getting "better, better, better . . . all the time."

"We got our ideas off the street," Lennon said, at a time when the street ruled. The Beatles took the anxieties and aesthetics of the day and transformed them into an ecstatic experience. In search of their musical and personal identities, they flirted with mysticism and drugs, those symbolic rebirths that typified the era's desperate retreat from a death-dealing society. The Beatles caught the numbness behind the age's reckless bravado—"She said I know what it's like to be dead"; "I read the news today, oh boy"—and also the idealism behind its relentless role-playing. These dropouts–turned rockers–turned movie stars–turned poet-priests–turned business tycoons celebrated the myth of transformation that the "changes" in their own lives reflected:

> There's nothing you can do that can't be done . . .
> Nothing you can make that can't be made
> No one you can save that can't be saved
> Nothing you can do, but you can learn how to be you
> in time . . .

"We were descendants of rock 'n' roll," Lennon explained, after the group had strayed far from its origins and discovered its own musical identity. "We sort of intellectualized it for white folks." The generation's search for new imagery was successfully evoked in the visual and aural innovations of their masterful album *Sgt. Pepper's Lonely Hearts Club Band*. The record cover's Pop Art collage, with the Beatles in the foreground surrounded by scores of their intellectual and personal influences, broadcast the era's eclecticism, which had its musical correlative in the new Beatles pastiche. *Sgt. Pepper* was a majestic record in which the Beatles broke out into a whole new realm of musical sophistication. It consolidated the experiments made in earlier records: the sound effects of "Yellow Submarine"; the surreal juxtaposition of words to create vivid new images in "Strawberry Fields" ("Living is easy with eyes closed/Misunderstanding all you see"). *Sgt. Pepper* was a gallimaufry of new and nostalgic sounds: Indian sitar and tabla, military bands, George Formby music-hall backing, electronic crescendo, to which were added barking dogs, canned applause, cock crows, a fox hunt. The songs ranged as widely as the sounds, turning the album into an expression of contemporary consciousness: working-class English life in "Lovely Rita" and in "When I'm 64," which conveys even the syntax of the shabby genteel world it describes; the ever-widening generation gap in "She's Leaving Home"; the inward-turning mysticism in "Within You Without You"; an acid trip in "Lucy in the Sky with Diamonds." In their acid vision, language is used as a collage of found objects to make surreal images: "a girl with kaleidoscope eyes," "newspaper taxis," "rocking-horse people." Although this poetic self-consciousness has not worn well with time, their effortless evocation of the small dramas of daily life remains poetic:

> Woke up, fell out of bed
> Dragged a comb across my head . . .

Even the great finale of the *Sgt. Pepper* album, "A Day in the Life," is a collage of two different songs with two opposing moods, which creates at once the sense of escape and the sense of terror that dominated the time.

The Beatles' musical flowering reflected the experiments and

the innocence of their age; and their breakup in 1970 foreshad-
owed the coming disenchantment. "Nothing happened except
that we all dressed up," Lennon said later in his self-imposed
American exile. "The same bastards are in control. The same
people are runnin' everything, it's exactly the same. They hyped
the kids and the generation." In their naiveté, the Beatles had
only reinforced the system they fondly thought they were changing. (Even their company, Apple Records, was conceived, they
said, as a form of "Western Communism.") But fame makes the
myths of capitalism glorious, and the stars are the performing
workhorses of free enterprise, who are trotted out to prove that
the system works. The Beatles scorned the bourgeoisie, only to
find they were the new hipoisie. In Lennon's apt and angry
words, the Beatles were "fab, fat myths."

"It was awful being on the front page of everyone's life, every
day," George Harrison says in his modest but elegant catalogue
of songs and Beatle memories, *I Me Mine.* As the ironic title taken
from one of his songs suggests, Harrison has followed the path
of Eastern mysticism toward nonattachment, a route somewhat
belied by the book and his baronial Oxfordshire estate from
which he "watches the river flow." McCartney, the most conservative of the group, has followed fame's line of least resistance
and become still more rich and famous with his second band,
Wings. Ringo good-naturedly wanders the world as actor/
singer/drummer, following no particular path. And until Lennon
was murdered by a fan, his path had been the most tortuous and
musically the most rewarding. He spent much of the 1970s trying
to disenchant the public—in songs like "God"—of its appetite for
magical solutions. "The Beatles is another myth," he said. But so
far, the Beatles myth has proved stronger than the men who
made it. As soloists, none of the former Beatles has attained the
impact or the excellence of the group. The genesis of that music
and the real lives of the group remain shrouded by the ill-written
hagiography about them. The books gloss the orgies and the
outrageousness. "Fuckin' big bastards, that's what the Beatles
were," John Lennon said in *Lennon Remembers,* the only book that
rings true about the monstrous greed that fame engenders in the

most modest heart. "You have to be a big bastard to make it."
Even when the ugliness of Lennon's own megalomania is frankly
exhibited in *Lennon Remembers*, the Beatles legend keeps its bru-
tality from being seen for what it is. "They can't feel," Lennon
said, speaking for the public and spouting the blinkered romantic
notion of the superiority of the artist. "I'm the one that's feeling
because I'm the one expressing. They live vicariously through me
and other artists, and we are the ones. . . ."

Listening to the Beatles' records again from the long corridor of
middle age, the spell is gone. The songs are still delightful, but
the thrill surrounding them has vanished as imperceptibly as
youth itself. Each lyric conjures automatically the Beatles sound.
Each sound recalls the definitive phrasing the Beatles gave to
their words. Their three-minute epiphanies were, for many, how
time was measured and history recalled in the 1960s. Were the
Beatles the Schuberts and Bachs of contemporary music? Such
lavish comparisons were made, but they hardly seem to matter.
Then, as now, the songs renovated life with their articulate energy. Familiarity has robbed the music of its astonishment, but
the songs still have the power to tap ancient longings. "Once
there was a way to get back homewards," Paul's sweet voice
intones, with a sense of loss that hits hard in adulthood. The
sound of a hard-driving Beatles song, heard as you are inspecting
the crows' feet and the other crenulations of age in the bathroom
mirror, can get you moving, mouthing the magic of an earlier
time to banish the fear of death. "Yeah, Yeah, Yeah." Once again,
the old and good times roll. The Beatles' music makes joy; and
that joy, once felt, is never easily forgotten.

9

Joe Orton

All classes are criminal today. We live in
an age of equality.

Funeral Games

Like all great satirists, Joe Orton was a realist. He was prepared
to speak the unspeakable; and this gave his plays their joy and
danger. He teased an audience with its sense of the sacred, flaunt-
ing the hard facts of life people contrived to forget. For Orton,
there were no "basic human values." Man was capable of every
bestiality; and all moral credos were heroic daydreams, the luxury of affluence. Orton's inspired megalomaniacs depict life as a
vicious and hilarious evasion of man's death and death-dealing.

With *Loot* and *What the Butler Saw,* Orton became the master
farceur of his age. His laughter was etched in the despair, isolation, and violence of modern life and offered instead of stasis the
more apt metaphor of frantic activity. Farce allowed Orton to
make a spectacle of disintegration. He showed man dummying
up a destiny in a meaningless world by making panic look like
reason. "In a world run by fools," Orton wrote, taunting the
readers of the *Radio Times* about his first play, *The Ruffian on the
Stair* (1963),

the writer can only chronicle the doings of fools or their victims.
And because the world is a cruel and heartless place, he will be

accused of not taking his subject seriously. . . . But laughter is a serious business, and comedy a weapon more dangerous than tragedy. Which is why tyrants treat it with caution. The actual material of tragedy is equally viable in comedy—unless you happen to be writing in English, when the question of taste occurs. The English are the most tasteless nation on earth, which is why they set such store by it.

Orton was a connoisseur of chaos, the first contemporary playwright to transform the clown's rambunctious instincts from the stage to the page. Like all pranksters, Orton was an enemy of order who adopted many protean disguises for his anarchic fun, including the *noms de plume* of Edna Welthorpe (Mrs.), with which he fanned the scandal of his plays by condemning them in the press, and Donald H. Hartley, which he used to praise himself. Orton also had a prankster's instinct for phallic mischief. "I'm to be at King's Cross station at eleven. I'm meeting a man in the toilet," Mike explains at the beginning of the the revised version of *The Ruffian on the Stair* (1967). Joyce replies: "You always go to such interesting places." Orton's plays put sexuality back on stage in all its exuberant, amoral, and ruthless excess. He laughed away sexual categories. "I'm a heterosexual," protests the psychiatrist, Dr. Prentice, in *What the Butler Saw.* Dr. Rance counters: "I wish you wouldn't use these Chaucerian words." A penis ("the missing parts of Sir Winston Churchill") is held aloft in the penultimate image of *What the Butler Saw,* an archetypal comic symbol of Orton's life and his art. Orton's plays goosed his public. "Sex," he noted in his diary, reminding himself to "hot-up" *What the Butler Saw* in the rewrite, "is the only way to infuriate them. Much more fucking and they'll be screaming hysterics in next to no time."

Orton's plays are a flamboyant dance with the death he found in life. He liked being "the fly on the wall" who registered the idiom, the lives, and the longings in his many anonymous subterranean encounters. Hunger and how it disguises its craving was what amused him. His sexual adventuring taught him to suspect every show of normality: "After walking for a long while I found a gent's lavatory on a patch of grass near a church," Orton wrote in his diary about a walk in Brighton while visiting his producer, Oscar Lewenstein.

> I went in. It was v. dark. There was a man in there. Tall, grand, and smiling. In the gloom he looked aristocratic. When the lights were turned on (after about five minutes) I could see that he was stupid, smiling and bank-clerkish. He showed his cock. I let him feel mine. "Oo!", he gasped, not noticing the sinister sore that had developed on the end over the last week or so, "Oo!". I asked if he had anywhere to go back to? "No," he said, "I don't have the choice of my neighbours, you see. They're down on me and I couldn't take the risk." He nodded to a dwarf skulking in the corner of the lavatory. "He'll suck you off, though. I've seen him do it." He made a motion to the dwarfish creature, rather as someone would call a taxi. The dwarf sucked me off while the other man smiled benevolently and then, I suppose, went back to his neighbours refreshed . . .

"I'm an acquired taste," Orton explained in 1967.

> That's a double entendre if there ever was one. Oh, the public will accept me. They've given me a license, you see. What they'll do is say "Joe Orton can do these things" if I'm a success. But I'm a success because I've taken a hatchet to them and hacked my way in. I mean it wasn't easy. *Sloane* wasn't easy. It wasn't the enormous success that people seem to think. . . . It's always a fight for an original writer because any original writer will always force the world to see the world his way. The people who don't want to see the world your way will always be angry.

Long before Orton found his comic voice, he was dreaming of conquest. In *The Vision of Gombold Proval* (1961), a novel published posthumously as *Head to Toe* (1971), Orton set down a battle plan carried out by his plays:

> To be destructive, words must be irrefutable. . . . Print was less effective than the spoken word because the blast was greater; eyes could ignore, slide past, dangerous verbs and nouns. But if you could lock the enemy into a room somewhere, and fire the sentence at them, you would get a sort of seismic disturbance . . .

Orton's comic salvos were devastating. "It's Life that defeats the Christian Church. She's always been well-equipped to deal with Death." (*The Erpingham Camp*) "God is a gentleman. He prefers blondes." (*Loot*) "Marriage excuses no one the freaks' roll-call." (*What the Butler Saw*) "Being a man of good will I'm well prepared for violence." (*Funeral Games*) Orton always wanted to shine. He polished the wit of his plays with the same delighted concentration that he rubbed baby lotion on his face to make it gleam. The result, in both cases, was dazzling.

Style is an expression of body as well as spirit. Orton built up his mind and body from its skimpy, undernourished Leicester boyhood to an appealing and lethal maturity. "The style isn't superimposed. It's me," he explained in the Royal Court program for *Crimes of Passion* (1967).

> You can't write stylised comedy in inverted commas, because the style must ring of the man. If you think in a certain way and you write true to yourself, which I hope I am, then you will get a style, a style will come out. You've only got to be sitting on a bus and you'll hear the most stylised lines. People think I write fantasy, but I don't; some things may be exaggerated or distorted in the same way that painters distort and alter things, but they're realistic figures. They're perfectly recognisable. I don't like the discrimination against style that some people have. Every serious writer has a style. I mean, Arnold Wesker has a style, but people don't normally think of him as a stylist, in the same way they think of Wilde, Firbank or Sheridan. Style isn't camp or chi-chi. I write in a certain way because I can express things that I couldn't express in naturalistic terms. In the whole naturalistic movement of the 20s and 30s you can't ultimately do anything except discuss teacup things, you know—Mavis' new hat. In a naturalistic style I couldn't make any comment on the kind of policeman Truscott is, or on the laws of the Establishment. Oscar Wilde's style is much more earthy and colloquial than most people notice. When we look at Lady Bracknell, she's the most ordinary, common, direct woman. She's not an affected woman at all. People are taken in by the "glittering style." It's not glitter. It's just that the author can express things more by style. Sheridan is the same. *The Rivals.* If you read *The Rivals*, it's most real.

Congreve too. It's a slice of life. It's written very brilliantly but it's perfectly believable. There's nothing incredible about it.

Dubbed by the *Observer* "the Oscar Wilde of Welfare State gentility," Orton did something special with the English language. His dialogue was a collage of the popular culture. He assimilated advertising jargon, the shrill overstatement of tabloid journalism, the stilted lusciousness of B-movies and fused them into his own illuminating, epigrammatic style. "I think you should use the language of your age, and use every bit of it, not just a little bit," Orton told the BBC in 1964. "They always go on about poetic drama and they think that you have to sort of go into some high-flown fantasy, but it isn't poetic drama, it's everything, it's the language in use at the time. I have to be very careful in the way that I write, not to let it become sort of a mannerism, it could very easily become a mannerism." Orton's dialogue forged a poetry from words debased and thrown away by the culture. Orton added his own brand of irony to the colloquial. "My uterine contractions have been bogus for some time." The pitch and roll of Mrs. Prentice's declaration in *What the Butler Saw* has all the playful strut and surprise that Orton loved in language. In his diary he noted:

> I read Genet's *Querelle of Brest,* an interesting book, but unformed. A first draft of rough jottings for a masterpiece. Undoubtedly Jean Genet is the most perfect example of an unconscious humorist at work since Marie Corelli. I find a sentence like: "They (the homosexuals of Brest) are peace-loving citizens of irreproachable outward appearance, even though, the long day through, they may perhaps suffer from a rather timid itch for a bit of cock" irresistibly funny. A combination of elegance and crudity is always ridiculous.

"Words," Orton wrote in *Head to Toe,* "were more effective than actions; in the right hands verbs and nouns could create panic." Orton's hero, Gombold, "looked up more books, studied the propagation of idiom and found pages on the penetrative power of faulty grammar." Orton made the same study. From his earliest writing efforts in 1954 up to his breakthrough with *Enter-*

taining Mr. Sloane in 1964, his notebooks show him experimenting with words and analyzing idiom:

> Are both, perhaps
> Which is always
> Remaining a
> Have has what
> Towards the never
> All is what
> Very much what
> I can only say how
> I cannot say where
> Be no
> Except for now

Orton, like Gombold, was looking for a way to "kill" with language. The instinct is built into the comedian's language for success, a language of annihilation where laughter "knocks them dead," "lays them in the aisles," "slaughters them." Orton's laughter aspired to drive an audience crazy with pleasure. Orton offered his audience grotesques which, like the gargoyles of a medieval cathedral, forced the public to imagine Hell and re-define Heaven. He was the pure comic spirit—angry, impish, and articulate. The impact of Orton's distinctive vision in his brief literary career between 1964 and 1967 is seen in the word "Ortonesque," which worked its way into the critical vocabulary as a shorthand for scenes of macabre outrageousness.

The comedian is a marginal man, someone who lives outside the boundaries of conventional life and acquires power (and danger) precisely because he can't be controlled by society. Laughter is the message sent back from his cultivated isolation. Orton was a survivor whose brutal laughter was a vindictive triumph over a drab and quietly violent working class world. About a production meeting with his producers, Oscar Lewenstein and Michael White, to discuss the Broadway cast of *Loot*, Orton wrote:

"You look very pretty in that fur coat you're wearing," Oscar said, as we stood on the corner before going our separate ways. I said, "Peggy [Ramsay] bought it me. It was thirteen pounds nineteen." "Very cheap," Michael White said. "Yes, I've discovered that I look better in cheap clothes." "I wonder what the significance of that is," Oscar said. "I'm from the gutter," I said. "And don't you ever forget it because I won't."

Orton's laughter never forgot his origins. He was born John Kingsley Orton in Leicester on January 1, 1933, the first of four children. His mother, Elsie, was a machinist who, because of failing eyesight in later years, became a charwoman. His father, William, a timid wisp of a man, was a gardener. They were an unaffectionate family. The struggle to scrape together a living left the Orton children isolated from their parents as well as from each other. They lived off the scraps of life and of emotion. "I never thought of myself as ordinary," Orton said. Asthmatic as a child and frequently absent from school, he failed his eleven-plus examination and was sent at great cost by his status-conscious mother to the local Clark's College under the misguided impression that she was paying for a liberal education. She wasn't. The "college" was primarily a secretarial school, where Orton learned Pitman's shorthand and accounting. His teacher remembers that, at fifteen, "he was semi-literate. He couldn't spell. He couldn't string a sentence together. He spoke very badly. He had a lisp."

Orton tried to educate himself. An avid reader, he also listened to classical music and took up amateur dramatics. Theatre, especially, appealed to him. It was a way to get out of a gloomy council house and belong to a community where he could invent possibilities for himself that were depressingly absent from his workaday world. "I was sacked from all the jobs I had between sixteen and eighteen because I was never interested in any of them," he said. "I resented having to go to work in the morning." His adolescent diary recounts the tedium of a work routine whose deadening ethic he would satirize in *The Good and Faithful Servant*.

"Thank God it's Friday again," he wrote on January 14, 1949.

"I wish I belonged to one of the idle rich and didn't have to work."

Theatre and the promise of productions thrilled him. They were an antidote to his stalled life. His fantasy of theatrical success was as desperate and unfounded as the rest of his aspirations. Even before Orton had ever performed in a play (his parts were, to his never-ending annoyance, usually small), he dedicated his life to the stage:

> It's nearly 12 noon. I am writing this on paper at work. I know I am slacking but I don't feel like work. I am longing for dinner time to come because then the time whizzes by and it's soon 6-30. I will work really hard this afternoon and forget the theatre for a while at least. Last night sitting in the empty theatre watching the electricians flashing lights on and off the empty stage waiting for rehearsals to begin, I suddenly knew that my ambition is and has always been to act and act. To be connected with the stage in some way, with the magic of the Theatre and everything it means. I know now I shall always want to act and I can no more sit in an office all my life than fly. I know this sounds sentimentali [sic] and soppy but it is all perfectly true.

Orton got the idea of going to the Royal Academy of Dramatic Art (RADA). He took voice lessons to eliminate his lisp and his prominent Leicester accent. To the amazement of his voice coach, Orton won a place at RADA and a Leicester Council grant. "It was rather extraordinary," he recalled.

> I did a piece from Peter Pan between Captain Hook and Smee. I think I was both at the same time—a schizophrenic act. It was quite alarming. I don't know how I did it. It impressed the judges. I didn't have a very good time at RADA . . . I actually expected to be taught something. It was complete rubbish. I was more enthusiastic and knew more about acting at the beginning of my first term than I did at the end. I had two years there. I completely lost my confidence and my virginity.

A month after Orton left for RADA, he met and moved in with Kenneth Halliwell. They were a strange combination. Halliwell, seven years Orton's senior, had been a classics scholar at the

Wirral Grammar School. He had given up a promising academic
career for what he saw as the greater glory of the Artistic Life.
Orphaned as a teenager, by 1953, when he was twenty-three,
Halliwell was bald, grave, pretentious, and abrasive in his egoism.
Orton provided the zest, beauty, and companionship Halliwell so
painfully lacked. And Halliwell offered his independent means, a
literate dialogue, and the paternal authority that had been absent
from Orton's boyhood. They became lovers, and their relationship lasted their lifetime. Neither of them was happy at RADA
and neither did as well as he'd hoped. After a brief stint at Ipswich
Rep ("What I learned from that was not to write in too much
business with drinks or telephones because it was awfully hard on
the assistant stage manager to fix all those things"), Orton returned to London to live with Halliwell and to write. It had never
been Orton's ambition to write; but Halliwell had written a few
plays before attending RADA and was working on a novel, which
Orton judiciously typed while they were still at acting school.
Writing was Halliwell's dream, and he invited Orton to share it.

Halliwell introduced Orton to the works of Ronald Firbank.
Together, he and Orton made collages, which, in time, would
feed Orton's comic style. Firbank, to Orton, was the master of
English comic prose. "I've read *Black Mischief*," Orton notes in
his diary, "(patchy—Waugh isn't up to Firbank: the source)."
Firbank was a conspicuous influence on the series of unpublish-
able novels that Orton and Halliwell wrote together: *The Silver
Bucket, The Mechanical Womb, The Last Days of Sodom, The Boy Hair-
dresser*. Orton took Firbank's fluting mischievousness and
brought it down to earth:

—Claude's such an extremist, you know. They say that when he
  kissed the Pope's slipper he went on to do considerably
  more. . . .

—His Hellenism once captivated me. But the *Attic* to him means
  nothing now but servants' bedrooms.

—Have you taken up transvestism? I'd no idea our marriage
  teetered on the brink of fashion.

Only the last joke is Orton's *(What the Butler Saw);* the others are from Firbank's only play, *The Princess Zoubaroff.* Orton's humor was more robust and gregarious than Firbank's rarefied fantasies. But he shared Firbank's obsessions and adapted many of Firbank's comic maneuvers to a much more aggressively popular dramatic form.

The Last Days of Sodom (1955) attracted the attention of Faber & Faber. It was a recherché joke, which reversed the current sexual and social norms. Although never published, Orton and Halliwell felt the gates of the literary world squeak open when Charles Monteith of Faber and Richard Brain, then of Hamish Hamilton, asked to meet them. "They hardly ever met other human beings. This was the first time, they told us, they'd met strangers by arrangement," Charles Monteith recalls. "I had a very clear impression at that first meeting that Kenneth was the one that did the writing. Kenneth's talk, his appearance, his age *vis-à-vis* Orton certainly gave the impression that Kenneth was the literary figure. I thought that John was—quite simply—his young, pretty, and rather vivacious boy friend."

Orton and Halliwell lived an isolated life. They wrote in the mornings and read in the afternoons. When the weather was good, they sunbathed. In order to save electricity, they rose at sunrise and went to bed at sunset. When Halliwell's small inheritance ran out, they set about working for six months to save up enough money for half a year of uninterrupted writing. Under Halliwell's guidance, Orton read the classics. "I admire Voltaire, Aristophanes. I read him in prose translations," Orton said. "I like Lucian and the classical writers, and I suppose that's what gives my writing a difference, an old-fashioned classical education! Which I never received, but I gave myself one, reading them all in English, for I have so little Latin and less Greek."

With a few exceptions, Orton wrote independently of Halliwell after 1957. Neither had any success. "I don't know if you have any convictions about the way life is run: its inexorable rules and so on," Halliwell wrote to Charles Monteith after a refusal of his novel *Priapus in the Shrubbery* (1959). "Personally, I am convinced that 'what you lose on the swings, you gain on the roundabouts' and vice versa. So it wouldn't, quite frankly, be in the logic of things for John or I to have much success in any sphere. We live much too comfortably and pleasantly in our peculiar little way."

Their Islington bedsitter was decorated from floor to ceiling with illustrations stolen from library art books. The decoration shrank an already small space. Everyone who visited their austere and tidy flat came away with a sense of its startling claustrophobia. Orton's fictional alter ego, Gombold, imprisoned and lost in a behemoth body, expresses Orton's despair at his literary failure and the oppressive isolation of his life:

> One day Gombold made a paper dart of another poem: it was the kind of writing he had never done before, indeed he was convinced it was of a type no one had ever attempted in any language. After a second or two the dart was returned unopened. His heart sank. There seemed no one here either to appreciate his writing and engineer his escape.

In *Head to Toe*, Gombold prays: ". . . Cleanse my heart, give me the ability to rage correctly." Orton's anger then was more articulate in his pranks than in his writing. Since 1959, Orton had been stealing books from libraries and taking humorous revenge on "all the rubbish that was being published" by altering the bookjackets and blurbs, then replacing the books on the shelves. "The thing that put me in a rage about librarians was that I went to quite a big library in Islington and asked for Gibbon's *Decline and Fall of the Roman Empire*. They told me they hadn't got a copy of it. They could get it for me, but they hadn't one on their shelves. This didn't start it off, but it was symptomatic of the whole thing. I was enraged that there were so many rubbishy novels and rubbishy books." Orton turned the library into his private theatre, planning his mischief and then watching surreptitiously while others perused the books he'd doctored:

> I did things like pasting a picture of a female nude over a book of etiquette, over the picture of the author who, I think, was Lady Lewisham. I did other things, very strange things. There was the business when I got the biography of Sir Bernard Spilsbury and

there was an illustration which said, "The remains discovered in the cellar at number 23 Rosedown Road." I pasted over the illustration, which was a very dreary one of a lot of earth, David's picture of Marat dead in his bath. It was in black and white. I left the original caption underneath so that it really did look like what it said, "The remains discovered in the cellar at number 23 Rosedown Road." The picture of the corpse in the bath had quite an effect on people who opened the book. I used to write false blurbs on the inside of Gollancz books because I discovered that Gollancz books had blank yellow flaps and I used to type false blurbs on the insides. My blurbs were mildly obscene. Even at the trial they said they were only mildly obscene. When I put the plastic covers back over the jackets you couldn't tell that the blurbs weren't printed. I used to stand in corners after I'd smuggled the doctored books back into the library and then watch people read them. It was very funny, very interesting. There was a biography of Sybil Thorndike in which there was a picture of her locked up in a cell as Nurse Edith Cavell. I cut the caption from another picture and pasted it under the picture, so that it read: "During the war I received many strange requests." One of the interesting things at the trial was that the greatest outrage, the one for which I think I was sent to prison, was that I had stuck a monkey's face in the middle of a rose, on the cover of something called *Collins Book of Roses.* It was a very beautiful yellow rose. What I had done was held as the depth of iniquity for which I should probably have been birched. They won't ever do that so they just sent me to prison for six months.

On May 15, 1962, Orton and Halliwell (who assisted him) were charged with malicious damage to 83 books and removing 1,653 plates from library books. Besides earning both men a jail sentence, the prank also brought them public attention. The *Daily Mirror* headlined the story: GORILLA IN THE ROSES. What the magistrate found objectionable was later picked up by *Reader's Digest* as good family fun. Orton was not contrite; but success allowed him to admit in retrospect that "they said something about resentment at being a failed writer at the trial, and they were probably right." Prison changed Orton. It was the first time he'd been separated from Halliwell for any extended period.

"Before, I had been vaguely conscious of something rotten somewhere; prison crystallized this," Orton said. "The old whore
society lifted up her skirts, and the stench was pretty foul. Not
that the actual prison treatment was bad; but it was a revelation
of what really lies under the surface of our industrialized society."
Within a year of his release, the BBC accepted the radio version
of *The Ruffian on the Stair;* and Orton, buoyed by his first acceptance in a decade, began a full-length play, *Entertaining Mr. Sloane.*
"Being in the nick [prison] brought detachment to my writing. I
wasn't involved any more and it suddenly worked." His writing
took on a playful antic quality of a man who, now a "criminal,"
had nothing to lose from society.

When *Entertaining Mr. Sloane* opened at the New Arts Theatre in
May 1964, it was clear that Orton's voice was an exciting and
unusual one. Sir Terence Rattigan, responding to the play's language and its careful construction, proclaimed it "the best first
play" he'd seen in "thirty odd years." It would be performed all
over the world, made into a film and a television play. According
to *The Times,* "*Entertaining Mr. Sloane* made more blood boil than
any other British play in the last ten years." Orton had launched
himself in the style of his laughter—with a vengeance.

Sloane was the first play to dramatize the psychopathic style of
the sixties: that ruthless, restless, single-minded pursuit of satisfaction transformed by drugs and rock music into myth. "In
Germany," Orton wrote to the director of the Broadway production, Alan Schneider, "Eddie was the central pivot of the play. His
stalking of the boy's arse was as funny and wildly alarming as
Kath's stalking of his cock. Unless this is so—you're in trouble."
In following the rapaciousness of his characters' needs—their
ignorance and their unwitting violence—Orton was not being
heartless, merely accurate. Sloane has killed one man when he
walks into Kath's house looking for a room to let. By the time the
play is over, he will have dispatched a second, Kath's father, only
to be blackmailed into bed by Kath and her brother, Ed. Sloane
feels no guilt, and his refusal to experience shame is what dis-

turbs and amuses audiences. Sloane is a survivor whose egotism is rewarded, not punished. Orton wrote to Schneider:

> I don't know what you mean about the Eddie-Sloane relationship. Quite clear. Sloane knows Eddie wants him. He has absolutely no qualms about surrendering his body. None. He's done it many, many times. Sloane is no virgin. He's been in bed with men and women in the past. But he isn't going to give in until he has to. And while he can get away with . . . riding around in cars, just fucking Kath a couple of times a week, getting paid a good salary, why should he give up his trump card. Eddie, naturally, doesn't know how amoral Sloane is. He imagines that he has a virgin on his hands. He thinks he can get Sloane. Sure he can. But it may take a bit of time—cause Sloane is such a nice kid. Where's the problem? . . .

When the play transferred to Wyndham's Theatre in June 1964, impresario Emile Littler and Peter Cadbury, chairman of London's biggest ticket bureau, joined forces in an attack hotly reported in the press, damning *Entertaining Mr. Sloane* as a dirty highbrow play which should never have been allowed in the West End. Orton savored the outcry and let Edna Welthorpe throw more fat in the fire with one of "her" letters to the *Daily Telegraph*, which sent up the violence beneath the calls for propriety.

NAUSEATED

As a playgoer of forty years may I sincerely agree with Peter Pinnell in his condemnation of *Entertaining Mr Sloane.*

I myself was nauseated by this endless parade of mental and physical perversion. And to be told that such a disgusting piece of filth now passes for humour.

Today's young playwrights take it upon themselves to flaunt their contempt for ordinary decent people. I hope that ordinary decent people will shortly strike *back!*

Yours sincerely,
Edna Welthorpe (Mrs)

The only brickbat that angered Orton was the grudging praise of his play as "commercial" from John Russell Taylor in his introduction to it in Penguin's *New English Dramatists* 8. "Living

theatre needs good commercial dramatists as much as the original artist," Taylor wrote. Orton was furious at such critical stu-
pidity. "Are they different, then?" he asked, quoting John Russell
Taylor's distinction between commercial success and art to his
agent and asking to withdraw the play from the volume. "*Hamlet*
was written by a commercial dramatist. So were *Volpone* and *The
School for Scandal* and *The Importance of Being Earnest* and *The Cherry
Orchard* and *Our Betters*. Two ex-commercial successes of the last
thirty years are about to be revived by our non-commercial
theatre: *A Cuckoo in the Nest* and *Hay Fever*, but if my plays go on
in the West End, I don't expect this to be used as a sneer by
people who judge artistic success by commercial failure. There
is no intrinsic merit in a flop."

The radio version of *Ruffian* had grafted Orton's obsessions
onto a structure borrowed from Pinter, who, along with Beckett,
was the only contemporary playwright besides himself Orton
respected. The opening of *Ruffian* was lifted from the opening of
The Birthday Party, a steal that Orton eschewed two years later
when, successful and in control of his talent, he rewrote the play
for the stage. "Everything the characters say is true. . . . The play
mustn't be presented as an example of the now outdated 'mystery' school—*vide* early Pinter," Orton noted for the Royal Court
production. "Everything is as clear as the most reactionary *Telegraph* reader could wish. There is a beginning, a middle and an
end. . . . The play must be directed without long significant
pauses. Any pauses must be natural pauses. Pace, pace, pace as
well. Go for the strong and the natural climaxes. Everything else
should be simple." In Orton's theatre there was no need for
obfuscation. "The number of humiliating admissions I've made,"
says Joyce in *Ruffian*. "You'd think it would draw me closer to
somebody. But it doesn't." The line is more than a good joke; it
contains a vision of desolation whose centripedal force only farce
could evoke. In farce, people are the victims of their momentum.
Survival and identity are at stake: characters state their needs, but
in the panic of events, their words go abused or unheard. The
body and mind are pulverized in their pursuit of order. Unheed-
ing and frantic, characters rebound off one another, groping for

safety. Orton's plays aimed at evolving a form that celebrated both the joy and the terror of this disenchantment.

The cut-and-thrust dialogue in *Entertaining Mr. Sloane*'s third act had a potential for mayhem that never got beyond the vaudeville of language to movement. Orton wanted to create visual as well as verbal anarchy; and he knew the limitation of his first full-length play. "What I wanted to do in *Sloane* was to break down all the sexual compartments that people have. It didn't entirely succeed because it's very difficult to persuade directors and actors to do what you want. When *Sloane* had been running for a while, it had got into compartments, so that Madge [Ryan] was the nympho, Peter [Vaughan] was the queer and Dudley [Sutton] was the psycho. Which wasn't what I wanted and which wasn't what I intended at all, but people *will* put things into compartments. It's very bad in class, in sex, in anything." Orton set about forging an unequivocal style, the theatrical equivalent of a shout to the hard of hearing. "The new full-length play," Orton told the BBC in 1964, speaking of *Loot*, "is an advance. Of course you can't tell until you've written it. But I think it's an advance."

The transition from *Sloane* to *Loot*, from the innuendo of a comedy of manners to outrageous farcical explicitness, was *The Good and Faithful Servant* (1964, televised in 1967). In this poignant, angry TV play about a worker, Buchanan, retiring from his firm after fifty years of service, Orton's outrage at the violence of authority and the lifesleep of the credulous starts to take on a more aggressively macabre form. Buchanan has lost an arm on the job. His body, like the toaster and clock the firm give him, is on the verge of breaking down. When he visits a lady friend on the evening of his retirement, she's shocked at the sight of a whole man:

EDITH: Your arms! Where has the extra one come from?
BUCHANAN: It's false.

EDITH: Thank God for that. I like to know where I stand in relation to the number of limbs a man has.

Orton's laughter begins to display its jugular instinct as it tilts directly against sources of oppression. Buchanan tries to talk his layabout grandson, Ray, into the same work routine that has eroded his own life:

RAY: I don't work.
BUCHANAN: Not work!? *(He stares, open-mouthed)* What do you do then?
RAY: I enjoy myself.
BUCHANAN: That's a terrible thing to do. I'm bowled over by this, I can tell you. It's my turn to be shocked now. You ought to have a steady job.
EDITH: Two perhaps.

Orton's skepticism about authority was as profound as his hatred of the slavish routines by which man gives up the responsibility for his own life. The grotesque would become his theatrical means of shocking the public into a renewed sense of its own life. In *The Good and Faithful Servant,* Orton's withering irony was concentrated on exploring how that life was wasted. "An affirmation of anything is cheering nowadays," says Mrs. Vealfoy, the firm's public relations officer who, like her name, is the voice of faith. "Say 'Yes' as often as possible, Raymond. I always do. *(Laughs).* Always. *(Smiles)* . . ."

The Good and Faithful Servant follows Buchanan from retirement to death, analyzing the emptiness of company allegiance as well as the social pressures that force the young into the same stifling work routine. For all the fervor of the play, the blast of its laughter is curiously muted by its naturalistic format. *Loot,* completed in October 1964, four months after *The Good and Faithful Servant,* breaks away from earnestness into manic frivolity as a barometer of disgust. The issues become larger than life and the method of attack more freewheeling and dangerous. *Loot,* whose original title was *Funeral Games,* sports with the culture's superstitions about death as well as life. "It's a Freudian nightmare," says the son, Hal, who is about to dump his mother's corpse into the wardrobe in order to hide stolen money in her coffin. And so it is. Comedy always acts out unconscious wishes suppressed in daily life. Orton seized this liberation with gusto. "You're at liberty to answer your own doorbell, miss," says the notorious Detective Truscott. "That is how we tell whether or not we live in a free country." Orton's laughter was offensive, elegant, cruel, shocking, monstrous, hilarious—and smart. "Your style is simple and direct," says the oafish Detective Truscott, of the nurse's confession of foul play. "It's a theme which less skilfully handled could've given offence." The joke lampoons the critical appraisal of Orton's style, disarming an audience while sticking the boot further in.

Loot was launched with an all-star cast (Geraldine McEwen, Kenneth Williams, Duncan Macrae, and Ian McShane) and directed by Peter Wood. It was scheduled for a short provincial tour and a West End run. But the plans came a cropper. The combination of frivolity and ferociousness which Orton had discovered as his mature comic manner was new to the English stage and it was difficult for any troupe to find the correct playing style. The confusion in Peter Wood's concept was immediately visible in the elegant but cartoonish black-and-white sets; Kenneth Williams's outrageous mugging as Detective Truscott; and the continual demand on Orton for rewrites, which never allowed the performers the security of the same script from one day to the next.

Loot, which opened in Cambridge in February 1965 and closed in Wimbledon in March, was a notorious flop. No West End theatre would take it. "The play is clearly not written naturalistically, but it must be directed and acted with absolute realism," Orton wrote about the stage production of *Ruffian* with the experience of *Loot*'s failure still vividly in his mind. "No 'stylization,' no 'camp.' No attempt in fact to match the author's extravagance of dialogue with extravagance of direction." The first production of *Loot* suffered and sank because of these excesses. "*Loot* is a serious play," Orton wrote to his producers. "Unless

Loot is directed and acted perfectly seriously the play will fail. As it failed in its original touring version. A director who imagines that the only object is to get a laugh is not for me."

Orton was angry and shattered by *Loot*'s failure. In the rest of 1965, he produced only one television play, his version of *The Bacchae*—a fun-palace revolution set in a Butlin's holiday resort, *The Erpingham Camp*. The play was part of an ITV series on "The Seven Deadly Sins," and *The Erpingham Camp*, like all Orton's farces, satirized Pride. Orton had explored the notion as a film treatment for Lindsay Anderson and then developed it as a Brechtian epic, complete (in early drafts) with illustrative banners such as SCENE 5: AN EXAMPLE OF THE ACTIVE LIFE OF THE CHURCH. ERPINGHAM PREPARES HIMSELF TO MEET THE PEOPLE. THEOLOGY DISCUSSED. THE PADRE PROVES THAT CHRISTIANITY IS ESSENTIAL TO GOOD HEALTH. The television play, which was aired in 1966, was a tepid version of the drastically rewritten and dazzlingly epigrammatic Royal Court production in 1967. "*Erpingham* is the best play of mine performed so far," Orton noted in his diary after the ragged dress rehearsal. "If only Arthur Lowe were playing Erpingham they'd all be raving."

Besides the television play, Orton made his first visit to Morocco, where, in spite of boys and hash, he continued to brood about the fate of *Loot*. He wrote to his agent, Peggy Ramsay, who was having difficulty arranging another London production for the play:

> I think it's disgusting with so much utter shit put on in both the commercial and subsidized theatres that a play like *Loot* should have this difficulty. I'd understand it after Wimbledon, but not after a really pretty average Rep production which succeeded in attracting a glowing notice in the *Telegraph*. I'm sick, sick, sick of the theatre. . . . I think you'd better warn Oscar [Lewenstein] that if the *Loot* option runs out in January with no signs of the play being put on I shan't renew the option. I shall throw the play on the fire. And I shan't write a third stage play. I shall earn my living on T.V. I'm really quite capable of carrying out this. I've always admired Congreve who, after the absolute failure of *The*

Way of the World, just stopped writing. And Rimbaud who turned his back on the literary world after writing a few volumes of poems. . . .

However, Orton did see his play remounted in London, by Charles Marowitz. On September 27, 1966, at the Jeanetta Cochrane Theatre, *Loot* reopened; both the times and Orton's luck had changed. The play was an overwhelming hit.

> Well, the sound of fury is over [Orton wrote to an American friend]. And *Loot* and *Joe Orton* (as you can see from the reviews) are a great success. I feel exhausted. 18 months of struggling to vindicate the honour of my play (my own is beyond vindication) have left me weak at the knees.
>
> There were other reviews which I haven't enclosed because I can't lay my hands on a spare copy. The *Express,* for instance, is a rave. Which pleases the management; it's supposed to sell a lot of tickets. The *Financial Times* was excellent. We had two bad ones. The *Mail* (not exactly bad, but sniffy) and the *Birmingham Post* (which doesn't sell a seat anyway, but was furious . . .). But who cares. We've scooped the pool with the rest.

Loot won the Evening Standard Award and Plays and Players Award for the best play of the year. Orton was, to his delighted surprise, a new star. "I'm now engaged in writing a film [*Up Against It,* commissioned by the Beatles but unproduced] for which I'm being paid (the equivalent) of 30,000 dollars," Orton wrote to a friend in 1967. "I'm going up, up, up." Despite *Loot*'s success, Orton was never thrilled with the production. To his producers, about *Loot*'s forthcoming Broadway production, he wrote:

> In general the tone of the London production is OK. Of course a lot of lines are muffed. This is the fault of having inexperienced actors in the parts. . . . The way it was done was on the right lines. Ideally, it should be nearer *The Homecoming* rather than *I Love Lucy.* Don't think I'm a snob about *I Love Lucy.* I've watched it often. I think it's very funny. But it's purely aimed at making an audience laugh. And that isn't the prime aim of *Loot.* . . . I also think it might be wise to reconsider Marowitz as a director. God

knows I'm not a fan of his. I think a lot of the direction in *Loot*
is atrocious. But on the principle of better the Devil you know
than the Devil you don't, I'd think about it. With a stronger cast
his direction wouldn't stick out so much. And it is a success in
London!! Remember that.

In its capering with "human remains" and its gleeful celebration of police corruption, *Loot* attacked the most deep-seated
myths of English culture. "I never understand why [people are
offended]," Orton said mischievously. "Because, if you're absolutely practical—and I hope I am—a coffin is a box. One calls it
a coffin and once you've called it a coffin it immediately has all
sorts of associations." As his diary recounts, Orton's art had a
curious way of haunting his life. Reality was the ultimate outrage:

Monday 26th December. I began writing *What the Butler Saw* at
eleven o'clock this morning. At twenty past the telephone rang.
It was from a call-box and the caller had difficulty getting
through. When they did it was George [Barnett, Orton's brother-
in-law]. He said, "I've rung to tell you that your Mum died this
morning. It was very quick. She had a heart attack." He didn't say
anything else.

My father, who has just come out of hospital having been run
over by a car, is staying with Leoni [Barnet, Orton's youngest
sister]. The funeral is Friday. . . .

Tuesday 27th December . . . Leoni hasn't rung. I'll have to send a
telegram to find out details of my mother's funeral. I can't go
home if there's nowhere to sleep.

And I don't fancy spending the night in the house with the
corpse. A little too near the Freudian bone for comfort. . . .

Wednesday 28th December . . . Leoni rang about six. I'd sent a
telegram earlier today. She'd just got in from work. She said that
Dad has gone back home. Sleeps in my mother's bed downstairs
with the corpse. After his accident he can't piss straight and
floods the lavatory with it whenever he goes. She said, "Well, I'm
shocked by our Marilyn, you know." I said, "Why, what's she
done?" Leoni said, "Oh, you know, she behaves very ignorantly
all round. And when I told her Mum was dead all she said was
—'I'm not surprised.' Well, you know, what kind of a remark is

that?" Dougie [Orton's younger brother] was upset. Remarkable how those without hearts when young suddenly develop them in later life.

I promised to go home tomorrow. Leoni and George will come round in the evening. As the corpse is downstairs in the main living room it means going out or watching television with death at one's elbow. My father, fumbling out of bed in the middle of the night, bumped into the coffin and almost had the corpse on the floor.

Peggy Ramsay said how dreadfully reminiscent of *Loot* it all was.

Thursday 29th December. I arrived in Leicester at four thirty. I had a bit of quick sex in a derelict house with a labourer I picked up. . . .

I got home at five-thirty. Nobody in the house. My father was across the road with friends. He can't see now. The accident has affected his walking. He trembles all the time. I said I'd take him to the doctor's tomorrow. He should be in a hospital. Later on George and Leoni came round. We went to see Mum's body. It isn't at home as I supposed. It's laid out in a Chapel of Rest. Betty [Orton, his sister-in-law] came round with Susan and Sharon [his nieces]. Both very giggly. Dougie also with them. He wasn't coming to see the body. He said he'd lifted Mum from the chair where she died and put her into the bed. He didn't want to see her again.

We all went to the Chapel of Rest. It's a room, bare, white-washed. Muted organ music from a speaker in the corner. The coffin lid propped up against the wall. It said "Elsie Mary Orton aged 62 years." Betty said, "They've got her age wrong, see. Your Mum was 63. You should tell them about that. Put in a complaint." I said, "Why? It doesn't matter now." "Well," said Betty, "you want it done right, don't you? It's what you pay for."

Mum quite unrecognizable without her glasses. And they'd scraped her hair back from her forehead. She looked fat, old and dead. They'd made up her face. When I asked about this the mortician said, "Would you say it wasn't discreet then, sir?" I said, "No. It seems all right to me." "We try to give a lifelike impression," he said. Which seems to be a contradiction in terms somehow. I've never seen a corpse before. How cold they are. I felt Mum's hand. Like marble. One hand was pink, the other white. I suppose that was the disease of which she died. The death certificate said, "Coronary thrombosis, arteriosclerosis and hyper-tension."

Great argument as we left. The undertaker gave Marilyn a small parcel containing the nightgown Mum was wearing when she died. Nobody wanted it. So the undertaker kept it. Not for himself. "We pass it on to the old folks," he said. "Many are grateful, you know."

Didn't sleep much. Awful bed. Damp. And cold. House without Mum seems to have died.

Friday 30th December. I got up at eight o'clock. I went downstairs to the kitchen. My father appeared in the doorway of the living room dressed only in a shirt. He looks thin and old. Hardly more than a skeleton. He weighs six stone four. I said, "Hallo." He peered blindly for a second and said, "Hallo." After a pause he said, "Who are you?" "Joe," I said. He couldn't remember I'd come last night. Then he said, "D'you know where my slippers are?" I said, "What do you mean—where are my slippers?" He got down on his knees and began feeling around. "I can't find my slippers," he said. "They're on your feet," I said. And they were. He'd been wearing them all the time.

. . . At ten the undertaker arrived. "What about the flowers?" he said. I said I'd no idea what to do with the flowers. "Where's father's tribute?" he said. "I think just father's tribute on the coffin." He found my father's wreath and put it on the coffin. Then we all got into the cars. My aunt Lucy was upset because strict protocol wasn't observed. "They're all walking wrong," she said. "They shouldn't be with husbands and wives. Just immediate circle should be in the first car." Several women were at their garden gates as the cortege passed. I noticed two old women weeping on each other's shoulders.

At the chapel in the cemetery they held a brief burial service. They didn't carry the coffin into the chapel. They wheeled it in on a trolley. The vicar, very young and hearty, read the service in a droning voice. And then the coffin was wheeled out and to the graveside. It was a cold, bright morning. My mother's grave was a new one. Her last wish was to be buried with Tony my nephew who was drowned aged seven, eighteen months ago, but

Peter and Marilyn refused to have the grave reopened and so my mother's last wish was ignored.

The coffin was lowered. The vicar said his piece. The earth was sprinkled over the coffin. My father began to cry. And we walked back to the waiting cars. Immediately the mourners left the graveside a flock of old women descended on the grave, picking over the wreaths and shaking their heads.

We got back home at half-past ten. Sandwiches had been prepared by a neighbour. The party got rather jolly later. . . . My father sat through the party looking very woebegone. The only person who seemed to be at a funeral, Mrs Riley, Mum's lifelong friend, was crying quietly in a corner and drinking endless cups of tea. "I don't expect I'll see you again," she said as she left. "Your mother was very dear to me. I've known her all my life. I shan't come up here now she's gone. Goodbye," she said, kissing my cheek. "I hope you have a happier life than your Mum did."

Leoni and I spent part of the afternoon throwing out cupboardsful of junk collected over the years: magazines, photographs, Christmas cards. We burnt eight pairs of shoes. I found a cup containing a pair of false teeth and threw it in the dustbin. Then I discovered that they belonged to my father. I had to rescue them. I found my mother's teeth in a drawer. I kept them. To amaze the cast of *Loot*. . . .

Monday 2nd January. Spent the day working on *What the Butler Saw.* In the evening Peter Willes [Yorkshire Television producer] rang. . . . I told him about the funeral. And the frenzied way my family behave. He seemed shocked. But then he thinks my plays are fantasies. He suddenly caught a glimpse of the fact that I write the truth. . . .

Wednesday 4th January . . . I'd taken my mother's false teeth down to the theatre. I said to Kenneth Cranham [who played Hal], "Here, I thought you'd like the originals." He said, "What." "Teeth," I said. "Whose?" he said. "My Mum's," I said. He looked very sick. "You see," I said, "it's obvious that you're not thinking of the events of the play in terms of reality if a thing affects you like that." Simon Ward [who played Dennis] shook like a jelly when I gave them to him. . . .

Buoyed by *Loot*'s success, Orton wrote with new verve and complexity. His idiom and stage effects became more brazen. It was an exciting, fecund period in his writing career, fed also by the emotional turmoil between himself and Halliwell, who was oppressed by his own inadequacy and increasingly distressed at Orton's celebrity. Between October 1966 and August 1967, Orton wrote his ghoulish capriccio about the Church, *Funeral Games*, for television; a film script; the major revisions for *Ruffian* and *Erpingham*, published as they were produced under the title *Crimes of Passion*; and his farce masterpiece, *What the Butler Saw*. *Butler* consolidated all the verbal and visual experiments Orton had made haltingly in his one-act plays. Originally, he had subtitled *Loot* "A Farce" but edited out the phrase from the final script. *Butler* had the frenzy and arithmetical logic that finally achieved the kind of ferocious playfulness he'd always envisioned. "Why are there so many doors?" asks the inspecting psychiatrist, Dr. Rance, as he stalks through the garden into Dr. Prentice's clinic. "Was this house designed by a lunatic?" Orton parodied farce (and himself) in the play and used its conventions for his own serious and sublime comic ends. He made comedy out of the ideas behind the farce form. Violence was enacted, and the resulting psychic numbness became a statement about life. A bellboy caught up in the carnival chaos confronts Dr. Rance and points to his bleeding shoulder:

NICK: . . . Look at this wound. That's real.
RANCE: It appears to be.
NICK: If the pain is real I must be real.
RANCE: I'd rather not get involved in metaphysical speculation.

"As I understand it, farce originally was very close to tragedy and differed only in the *treatment* of its themes—themes like rape, bastardy, prostitution," Orton remarked. *What the Butler Saw* put these subjects back on stage with a robust delight in human animality. "Oh this is a madhouse," shrieks Mrs. Prentice. "You must help me, doctor. I keep seeing naked men." Orton raised the stakes of farce's game: never had the genre shown movement complemented by such crystalline wit. "Reject any para-normal phenomena," says Dr. Rance. "It's the only way to remain sane." And where Orton's earlier plays had lacked the scenic surprise to match the jolt of his lines, he was now using the stage with an inventiveness that no modern comic playwright had dared. At one point in Act Two, the psychiatrists declare each other insane at gunpoint. An alarm is pressed. Metal grilles fall over the doors and windows, which clang down with an impressive thud. The sound is at once terrifying and funny; the bars are a stunning image of spiritual stalemate. Orton's *coup de théâtre* elevates his farce onto an imaginative level unique in contemporary theatre. He had worked the same kind of magic into the rewrite of *Erpingham Camp*'s ending:

> I had an inspiration on the end. In the original television play Erpingham falls from a high-diving board. I'd rather clumsily made this possible for the stage by making him fall out of the window. This isn't good. I'd been trying to think of some way to kill him swiftly, dramatically, not involving too many production difficulties and possible on the stage, also ludicrous. I had a vision of him shooting up into the air. This wasn't practical—how could someone do that? And then I got it—he must fall through the floor! . . .

"And when I beheld my devil, I found him serious, thorough, profound, solemn," wrote Nietzsche in *Thus Spake Zarathustra*. "It was the Spirit of Gravity, through him all things are ruined. One does not kill by anger, but by laughter. Come let us kill the Spirit of Gravity." Laughter's disdain for boundaries also contained a yearning for an impossible freedom. Orton's plays wanted to defy gravity (in both senses of the word). *What the Butler Saw,* better than any of his other plays, found the visual correlative for this antic spirit. In its send-up of a Euripidean ending, Orton's final image acts out the comic hope of transcendence. A rope ladder descends from the skylight with Sergeant Match still pursuing the missing parts of Sir Winston Churchill. *"They pick up their clothes,"* Orton's stage directions read, *"and weary, bleeding, drugged and drunk, climb the rope ladder into the blazing light."*

Orton finished typing out the final copy of *What the Butler Saw* from the single-space pages of his rough draft on July 11, 1967. Both he and Halliwell were pleased with it:

> Yesterday Kenneth read the script and was enthusiastic—he made several important suggestions which I'm carrying out. He was impressed by the way in which, using the context of a farce, I'd managed to produce a "Golden Bough" subtext— even (he pointed out) the castration of Sir Winston Churchill (the father figure) and the descent of the god at the end—SER-GEANT MATCH, drugged and dressed in a woman's gown. It was only to be expected that Kenneth would get these references to classical literature. Whether anyone else will spot them is a different matter. "You must get a director who, while making it funny, brings out the subtext," Kenneth said. He suggests that the dress MATCH wears should be something suggestive of leopard-skin. This would make it funny when NICK wears it and gets the right "image" for the Euripedean ending when MATCH wears it.

Orton's final polishing of the farce was completed on July 16. "I added very little on this version (just incorporated Kenneth's suggestions which were excellent), except the description of the light from the garden when the lights in the room go out. And stressed the leopard spotted dress of MATCH," he wrote in his diary. "The Euripedean ending works, surprisingly, as 'all is forgiven'—just as in the later Shakespeare plays." The excited reaction to *What the Butler Saw* was immediate. Within a fortnight, Orton and Halliwell were visiting Orton's producer, Oscar Lewenstein, to discuss production plans for the play. Lewenstein was worried about the Lord Chamberlain's reaction to incest and the flourishing of the cock from the statue of Sir Winston Churchill. Orton agreed, if necessary, to change the figure of authority, but never the incest.

> "What am I saying about Churchill, though?" I said. "You're saying he had a big prick," Oscar said. "That isn't libellous, surely?" I said. "I wouldn't sue anybody for saying I had a big prick. No man would. In fact I might pay them to do that."

Lewenstein thought it might be fun to stage Orton's play with Binkie Beaumont at the Haymarket, the very bastion of bourgeois "enchantment" Orton was satirizing. "That would be wonderful," Orton said. "It'd be a sort of a joke even putting *What the Butler Saw* on at the Haymarket—Theatre of Perfection." Lewenstein also suggested Ralph Richardson for Dr. Rance. "Although I admire Richardson," Orton wrote, "I'd say he was a good ten years too old for the part. And he isn't primarily noted for his comic acting. . . . Both Kenneth and I thought Oscar misguided in suggesting Richardson."

By the time *What the Butler Saw* opened in the West End on March 5, 1969, there was no Lord Chamberlain to censor the play. But Orton's phallic fun was edited out just the same and the missing part of Sir Winston Churchill was turned into a cigar. The change found its way into the script and was printed in the first published version. What was intended as an image of triumphant and mischievous stage anarchy (RANCE: "How much more inspiring if, in those dark days, we'd seen what we see now. Instead we had to be content with a cigar—the symbol falling far short, as we all realize, of the object itself") turned into a giggle. Although launched with a star-studded cast (Richardson, Stanley Baxter, Coral Browne, Julia Foster), the production was a fiasco. On opening night, the gallery barracked the farce with cries of "Filth!" Critics mistook the flaws in the production for limitations in the play, and Orton's best work became the most underrated. Today, the play has become part of the repertoire of modern theatre. Not until Lindsay Anderson's brilliant revival at the Royal Court in 1975 was Orton's comic business and the reputation of his finest farce restored.

"We sat talking of how happy we felt," Orton wrote in his diary from Tangiers in late May 1967,

and how it couldn't, surely, last. We'd have to pay for it. Or we'd be struck down from afar by disaster because we were, perhaps, too happy. To be young, good-looking, healthy, famous, comparatively rich *and* happy is surely going against nature, and when to the list one adds that daily I have the company of beautiful fifteen year old boys who find (for a small fee) fucking with me a delightful sensation, no man can want for more. *"Crimes of Passion* will be a disaster," Kenneth said, "that will be the scapegoat. We must sacrifice *Crimes of Passion* in order to be spared disaster more intolerable."

But it was Orton himself, not Orton's play, who would be sacrificed for his glorious talent. On August 9, 1967, in the early morning, Halliwell beat Orton's brains out with a hammer and then swallowed twenty-two sleeping pills to kill himself. Halliwell achieved in murder the association with Joe Orton that he'd been denied in life. At the time, Orton's death was more famous than his plays. But the years have reversed this situation. Orton is now seen, along with Harold Pinter, as the most influential writer of his era. Nobody came closer than Orton to reviving the prankster's violent outrageousness on the English stage. In the process, Orton created the purest (and rarest) of drama's by-products: joy. In showing us how we destroy ourselves, Orton's plays are themselves a survival tactic. Orton expected to die young, but he built his plays to last.

II

10

Hog Heaven:
Scenes from Dallas

Prophet Calhoun was standing under the marquee of Dallas's most renowned store, Neiman-Marcus. He was taking a short breather. The humid heat of the Texas summer is enervating. Life seems to wilt in the oppressive brightness. On the prairie, cows hide from the sun under mesquite trees; in town, people stay close to their air conditioners. A strange lassitude pervades the long, uneventful grid of streets that makes up downtown Dallas. At night and on weekends, the wide pavements are empty and filled with the doom of a ghost town. On weekdays, people walk only if they have to, and then just to hurry to their destinations and to shade.

But Prophet Calhoun stood on the southwest corner of Main and Ervay mopping his brow with a white handkerchief. Indifferent to his comfort, he was wearing a black skullcap, a black suit, a black vest, and black patent leather shoes that caught the glare from the skyscrapers. He was readying himself to outshout the message of the Dallas skyline, which rises up out of the flatlands like a bar graph of profits. What dominates the skyline is what dominates life: banks and insurance companies. The newest Dallas buildings are designed with reflective glass, which throws the city back on itself. Nothing so epitomizes the city's desire to shine and be seen as the colorful, often blinding, glare off these buildings. Before sunset, the buildings reflect only the azure sky and seem like airy, empty scaffolds.

Prophet Calhoun was there at midday to remind Dallas of the emptiness: "Hog Heaven ain't God's Heaven." He had been prophesying for fifteen minutes without rest. It was hard work convincing Dallasites there was anything wrong with their contentment. The latest issue of *Dallas* bannered the headline: DALLAS: THE MARKET CENTER—FOLLOWING THE YELLOW BRICK ROAD TO EMERALD CITY. The editor's page asked: "Do we know how important we've become?"

Prophet Calhoun, his body stiffening like a fighter rising to the bell of a new round, lurched out from underneath the marquee onto the street corner. "Don't need no charge card," he shouted. "Don't need no NEIMAN-MARCUS charge card!" He thumped the iron newspaper dispensers with both hands to make his point. The clatter and the shouting brought the young hustlers hanging around the pay phones at H. L. Green's out onto the curb.

> Don't need no bank book
> Don't need no food stamps
> Don't need no social security
> Cause you're paid up with Jesus!
> When Christ is on your mind
> Then you're born again.
> IT'S GOODBYE WORLD—OOOEEEE!

In a community spellbound by its own abundance, it is not surprising that the real downtown landmark is a store, not a cathedral. If the enchanted needed an Aladdin's cave, Neiman-Marcus would be it. Here greed is made glorious, and the wealthy can flex their purchasing muscles. Displayed in hushed elegance, Neiman-Marcus's seven-story building features such items as a $1,200 stuffed elephant and an $8,000 Galanos evening dress. On the third floor, china bowls are set out like museum displays on pedestals with citations:

CHING DYNASTY
(c. 1662–1772)
CELADON BOWL.

There is no price tag.

"They'll think it's strange," Prophet Calhoun shouted. "Oh yes, they'll think it's strange." The shoppers emerging from the tranquility of Neiman-Marcus hurried away in the opposite direction. A motorcyclist in a red T-shirt saying EVERYTHING ALL THE TIME revved his BSA 3000 and peeled off a strip as the light changed. People watched Prophet Calhoun from passing cars but never opened their windows to let in the hot air or his voice.

Dallas works hard at promoting complacency. Dial the time, and, courtesy of Republic National Bank, every minute praises the city. "Dallas: the city without limits. Republic Bank Time 4:34. Dallas is the good life. Republic Bank Time 4:35. Thanks Dallas for helping our city grow and prosper. Republic Bank Time 4:36. Thanks Dallas for your great educational facilities. Republic Bank Time 4:37." Turn on the radio and you'll hear "Dallas is to money what New York is to fashion." Open the slick, prosperous city magazine *D,* which analyzes the minutiae of Dallas's power, wealth, and celebrity, and you'll read tall talk. DALLAS, THE CITY OF CONFIDENCE is the headline over the publisher's page of the June 1979 issue. It goes on:

> Is Dallas a boom town? Yes. Will the boom last, given the turbulence and hesitancy of the U.S. economy? Undoubtedly . . . Dallas is becoming a *strong* city. I've never applied that adjective to a town before, but it fits. We're feeling our strength. . . . Confidence is in the air around us.

Over the previous two decades, Dallas has dubbed itself the City of Excellence, Athens of the Alfalfa Fields, the All-American City. But Dallas's whoopee was about economic growth—the "right to work" laws, the low corporate and personal income tax that gave Dallas the best business climate in America. And what Prophet Calhoun was stomping the pavement about was spiritual growth.

Don't care if you a high-roller
Don't care if you a low-rider
Remember one thing:
The Judgment is set
The Judgment is SET!

Long before there were voices like Prophet Calhoun's preaching
in the wilderness, there was the Texas wilderness. On the flat,
sunbaked earth—prone to brush fires in summer and flooding in
spring and winter—there was no apparent wealth. The Conquis-
tadors, led by Francisco de Coronado, left the land to the Caddo
Indians in 1542 when they crossed the prairie looking for the
fabled land of gold. When Dallas's founder, John Neely Bryant,
arrived in 1841 to establish a trading post, he was filled with
entrepreneurial schemes to wrench profit out of emptiness. He
first wanted to exploit Indian trade, then the Trinity River as a
trade route, then a highway he was assured was coming through
the area. All these plans came a cropper. There was no reason for
a town to exist in this inhospitable locale; so Bryant set about
inventing one. From the outset, Dallas tried to accentuate the
positive. Homesteaders bushwhacked across America buoyed by
Bryant's ballyhoo of the area's rich black land and reputedly
navigable river. John Billingsley, one of the first settlers, arrived
"in the great city of Dallas" in 1842 to find two cabins:

> We had heard a great deal about the three forks of the Trinity
> River and the town of Dallas. This was the center of attraction.
> It sounded big in the far-off states. We had heard of it often, yes,
> the place, but the town, where was it? Two small log cabins.
> . . . This was the town of Dallas, and two families, ten or twelve
> souls, was its population. . . . After taking in the town the next
> thing to see was the river. A few yards away and we were on its
> banks.

Gradually Dallas, which appeared to one settler in 1847 as "a
sort of doll village," was, by 1875, according to an Eastern historian, growing "like an enchanted castle in a fairy tale." Dallas was

landlocked and lacked any major mineral or agricultural re-
source, but the city leaders turned this limitation into an asset.
They capitalized on its location in almost the center of the continent, poised between the West and the Deep South, and turned
Dallas into a regional marketplace. Crucial to their dreams of
riches was transportation. They fought to get it to Dallas: first the
stagecoach, then the railroads, and in 1978 an international airport, within a year already the third busiest in the world. A city
of entrepreneurs, Dallas adapted to each new business wave and
rode it straight to the bank: cotton, buffalo hides, cowhide, bank-
ing, oil, fashion, electronics.

Because of its diverse economy, Dallas is now growing at
three times the national average. Five hundred new residents
arrive each week. The city is in the black. Dallas, the local saying
goes, "wasn't created, it was made." The will of man has tri-
umphed over the will of nature, but the city cannot rest. In Dallas,
the stories are not about how the West was won, but of how it
was sold. "Not long ago," begins the *Dallas* tale called "Trammel
Crow: Lord of the Realms," "Crow and a friend were driving
along Stemmons Freeway, close to where Crow has built the
world's largest wholesale merchandising mart. Suddenly the developer seized his portable dictating machine. 'Memo to Self,' he
said tersely. 'Buy Cobb Stadium.'"

Dallas has a longing for perfectibility and a hunger for profit,
and the two give the city a protean, schizophrenic personality. It
produces a handful of films and calls itself "The Third Coast";
it builds an extraordinary airport and becomes "The International City." This year [1979] for the Neiman-Marcus Fortnight,
the Union Station was transformed into Paddington Station. It
was rumored that the Queen and Prince Philip would attend the
ball. Overtures were made to Princess Margaret. But no royalty
showed up to fulfill the city's booster dream. The Old World
would have danced to the tune of the New. And Dallas would
have made her debut in high society only a stone's throw from
Grassy Knoll.

*

Dallas currently houses 675 corporate headquarters, each with a net worth of more than $1 million, which makes it the third largest major corporate city in the country. Football is a paradigm of the corporate struggle, and naturally plays a big part in the fantasy life of the city. The game is about specialized functions and teamwork, about strategy and exact execution, about controlled violence and victory, about one bureaucracy intimidating and outwitting another.

From the Dallas Cowboys to the pee-wee leagues, watching football is as close as most people in the city come to a religious experience. They are fanatical about the game. Dallas Cowboy fans gladly pay $50,000 for twelve-seat boxes at Texas Stadium and decorate them in styles that vary from Louis XIV drawing room to Grecian plush. In October when Texas plays Oklahoma University, 72,000 people converge on the Cotton Bowl. As they say in Big D, "I love my wife, but OU Weekend."

Coach Frank Beavers preaches the gospel of football at Highland Park High School. He's good at his job—and he has to be. Success has built this leafy suburban showplace of North Dallas, and winning is important. Highland Park's wealth has eliminated every abrasion and ugliness to give the suburb a sense of fairytale ease; even the fire hydrants have been painted into red, white, and blue toy soldiers. At Beavers's level, football may not be big business, but he sees the connection. "There's a definite link between the work we do with these kids and their ability to move into corporate life. 'Cause if you learn the rules here, the same rules apply in business. Respect for each other. Playing by the rules. Functioning and getting along well. Blending in.

"We stress things like loyalty. A guy's got to be loyal to his assignment, to our team, to our school, and to our community. Nothing tears you apart quicker than someone who's disloyal. In business, if you don't stick together and you start nitpicking within the team, it falls apart. That's why we stress loyalty to the system. In business you got to dedicate yourself to a cause. We keep anybody who can make a contribution.

"Winning is very important," Beavers adds; "you have to

develop the spirit of winning. Kids can tell. They know when you're confident and not confident.

"We run a positive program. I bust my ass trying to do positive things and I hate for it to be twisted just because a kid skins an elbow. Tomorrow's the last day of spring training. We're filming our last scrimmage at Texas Stadium tonight and the film will be ready an hour afterwards. The kids'll whip in around seven-thirty in the morning to look at them. And then, for those that need it, our teachers tutor 'em for thirty minutes before school starts at nine-twenty. It's a positive approach."

I found "positive" a favorite word in the Dallas vocabulary. The city's Performance Report for 1978 reads: "Dallas appeals to her citizens with positive and professional performance"; "The positive spirit in Dallas inspires unusual cooperation between public and private sectors." The Consultant's Guide to one of Dallas's legendary business successes, Mary Kay Cosmetics, has on the first page: "SET YOUR GOAL, PLAN YOUR WORK AND WORK YOUR PLAN! . . . THINK POSITIVELY! Reject all negative thoughts that will deter you from realizing your ambition." And later: "Too many people are defeated by the everyday problems of life. . . . Don't let dishes, floors and everyday things keep you from achieving greatness. Hire someone else to do the things that don't count. Success is here for the taking. . . ."

Mary Kay's Dallas headquarters is a newly designed $7 million building that glows like bullion. The reflective amber glass has been tested to withstand tornado winds of 150 miles an hour. Mary Kay is a matronly, bright-eyed lady of undisclosed middle age; her rinsed white bouffant looks as if it too could withstand winds of that speed. Her domain is built on vindictive triumph. In the reception room, a bronze acorn is mounted on a stand with the inscription: "It's not where you start but where you finish." And in her sumptuous office, above the Direct Selling Hall of Fame glass trophy (1976) is a framed sampler:

> I have a premonition
> that soon on silver wings

It is a dream of your accomplishment
of many wondrous things
I do not know beneath which sky
Nor where you will challenge fate
I only know it will be high
I only know it will be great

Mary Kay is the ideal whose image directors swear "to uphold
and project." She knows her opulent lifestyle inspires confidence
in corporate underlings. Her powder-pink Biarritz Cadillac, her
$350,000 circular house, her legendary sunken marble bath
where aspiring directors sometimes have themselves photo-
graphed are all part of the Mary Kay plan. Without tempting
glimpses of wealth, to use one of her Texas phrases, "The dog
won't hunt." Part of the company's sales pitch is to recount the
Mary Kay Success Story ("Follow the outline: THE DREAM THAT
CAME TRUE"). And much of the spirit behind her marketing innovations can be found in the frustrations and accomplishments of
her childhood.

Mary Kay was brought up with an invalid father; her mother
worked to support the family. "I never remember her being at
home," says Mary Kay, whose company motto is "God first, family second, job third." "She would leave every morning at five
A.M. and get home about nine P.M. At the age of seven I was
getting on a streetcar in Houston and going downtown to buy my
clothes. I never remember my mother in any conventional setting
you're supposed to. In my neighborhood, the child who lived
across the street was the exact opposite of me. She had doting,
well-to-do parents. I became her mentor. I had to be a model of
behavior so that her parents would think, 'Now, Dorothy, why
don't you behave like Mary Kay,' which was my ticket to being
able to go on their vacations and take part in their activities that
otherwise I had no access to. This set up a competitive thing in
my life which has become a very great asset." Her friend went on
to Rice University; without funds, Mary Kay went on to a bad
marriage. Mary Kay Cosmetics is a universe of happy competition
in which nobody loses—especially Mary Kay, whose consultants
pay cash on the barrel for the cosmetics. "No credit. No accounts

receivable, no accounts payable. Doesn't that blow your mind?" She smiles.

Mary Kay bought the cosmetics formula outright for about $2,000 from the family of a Dallas beautician who had tried and failed to market it. In September 1963, she went into business with eight consultants; now fifty thousand women sell her cosmetics in the United States, Canada, and Australia, and her company earns around $100 million a year. Mary Kay, who believes in Robert Schuller's "possibility thinking" and listens avidly to his Sunday TV *Hour of Power,* puts her success down to the positive idea behind it. "My objective was to help women build their confidence and make something of their lives." They do this by selling the thirty-one items of Mary Kay's skin-care plan to a pyramid of acquaintances, earning commissions not only on their own sales but on the sales of new recruits they bring into the company.

"You may want a diamond or a gorgeous mink," goes one company song, performed to the tune of "Put Your Arms Around Me, Baby":

> What you want you'll surely get
> It's how you think
> Oh, oh, success is on the way
> Selling Mary Kay.

The 1979 Queen of Sales, a New Jersey housewife, pocketed $45,000 working thirty-five hours a week, and two consultants have earned more than $1 million with the company. Mary Kay encourages competition with flamboyant bonuses of pink Cadillacs, mink coats, and diamonds. The Cadillacs are leased, not given, to those consultants or directors whose annual sales total exceeds $120,000. ("I discovered a long time ago that once you've driven a pink Cadillac, you can't go back to driving a buckboard.") Mary Kay also dispenses diamond bumblebee pins, the totem of the company's positive spirit. Aerodynamically the bumblebee is too heavy to fly, but still does. The pin symbolizes that the women have "found their wings."

The prizes are dispensed each year at Awards Night, the glitzy climax of the company's three-day seminar on selling. Eight thousand consultants and directors pay their way to Dallas for the jamboree, where the Queens of Sales and Recruitment are crowned, complete with scepters and capes. Here, too, the oil paintings of the "immortals" of Mary Kay selling are presented, later to be added to the lobby's Hall of Fame. Mary Kay has made the star system a crucial part of her marketing plan. The spectacle is a carefully stage-managed attempt to inspire both pride and envy. "Of course it's glamour," Mary Kay told the Dallas *Morning News* before the 1979 extravaganza. "That's what it's all about— glamour." Awards Night is the epiphany of the female psychology behind Mary Kay's company. "We're all *Vogue* on the outside and vague on the inside. We begin by giving them confidence. And the way we do it is to praise everything they do right. They fall on their faces and we tell them how gracefully they did it. We just praise, praise, praise. And confidence comes from one little success after another."

Awards Night allows the consultants to bask in their own glory and the reflected glory of the company's success. "I've given them a new lease on life, something to fight for, something to win, an opportunity that's almost unparalleled in America," Mary Kay says. And at Awards Night, the eight thousand sing "fight" songs made up in a contest among themselves to the blessings of Mary Kay Cosmetics and positive thinking. "Look what you do in high school, in church. Rah, rah, rah, right?" Mary Kay said, coming from behind her Regency desk. "There are 1,060 sales units in this company and each unit thinks theirs is the best, and they try to climb the ladder of success. We have one song we sing more than any other." In a voice more uncertain than her personality, she sings:

> I've got that Mary Kay enthusiasm
> Up in my head
> Deep in my heart
> Down in my feet.
> I've got that Mary Kay enthusiasm

All over me
All over me
To stay,
Hey!!

Dallas abounds with go-getters like Mary Kay, buoyantly pursuing profits and building monuments to their enterprise. A handful of new downtown skyscrapers, including the Plaza of the
Americas, which features a fifteen-story atrium and an ice-skating
rink, are under construction. The Trade Center and the Apparel
Mart, built in 1964 and 1974, respectively, are being massively
expanded. But plans are also under way for a new arts complex,
a central library, and a 750-seat additional theatre for the Dallas
Theatre Center. The Chamber of Commerce and land developers said, Let there be art for business's sake, and the community
said, Amen.

In 1977 the city brought development of the arts under the
umbrella of local government. It hired the puckish, shambolic
Richard Huff away from the State Arts Commission, where he was
Grants Officer. He now distributes $1.6 million among the eleven
major arts institutions in Dallas, as well as grants-in-aid to neighborhood groups and $1 million in facilities support. The sums
are small, but they are nonetheless the largest in Texas, which
gives less to the arts than almost any other state in the Union.
Sitting in one of the streamlined offices in I. M. Pei's new City
Hall, Huff peers out over the top of his wire-rimmed glasses and
offers his mischievous observations in a wry Texas drawl. "Goodness, Truth, Beauty, I love them dearly. But that is not why the
arts are gonna get here." Huff has no illusions about the new
interest in the arts. "American Airlines," he says. "It and other
major corporations are moving their headquarters to Dallas.
There has to be something here." In this last frontier of free
enterprise, winning—what Brecht called "that black addiction of
the brain"—is the only thing the community respects or understands. Huff knows it, and intends to parlay this spirit of civic
competition into a thriving arts community. "Dallas likes bigger,

better, more expensive. They're willing to put their money, time, and sometimes even their careers on the table, to come out on top. Declare something the best and Dallas has to have it. Have we got the best? I don't think so." He gives a Mr. Peepers smile. "But we will."

The city's wealth and its youth make Huff, like so many Dallasites, confident of success. "Dallas is so young that it doesn't know what it can't do. Therefore it assumes it can do anything. And more often than not, it pulls it off. We don't start from a negative but from a positive. 'What do you want to do? Let's find a way of doing it.' "

"You look at a thing like this as a journey. Is it fun? Can you make theatre important in a city where it hasn't been important?" Paul Baker is sitting with his legs lopped over the orange seats of Row K in the theatre Frank Lloyd Wright built in 1959 to house Baker's Dallas Theatre Center (DTC) on rocks behind Turtle Creek, one of the most beautiful areas in the city. At night, the creek's magic turns to menace and it is deserted, for Dallas leads the country in rape as well as growth. Baker has the strong leathery face of an outdoorsman. At social occasions, with his silvery-gray hair slicked handsomely back and his head bowed to hear with his good ear, Baker appears a shy, humble man. He is neither. He is a shrewd, tenacious optimist who has manipulated Dallas's booster zeal to create a laboratory for the expansion of his artists' creative imaginations. "Training someone merely because he is in theatre will not make a creative person out of him. It will not help him find within himself the creative imagination and the creative drives which he will need if he is to develop a new world for himself—a world that is individually his, expressed through his acting and writing, his design and directing."

Baker's theatre is unique among American repertory theatres, but the product hasn't always pleased the city fathers, who are more interested in results than process. "In the first years we had a lot of antagonism because we didn't fit into the commercial mold," says Baker. "Very poor audience. We barely made it

through the first two years. My God, it was tough. We did a lot
of experimentation, new techniques in producing plays. Experimental Shakespeare. Now our subscription is about eleven thousand and our five-hundred-seat house plays to eighty-five percent
capacity."

Baker is watching the crew swarming over the stage. They will
work until three in the morning getting the first show ready for
the third DTC Play Market, a three-day festival of nine DTC plays
for agents, producers, and theatre managers from around the
country, which begins the next day. The idea was inaugurated by
Baker with tremendous success in 1974. Even these stagehands,
who bang and clatter in front of him, are part of "Mr. Baker's"
plan, an extension of his philosophy of education, called "inte-
gration of abilities," first conceived when Baker was a graduate
theatre student at Yale in the thirties, and refined over decades
of teaching and directing at Baylor and Trinity University in
Texas. The man standing in the middle of the stage adjusting the
lights is Randy Moore, one of the company's finest actors but
lighting designer for this play, *The Firekeeper*, which Baker himself
will direct. The girl dismantling the set with a hammer is M. G.
Johnson, the author of the play now being struck, *Blood Money*.

"This building," Frank Lloyd Wright said in 1959, "will mark
the place where Dallas once stood." Wright wanted the building,
and not the scenery, to be the backdrop for the stage, and so
designed it with no adequate backstage space. Wright's professional uncooperativeness is not in keeping with the spirit of the
place. Baker's theatre is a radical about-face from the theatre's
usual celebration of self and specialization. "You only have a
certain amount of energy to devote to a particular task," he says.
"Quite often doing other kinds of work gives you another point
of view, and keeps you much happier. In most educational set-
ups, the music people don't talk to the art people, and the art
people don't talk to the writers. They get to be rigid, often antag-
onistic bureaucracies, which is fatal to growth. As a theatre person, it's important to feel a relationship to a number of areas.
I've done my best to encourage this, and break down the old
bureaucracies."

A conservatory and professional theatre, the Dallas Theatre Center trains seventy graduate students and also employs a resident company of about thirty-five. There are no unions: the theatre is run with the hard work of students and professionals doing a multiplicity of tasks that union regulations forbid. The result is an extremely adventurous and efficient program, which consists of a year-round children's theatre, summer-long shows in the Dallas parks, bus and truck tours, and three series of five plays on its main and studio stages, which feature a large proportion of new works. The cost of all this activity is only $1.3 million a year. Each member of the acting company is guaranteed a nine- or twelve-month contract of $280 to $460 a week. Whether they are teaching at the new Arts Magnet High School (run on Baker's principles and where he is also in charge), acting, writing plays, or working in the box office, everybody is fully employed and allowed a full life in the theatre. How many Equity actors have that?

Like every other Dallasite, Baker talks about growth, only to him growth isn't measured in dollars and cents. Baker has nothing but contempt for the blinkered specialization of the corporate man. "I believe with Sean O'Casey that the last part of the twentieth century belongs to the artists. In terms of imagination, the corporations are spiritually dead. The corporate man applies well-worn formulas, recollects, memorizes, improves standards and talents, develops cults. He projects systems whereby he can estimate how far below his own standards other people have fallen. He joins, dictates, slaps backs, smokes cigars in back rooms." Baker is the son of a minister, and his love of theatre and passion for dynamic imagination have a missionary zeal. Sometimes his words smack of the pulpit: "We will be criticized and ridiculed. The dull ones, the almost dead ones, will say ugly things about an alive, growing person and untried products; but making mistakes, fearless of the consequence, is the first prerequisite of growth."

The second prerequisite for such a large undertaking is money. The continuity Baker has struggled to create requires both time and abundance. "You must be committed to the work

of your people and not be afraid to back it," Baker says. If someone in his company writes a play, it's going to get done. The
process necessarily produces more misses than hits. "It takes a
long time for a writer to mature. Meanwhile he doesn't feel so
panicked or driven because he's going to get paid whether he's
a success or not." And that's where Baker's Play Market slots into
the scheme of things. It allows Baker to show off the talent and
range of the company, and the board and theatre volunteers to
celebrate their civic enthusiasm and their status.

In Texas, as on Broadway, the rules of the game are the same:
anybody with money can play. At the party opening the Play
Market, and also honoring the DTC's twentieth year, the bar in
the theatre lobby was hopping by five-thirty as board members
and volunteers arrived in evening dress, anxious to mix and
mingle with the assembled theatrical panjandrums. Baker was
spruced up, his director's tennis hat now discarded for a Western
suit in which he strolled bow-legged through the chattering
crowd. Near him at the front door, Dallas's handsome, square-
jawed mayor, Bob Folsom, was already working the room. Folsom was a former end at West Point and SMU, who counted
himself "a bit of a jock." He was standing soldier-straight in his
blue suit, waving hellos, flashing charm as golden as the em-
bossed insignia on his calling card. A land developer who report-
edly ran a $500,000 campaign to get elected on a growth and
prosperity ticket, Folsom earns $50 a year as mayor ("I have
people to take care of my business"). He was talking to an executive of Frito-Lay. They were laughing. "The Republicans think
I'm a Democrat and the Democrats think I'm a Republican,"
Folsom quipped.

"He's on the right side, even if he doesn't say which side he's
on," said the Frito-Lay executive with a wink.

In another part of the room the playwright Jerome Lawrence,
who co-authored *Inherit the Wind* and *Mame*, had been cornered
by two women about a literary matter. "We want to write a
biography about Linda Darnell. She's a Dallas story. In fact
they've got her in the Dallas Wax Museum," one lady said. Her
partner added: "We've done some research. We went down to

the Wax Museum. We even know the size of Linda Darnell's hands and feet."

At the Guest Table, the company's most famous playwright, Preston Jones, sat hardly noticed. He was sipping gin and tonics from a plastic cup and floating paper airplanes at a three-year-old boy, who laughed and heaved them back. Jones wasn't laughing. *Remember*, his offering for this Play Market, was just ending, and he was "sweating out the audience." In 1974, his *Texas Trilogy* began at the Play Market and went on to be an international success. Jones wrote his first plays between rehearsals and while working the box office. He was the finest flowering of Baker's philosophy ("Preston couldn't write if he wasn't acting"). Pressed to respond to the contention that he had the best deal of any contemporary American playwright, Jones looked down at his cowboy boots and said, "Yep."

[Tragically, he died in September 1979. He was forty-three.]

It was not Jones's play but that of another DTC performer, Mary Rohde, that scooped the pool. Its first showing was directly after the cocktail party. Mary Rohde sat at the back of the small studio theatre rubbing her hands together and waiting for the lights to go up on *Lady Bug, Lady Bug.* She was wearing a green party dress with a red sash, but she was hardly festive. "I don't mind people criticizing my acting," she said as the audience filed in. "But criticize my plays and it cuts deep." The actors were already inhabiting the replica of a small-town beauty parlor. Women shouted requests for hairdryers, the air conditioner hummed, and, swilling a Dr Pepper, a beef trust beautician ministered to her customers' needs for gossip and style.

It was a witty set and a clever play—the kind the DTC does well. Two hours later, Mary Rohde had a hit. There were no critics dashing up the aisles, no TV reviews, and at the party afterwards she was shoeless and serving canapes instead of taking bows. But the next day there were twenty-two requests for her play and she was signed by a New York agent. She also found herself with an invitation to dinner at Idelle Rabin's. She had arrived.

Idelle Rabin has a passion for theatre and for Dallas. She is third-generation Dallas. Her grandparents arrived in the 1870s, having traveled from Latvia to England and then up through Galveston on a textile boat. She's still in textiles. Her store, Delann's, has made her rich; but, honoring Jewish tradition, she has been taught the importance of community life and has taken on the theatre as one of her civic missions. Because theatre is not adequately subsidized in America, and especially in Texas, the DTC is beholden to the goodwill, generosity, and hard work of the many board members like Idelle Rabin who raise money and chip in some of their own. Even at its happiest, this is an uneasy alliance, since those who pay the piper do not, in Mr. Baker's theatre, call the tune. And tempers were frayed when Mr. Baker arrived for the grand finale dinner with his cargo of honored guests forty-five minutes late. Undaunted, Mrs. Rabin had her liveried servants bring back the main course, and sat everyone down beside the four-hundred-year-old Kabuki actor's robe that hangs like a tapestry in the gallery adjacent to her behemoth living room.

Mrs. Rabin helped design her new home on Royal Way, a well-named avenue in the far reaches of North Dallas. Her house is part of a self-contained settlement of millionaire dwellings surrounded by a large brick wall that share a private guard as well as a tennis court and swimming facilities. (The stockade style, on a much smaller scale, extends twenty miles north to the farthest boundaries of Richardson, where the steeply sloped roofs of the middle-income $100,000 homes are enclosed by wooden walls.)

"What Idelle wants," said her husband, Leon, "she usually gets." And what she wanted was a house whose living room is thirty-two feet high and whose fireplace has been replaced by a ten-foot-high stove hand-made in Florence from a shop on the Ponte Vecchio and airmailed to her. After the latecomers had polished off the crab cocktail, steak, and cake with their gold cutlery, Mrs. Rabin whisked them away on a tour of her house.

"When we stayed at the Savoy in London, I said to Leon, 'If we ever build another house, I want a bedroom like the Savoy,' " she remarked on entering her bedroom. "Now I have it." She strode across the large room and thumped the wrought-iron fireplace. "This is art history. It was shown at the Grand Crystal Palace in 1851." In the bathroom, beside the sunken bath, she pulled back a lithograph on the wall to reveal her pills. "I have this *thing* about medicine cabinets. I can't stand them. So I camouflaged mine." By the time we got to her study, Mrs. Rabin was exultant. "In the year 3000 they're gonna uncover Dallas and they're gonna put their hands on this wall and they're gonna say, 'My God, Ultra Suede for walls!' " She touched the soft gray wall and smiled: "Why not? I'm a fabric person. I'm in the trade."

Later that night, Idelle Rabin was back in the theatre lobby hosting one last cheese-and-wine wingding. As she sat watching volunteers set out her $700 of assorted cheeses, biscuits, and wine, Idelle Rabin thought about what she was celebrating: "You've given back to the community these actors—not just a transient population."

[In 1982, pressured by Idelle Rabin and other board members to turn the DTC into a "world-class theatre," Baker resigned to save the conservatory concept of his theatre.]

In its pursuit of the positive, Dallas is driven to deny the negative. When President Carter came to Dallas, his local advance men had the Texas Book Depository screened out of sight so that it was hidden from Carter's hotel room. Nobody talks much now about the event that made Dallas infamous. The assassination is memorialized on postcards and recalled in asides by local columnists. Dallas has put that infamy behind itself and is working for glory. But the fears of intellectual infection and the habit of evasion still persist. H. L. Hunt no longer sends each graduate of Dallas's high schools a Bible as he did in the sixties, but the twenty-six-member Dallas Motion Picture Board—the only one in America—meets weekly to impose its own ratings on Parental Guidance (PG) pictures.

The board meets at City Hall. The members see and assess

every commercial PG release, and either reject or accept it as suitable for young persons. The quasi-judicial board rates about 350 movies a year and is no stranger to litigation from film companies. It is empowered to add its own symbols of classification to indicate exceptions to a film's suitability. According to the Dallas City Code,

L means obscene language.
S means sexual conduct or explicit sexual conduct or defecation
   or urination.
V means infliction of serious physical harm to a person, animal,
   or inanimate object, or serious physical injury to a person.
D means use of harmful drugs or drug abuse.
N means nudity.
P means a perverse person such as a masochist, sadist, paed-
   erast, or other aberrant sexual person.

"You missed the worst part," Lea Hamilton was saying to Lucy Mabery, who claimed she'd been absent from the first few minutes of *Time After Time*. "He caught her in the alley and gave her a gold coin because she was a prostitute. She was backed up against the wall. She picked up her petticoat. You could see her underpants."

Ms. Hamilton was talking about Jack the Ripper (David Warner), who, thanks to a time machine, was killing prostitutes in San Francisco discotheques in 1979 and being pursued by H. G. Wells (Malcolm McDowell). The board had voted the film unsuitable, but one member had changed her vote. There had to be a recall. Mr. Surratt, one of the three men present, moved that it be "made suitable with the exception of Sex, Language, Drugs and Violence."

"Mr. Surratt," Sharlyn Majors said, her voice heavy with sincerity, "any female has that innate fear of being raped by some nut, especially in this day and time. I don't think the film was meant for children to see. I have been a little on edge ever since I saw it. I think it was a good film, but I'm an adult. I think those scenes would be lasting scenes in a young child's mind."

Nita Dodd added: "That last murder—showing dismembered parts of the body—was sufficient, quite frankly, to deprive any young person from seeing the film."

"It was only a hand," Honu Frankel said. And the group went on to the subject of drugs.

"I think Drugs should be withdrawn because they were never used," said Barbara Silberberg.

"Marijuana," countered Lucy Mabery, sharpish.

"Marijuana was shown but never used," said Barbara Silberberg.

"She rolled it and smoked it," said Lucy Mabery.

"She never smoked it," said Barbara Silberberg. "She was killed before she could smoke it."

"I don't mind taking Drugs off and changing my motion to Sex, Language and Violence," said Mrs. Adleta, the lady who'd changed her vote.

"Let's take a vote on it now." Mr. Surratt scowled.

"Only those members who were at the screening?" asked Honu Frankel.

"Only those I call out who were there," Mr. Surratt replied.

"Was it Sex, Language and Violence?" Honu Frankel asked.

"Sex, Violence and Language," Mr. Surratt said. "The movie is found suitable with the exception of Sex, Violence and Language." After the roll-call vote, the film was passed. The meeting had taken ten minutes. The Dallas Motion Picture Board adjourned.

While Dallas seeks to protect its community from perversion, it perversely glorifies other neurotic behavior. The TV series *Dallas* has elevated the barbarity of the city's competitive spirit into myth. In this world of high stakes, respect goes only to the victor. J. R. Ewing and the Ewing family machinations are an amalgam of psychopathic styles passed off as entertainment. The ferocity and low cunning of the sports field have their theatrical equivalent in the power plays of J.R., whose ruthless efforts to manipulate the oil market and destroy his opponents are not so different from the Hunts' real-life attempt to corner the silver market. All the characters in *Dallas* are monsters of competition whose will has been overdeveloped at the expense of intellect. These behemoths, like their prehistoric prototypes, are prodigiously successful at survival.

Rich beyond the dreams of avarice, the *Dallas* characters accurately depict the isolation of the wealthy from the world around them. They are hermetically sealed in comfort. Almost no black or Chicano ever appears in the story; no ugliness is ever shown in the landscape; and from watching the series, viewers would never realize that the shiny, confident skyscrapers in the show's establishing shots are surrounded on all sides by ghettos. Children, too, are hardly ever part of the eventful lives of the adults except as props or pawns in property wrangles. In the never-ending plot reversals, every dilemma has its immediate solution. There's no problem that can't be solved by buying the answer. It is the wealth, the ease, the access of the rich to power, and the viciousness of these characters' self-aggrandizement that has endeared them to the American public. As a picture of the shallowness of white upper-middle-class Dallas success, the show is accurate. The series makes the arid Ewing affluence fun. The problems of their wealth rebound only on the rich. But in life, things are different; other people pay the price for the rapacity of the rich. As a community, Dallas has avoided the shame of penury only to commit the greater sin of mercilessness.

Inez Sanchez arrived in January. For eight hours, she lay face down in the back seat of a car with a blanket over her body, terrified the police would stop the car, praying for the safety of her eldest son, José, left behind in Mexico City, and for her seven-year-old daughter, Maria, who was being taken by bus to Dallas with the *coyote* to whom she'd paid $600 to smuggle José, Maria, and herself into the country. The *tristeza* that seized her then is still with her, even though she is now reunited with the rest of her family and her "husband," Louis. She'd like to go back to Mexico to try to find one son who is still missing, but she can't go back. She is not married to Louis; she hasn't got proper papers. If she went back, there would be no guarantee of ever returning.

Inez speaks no English. For six months before she found a friendly Chicano lawyer to negotiate for her, the children could not go to school in Dallas. Each time she called the school, the voice at the other end of the phone was Anglo, and Inez hung up. She kept her children inside their one-room apartment in Oak Cliff all day, fearful that otherwise they'd be picked up as truants and the family sent back to Mexico.

But there is sufficient reason to be paranoid. They are in constant jeopardy of being discovered and returned to Mexico. Anyone who calls the Immigration and Naturalization Service after hours gets a recorded message saying: "If you have an illegal immigrant to report, the number to call is . . ." (The maids in many of the richest and most powerful Dallas homes are illegal.) It is not uncommon practice for illegal immigrants to be hired for a week, then turned in to the immigration authorities before payday. "The white people have treated us extremely well," Louis says. "But it shocked and hurt us that many of the Chicano community were ungenerous. Our fears of greatest betrayal came from them, and the paid informers who live among them."

The Sanchez family live near Singleton Boulevard, just three miles from downtown Dallas. The boulevard is the mainstreet of West Dallas, a five-mile stretch of dusty, potholed road. It's a mean, punishing road, as forgotten by the city as the people who live around it. The skyline gleams just across the Trinity River, but the city's grand dream has all but vanished here. On one side of the road are the fenced lairs of industry (Ryerson Steel, Austen, Atlas Metal); and opposite them, on the other side, are the gray, ramshackle warrens of the workers. Waste and the wasted are tumbled together, thrown up along the roadside like so much scrap. Auto parts, auto supply, metal shops, junk shops, garages are sandwiched between small groceries and specialty stores. There are no neon signs, no franchises, no shopping malls, no motels: nothing, in fact, that holds the promise of affluence or mobility.

Still the Sanchez family considers itself lucky to be in La Bajuda (the Low Place). The road on which they live was paved last year, and they now inhabit four rooms instead of one. Their apartment is scrubbed and airy. Inez has designed some of the things in her house, like the TV stand made from an orange crate and wrapped with green and red Christmas paper, and the knitted yellow doily, dress, and hat for the Mexican doll that stands alone on the living room table. To her son José, the living room's gold wall-to-wall carpet is the symbol of their new good life. In Mexico and in their first Dallas home, the floors were bare. Inez buses dishes at a restaurant; José chromes fenders at the auto shop that once employed Louis. Jobs keep them content and enslaved. But they live in hope of building a line of credit, a voting record, and establishing their place sufficiently in the community to apply for citizenship. Then, they will go home to Mexico.

The other barrios are named sardonically Barrio Cemento (Cement City), Barrio de la Aceite (Oil City), El Poso (The Hole). The oldest and most attractive barrio is Little Mexico, just a few minutes north of downtown Dallas. The first Chicanos were brought to Dallas as railroad workers and lived in boxcars near the city's Union Terminal. Little Mexico was just up the railroad tracks, the obvious place for a Chicano settlement. Formerly Dallas's red-light district, the Chicanos moved into the shacks after the city fathers had thrown the whores out. Dallas now sells Mexico Chiquito, with its quaint three-bedroom brick houses and its picturesque Mexican restaurants, as part of the city's distinctive character. But for a long time Little Mexico was remarkable only for its squalor. Now urban renewal has toned up and torn down much of the old neighborhood. When the highway cut through Little Mexico, it forced the exodus of many middle-class Chicanos. With an energy crisis looming, land close to downtown Dallas is becoming very valuable, and Little Mexico is sure to be eroded again by developers.

The dilemma of the Chicano in an Anglo society is as much spiritual as political. Octavio Paz has written: "North Americans want to understand and we want to contemplate. They are activists and we are quietists. They believe in hygiene, health, work and contentment, but perhaps they have never experienced true joy, which is intoxication, a whirlwind." *No tienen sabor* is a saying among Dallas Chicanos which pokes fun at the deadness of the Anglo world around them. To the Chicano, the Anglo's food, his music, his dances, his isolated suburban style of life have no *flavor*. The Chicano is ruled by neither the clock nor the dream of wealth. As Paz writes: "The North Americans consider the world to be something that can be perfected. . . . We consider it to be something that can be redeemed."

Nellie and Jessie Tafolla live twenty miles out of town, a few hundred yards over the city line in Mesquite. They have a comfortable corner house and a big yard for their five children. They moved out of downtown Dallas twelve years ago when they married. But they return most Sundays to Little Mexico for Jessie's mother's ritual Sunday morning breakfast of menudo, tortillas, and huevos rancheros. Jessie Tafolla has nine brothers, so there are often as many as eighteen at table. The Tafollas are typical of the new generation of white-collar Chicano workers in Dallas, committed both to making the Anglo system work for them and to keeping alive their own cultural traditions. It's a hard battle. Already Jessie's ninety-four-year-old grandfather, a former lampman for the Texas Pacific Railroad, listens to the educated inflections of sixteen-year-old Jessie Jr. and taunts him with *brolio* (white man). The grandfather tells Jessie Sr., who works for IBM in administration: "Stick all your money into this boy, educate him. But get your money out as quick as you can 'cause the boy's gonna leave you behind."

Nellie and Jessie are active in their community (Jessie polled one third of the votes when he ran for precinct chairman) and IBM encourages community work. But Jessie has discovered a snag. "All corporations say to their employees, 'We want you involved in community work because it represents the company.' But they don't mean it. You get passed over for promotion. You know you're due so you have a meeting with your manager. The response is: 'Jessie, to move up the ladder you got to give one hundred one percent.' That's true, you can't fight 'em on that. 'But twenty-five percent of your effort is going over here to the community, that means you're giving us seventy-five percent.' Hey, you've been burned. I'm just part of their statistics."

The Chicano is the invisible man of Dallas. As Jessie Tafolla says: "The only thing the Anglos can really identify us with is Mexican food. They think they understand us because they eat our food. It's the only area of expertise conceded to us. When President Carter came to San Antonio, he ate that tamale, the chuck [corn husk] and all. He was appealing to our vote and didn't know the first thing about our culture. The same goes for Dallas. Sure they eat at our restaurants, but they don't give us the courtesy of finding out who we are, what we're after. We're fighting to be able to be corporate executives and still eat tortillas with our fingers."

Although conservative estimates put the Chicano population at 15 percent of the city population, the Chicanos have no elected city official. They are totally disenfranchised.

Seventeen blocks from the famous Dallas skyscrapers is South Dallas, the city's black ghetto, where the tallest building is three stories high. Al Lipscomb is cruising his turf, District 6, in his black Buick. Every pedestrian who crosses his path gets a wave and a fist salute—"RIGHT ON! SOLID!" Lipscomb turns back. "A thousand salutes and you can't get twenty people to a meeting."

Lipscomb was born and works here as the head of the South Dallas Action Center. They call him "The Lip" because he speaks his mind; and his emotional outbursts have earned him something of a reputation as a clown to the white establishment, who don't conduct business that way. As the sad, mangy streets loom up before him in the windshield, his voice finds its edge. "We've had three hundred eight companies relocate in the metroplex here—three hundred eight. Not a damn one relocated in District six. Not *one!* The name of the game is economics, sir. Politics and a dab of education also. We been systematically culled out of the economic system of this city. We been niggerized.''

He points across Pennsylvania Avenue. "See there. The Negro Chamber of Commerce which I say is a misnomer because there is no commerce. Not one Abraham Brown penny have they ever generated in this community. They love to be sitting up at the Hyatt Regency with them millionaire whites and all.''

Lipscomb's Buick rolls past Pleasant Grove Baptist Church, then New Bethal Baptist Church. "Vultures. Just vultures. The preachers don't live in the area. They're vacuum cleaners, suckin' everything out, puttin' nothin' back in. Black people don't have no country clubs in Dallas, so the Baptist Church is our country club." Rain starts to fall. The streets are greasy. A boy dribbles a basketball along the divider line. "No education, no economics, no discipline,'' Lipscomb mumbles to himself and turns up toward Lincoln High School, his alma mater. "I don't see a damn thing different from when I graduated. Sure some gone to California, New York. They roll their r's. But there hasn't been any smoke from South Dallas. Dallas has been lulled into security.'' The car glides down Farragut Street. Lipscomb honks his horn and salutes an old couple who sit with their canary suspended above them on the porch. "Makes the day for them. It gets them up,'' he says.

Lipscomb pulls the car over to the curb in front of a sign that reads L. BUTLER NELSON MEMORIAL PARK. "This'll be a quickie, a quickie Jones." The long expanse of ragged, narrow land is divided by an aqueduct and bounded on one side by the Lincoln High School fence. Lipscomb strides out ahead, reading the headstones. "Perpetual care?" he says, pausing by one of the many gravestones that have been toppled and overrun with weeds. "The city said there'd be perpetual care for the bodies that are in here. The Jefferies and Lipscombs paid for the plots. Look here, they're gone.'' Graves have been washed away, one toppled headstone has FUCK spray-painted across it. Lipscomb walks faster into the high grass. He's looking for something beside the high-school fence. He's talking to himself. He points to a row of graves lined up beside the fence—TUCKER. LUCKIE. LADY LUCK. CUDDLES. TOTO. DOLLY (My Baby Always).

"Say, sir," Lipscomb says. "Are these animal graves?" He bends over one that reads:

> DUKE (1934–1952)
>
> Our darling boy
> Sleeps here apart
> But he is with us
> In our hearts

"In Dallas, the blacks and dogs were buried together," Lipscomb says. "When I was at Lincoln High School, we couldn't even get a goddamned second-hand textbook. The pages were ripped out. But you'd see some of your civic leaders out here, their handkerchiefs out, weeping over their dogs."

On his way back to the car, tin cans crunch underfoot. "You can't throw a cigarette butt by the Hyatt Regency," Lipscomb says. "Dallas, Texas, today? It's a great city as far as a growin' city. But as far as a human city? Great googamooga, man. Dallas is *known* to be the number-one racist city."

The sun has come out. Lipscomb turns on his car radio, a public service announcement: "Check out the library. It's full of success stories." Lipscomb turns the radio off. Blacks in tank tops, baseball hats turned back on their heads to keep the sun off their necks, beers in hand, lean against the side of the Twilight Lounge. "Hiya, Al!" they yell as Lipscomb shoots them the right-on sign and honks his horn. "RIGHT ON TIME!" he shouts to them.

Language is Lipscomb's only revenge; in it he salvages some sense of power and humor from the hopelessness around him. "I can stand on the dome of the Texas Stadium and see people who don't even have sewerage. At Fair Park, where they have the Cotton Bowl and the Texas State Fair—probably the richest state fair in America—there's just one link fence that divides it from abject poverty."

Lipscomb was the first black man in Dallas to run for mayor

(1971). He is fighting for complete desegregation of the Dallas school system ("We still got seventy one-way schools. Separate but unequal"). He is fighting the City Council; his suit challenging the at-large system and district sizes has prevented any city election from being held and is still being tested in the courts. ("Dallas can't hold no election. Hell, no.") He is fighting for Oliver Lee Davis, a young basketball star, sentenced to ninety-nine years for sodomy and aggravated assault against a white prisoner while awaiting trial for a robbery charge for which he was eventually cleared and despite the fact that the alleged inmate has testified that Davis did not attack him. He is fighting to get money into the community and drugs out of it. Everywhere there is struggle.

He waves to an old man using the beat-up front seat of a car for his porch chair. "RIGHT ON TIME!" Lipscomb leans on the horn. Showering the neighborhood with salutes, he's performing the small, sad rituals of pride. "Hopelessness. Dejection. Saving the world with rhetoric," Lipscomb says to himself, and salutes another passerby.

Military Parkway is a long, dusty, uneventful road that runs straight across the top of South Dallas on the outskirts of Lipscomb's turf. It's not far from the infamous Frazier Court, or Police Beat 341, the notorious twenty-block area bounded by the Santa Fe Railroad tracks and Grand Avenue on the west and Forest and Crest streets on the east, which has the highest murder rate in the city. In the sweltering morning brightness, the road is empty and unpromising until you come to the Palms Land and Cattle Co., a large yellow brick building set off from the road near Stan's Drive-In. There, neatly parked, are rows of Montecarlos, Eldorados, Trans-Ams, and stationwagons. Between 10:00 A.M. and 3:00 P.M., while their husbands are at work and their kids are in school, the white housewives of Dallas venture into this no-man's-land for a romantic flutter with the shift workers, truck drivers, and free-lance romeos of the town. Admission to Palms Danceland is $1.50; but women can come and drink for free.

Blinded by the perpetual night inside, the newcomer is seen long before he can see. Time enough to slip out the back if it's an unexpected husband or to size up the new talent. The dark is filled with the sounds of music, chatter, the click of pool balls. Only the red eyes of the Schlitz bull are clearly visible.

At the bar, Jim, who is moonlighting from his real estate job, says: "I'm new meat. I haven't been here often. If you ask five girls to dance, three or four are bound to accept. It's a percentage play. These women are all married. The relationships they have here can't go anywhere. They're here for a walk on the wild side for a few hours."

Tables are set out around the large rectangular dance floor. A jukebox is playing Tanya Tucker's "It's a Cowboy-Loving Night." Most of the men in the room are wearing straw cowboy hats; they wear them even while they dance. "These dudes with their fuckin' cowboy hats," Jim says. "They wouldn't know what side of a horse to crawl on."

The real party girls sit close to the dance floor; the shy ones hide in the shadows beside the bandstand or near the bar. Men cruise the tables, coaxing girls out of their seats to dance or sitting down to sweet-talk them. At the tables near the dance floor, there's a lot of kissy-face and groping going on. Jim says: "They call this place the pressure cooker. Most of the women rush home and throw some food in a pressure cooker for their family dinner."

At a table close to the dance floor, two petite blondes with short hair and in slacks are entertaining four men. One called Gwen says: "I'm gonna have to bring my typewriter here and set it up right in the corner. I ain't gettin' any work done if I come here and dance every day."

"How fast do you type?" asks the hulky man beside her.

"How fast do you do it?"

The man laughs and pulls Gwen up to dance. They dance the two-step, then the schottische. He holds her around the neck with her head in the crook of his arm; she holds onto his belt. Her friend Jean is sitting between two men. She is kissing one, while her right hand fingers the crotch of the other, who stares indifferently at the front door. A beautiful older woman wearing diamonds and a tailored pants suit enters, surveys the room, and moves into the shadows. The man gets up and makes his way toward her.

The waitress, sporting a blond beehive hairdo and butterfly glasses, comes to the table: "Can I get you-all anything?"

"Shiner's Long Neck," says the man whom they call Gus. He puts his arm around Jean.

"Long Necks and rednecks."

"Hush up, Twyla," Gus says to the waitress.

When Twyla comes back with the beer, Jean is sitting alone. Gwen is dancing with Gus. The band is playing "If I Say You Have a Beautiful Body, Will You Hold It Against Me?"

Twyla puts her tray down on the table and takes a seat. She follows Jean's gaze and stares out at the dance floor. "Is that girl snakin' your man?"

"Twyla, do me a favor? Don't piss on my shoes and tell me it's raining."

"Shoot, honey, just interested, that's all." Twyla takes a swig from the bottle of beer. "You're looking at a happy woman. I got a tankful of gas this morning."

"You're easy to please."

"We all know what you like, honey," Twyla says. "You've had more pricks than a used dartboard."

Gus and Gwen come off the dance floor laughing. Gus says: "What you two talkin' 'bout?"

"The energy crisis," Jean says.

"Hell, my engine's always full up." Gus humps Gwen from behind until she squeals and shoves him away. "Behave yourself, boy."

The band starts to play a Cottoneye Joe. With a hoot, Gus drags Gwen back up to dance. They move counterclockwise in a kind of chicken strut. Gus sashays Gwen from left to right around him as they skip with the other couples around the floor.

Twyla points to the beautiful older woman sitting alone in the corner. "She used to be a model. Married twenty-eight years before her husband divorced her. She just don't dance."

"Stupid to come here and not dance."

"Says she just likes to see people have a good time. I says to her, 'Dance, honey.' Know what she said? 'It's hard coming into this place. I was taught better.' "

"Some people are plumb stupid," Jean says. "Dallas is good for only two things—money and men. Not necessarily in that order. I told Duane, 'Okay, we'll stay here for your career. But I'm not gonna be buried in Dallas. No way. I'm putting it in my will.' "

" 'Nother drink?" Twyla says.

Jean pinches the ribbon of fat on her waist and declines. "Love-handles," she says. "Duane gets home and he expects me to eat with him. And that microwave cooks things so *fast*. You can't drink all day and eat at night and stay thin."

Gus and Gwen come back to the table and sit down. Twyla takes her tray off the table. "I heard a good one the other day. Do you know how to tell if you're really a fat person underneath?"

"Okay, Twyla, how do you tell?" Gus asks, sitting back with his hands around both women.

"Answer these questions for yourself. Do you know the meaning of 'too rich'? Do you know the meaning of 'spoil your dinner'? Do you know the meaning of 'full'?"

Gus looks at Gwen and Jean. They look at him.

"Nope." Gwen laughs.

Two handsome men in cowboy hats approach the table. And soon Jean and Gwen are standing up to dance the rest of the day away in Dallas.

III

11

Studs Terkel

But do other enchanted people feel as nervous
As I do? The stories do not tell.
STEVIE SMITH, *The Frog Prince*

Every society is built on a sense of collective mission, but the particular virulence of America's dreams had its origin in the promise of the New World. Zealots, malcontents, entrepreneurs, the early settlers were a self-selecting group of dreamers who implanted in the New World a sense of optimism and fierce ambition to make life in such inhospitable terrain equal to their dreams. It wasn't easy. "What could they see?" wrote William Bradford, an eyewitness to the landing of the *Mayflower* in 1620, describing the unpromising vista of the Promised Land, "but a hidious and desolate wilderness, full of wild beasts and wild men? and what multituds ther might be of them they knew not." Dreaming, not freedom and equality, was the first inalienable right of the settlers. From the outset, the nation's credo was: "I dream, therefore I am."

"America was meant to be everything," wrote an early English visitor, Harriet Martineau, implying that its space had become synonymous with hope. The vagueness of America's boundaries, the variety of its climates, the vastness of its territory, and its newness created an irresistible atmosphere of expectation. A society inventing itself, America was a laboratory for fantasies of freedom. "If New England be called a Receptacle of Dissenters, and an Amsterdam of Religion," wrote the Reverend Hugh Jones in 1724, cataloguing the range of experiments in the American dreamscape, "Pennsylvania the Nursery of the Quakers, Maryland the Retirement of Roman Catholicks, North Carolina the Refuge of Runaways, and South Carolina the Delight of Buccaneers and Pyrates, Virginia may be justly esteemed the happy Retreat of true Britons. . . ."

When the colonies became a nation, democracy tumbled the barriers of privilege and replaced them with the obstacles of competition. America's yearning was quickly channeled into a quest for status and well-being, wealth being the only recognized distinction in a society that had rejected the aristocratic distinctions of birth and profession. Having revolted against its parent, America built its society around a distrust of authority and a belief that each generation should surpass the preceding one in attainment. "No matter how many generations separate an American from his immigrant ancestors," says Geoffrey Gorer in *The American People*, "he rejects his father as authority and exemplar, and expects his sons to reject him." Thrown back on himself, compelled to surpass his parent, each new American is forced to recapitulate the American Dream of total individual transformation. The result is a society heavy with dreams of ambition and escape.

The American Dream required abundance to make it credible, and worked as an inspiration to achieve abundance. The Dream promised a payoff for hard work: pluck 'n' luck would yield the American reward of increased wealth, status, mobility, and financial security. There was a large component of fact in the fiction. The resources and technology could make a great number of these dreams come true and thus keep the populace enchanted by them. The land fostered the hope of freedom and equality even in the face of disillusion. If the immigrant was frustrated in his abilities to improve his lot, he could always move on. The land seemed to offer an endless second chance, and the American Dream goaded every citizen to test his freedom. The immigrant could leave his failures and his past behind him, rewrite his history, pursue the idea of perfectibility that seemed built into the continent and the Constitution. Tomorrow, he might find his fortune, his homestead, his roots.

America's abundance teased the imagination with a sense of blessing and also created an appetite for conquest. The country gained not only the daring and idealistic, but the rootless and unscrupulous. Then, as now, America was a percentage play. Gamblers and the feckless with nothing to lose thrived in such a climate of uninhibited self-assertion, adding their spirit of self-aggrandizement to the American character. As Philip Slater writes in *The Pursuit of Loneliness:*

> We gained an undue proportion of persons who, when faced with a difficult situation, tended to chuck the whole thing and flee to a new environment. Escaping, evading, and avoiding are responses which lie at the base of much that is peculiarly American —the suburb, the automobile, the self-service store, and so on.

But the combinations of courage and cunning, righteousness and ruthlessness were adaptations to the rigors of a dangerous, brutal, and unshaped continent. The Dream that first galvanized the country would come to spellbind it, at once an agent of inspiration and forgetfulness. If the Dream came true for everyone, it wouldn't be a dream. Within the American's fantasy of vindictive triumph was the fact of vindictive tragedy. (In 1660, the slave population comprised 8 percent of the population; by 1770, slaves represented 21 percent of 1.6 million new Americans.)

The dissonance between the society's democratic ideals and its practice forced white Americans to rationalize their ruthlessness by clinging tenaciously to their "manifest destiny." As Alexis de Tocqueville observed about the systematic annihilation of the Indians, "It is impossible to destroy men with more respect for the laws of humanity."

Dreams made the society great, and anticipation drove it crazy. When de Tocqueville toured America in 1831, he found "an agitated mass" who were "restless in the midst of abundance."

Even then, the Dream was entrenched and the populace spell-bound in its hurry for well-being. The abundance that inspired dreams of perfectibility also robbed Americans of peace of mind. They were in the thrall of expectation and in fear of disappointment. They fueled their nervous solitude with frantic activity. "Besides the good things that he possesses," de Tocqueville wrote, characterizing the restless insecurity that dreaming added to the American character, "he every instant fancies a thousand others that death will prevent him from trying if he does not try them soon. This thought fills him with anxiety, fear and regret and keeps his mind in ceaseless trepidation, which leads him perpetually to change his plans and abode." Dreaming made Americans more hopeful, but it also made them more insecure. The insecurity served the function of keeping the society at work.

With industrialization, the spellbound became a feature of the modern American landscape. Describing the new momentum of the twentieth century, Henry Adams wrote in his autobiography: ". . . all the new forces, condensed into corporations, were demanding a new type of man—a man with ten times the endurance, energy, will and mind of the old type."

The new metabolism had to be manufactured by raising the amperage of American dreams. With the frontier closed, with the exodus to the big cities, with mass production promising a democracy of objects while reducing man's labor to a series of movements, the dreaming's negative aspect became apparent. Dreaming was not only a spur but a refuge from the momentum and boredom of the new industrial rhythm. Daydreamers became a central theme of American culture. The dazed resilience of the silent-film clowns, those little men who bounced back from every act of violence while staunchly pursuing their goal, epitomized the spellbound triumphant. Edward Hopper painted the dreamy American self-involvement, people in a city landscape forever lost in thought and set apart in a melancholy dialogue with themselves. George Kelly's *The Show-Off* (1924) created the epitome of the spellbound's trance state in Aubrey Piper, who imagines every dream a reality, the psychopath who somehow manages to end on his feet.

Eugene O'Neill's *The Iceman Cometh* (produced in 1946) used the metaphor of a flophouse bar to evoke the spell: the dazed contentment of pipe dreamers with their "touching credulity concerning tomorrows." The characters talk of breaking free from the bar's safety, but they never stray. "It's a great game, the pursuit of happiness," says one of them sardonically. The weird security of the skid-row bar is a haven from the competitive dream: "No one here has to worry about where they're going next, because there is no farther they can go," Arthur Kopit's *Indians* (1968) portrays Buffalo Bill retreating from the reality of Indian annihilation into the daydream of heroism he helped create. And Sam Shepard's finest play, *The Tooth of Crime* (1972), is about the competition of two famous rock stars to remain in the enchantment of fame. Shepard is explicit about "the way things are"—"everybody's walkin' asleep eyes open." The winner of the rock-'n'-roll battle ends up praying for the enchantment to last. He sings:

> If I'm a fool then keep me blind
> I'd rather feel my way . . .
> Just keep me rollin' down
> Keep me rollin' down
> Keep me in my state a' grace. . . .

"If one could control the songs of a nation," John Dewey wrote, "one need not care who made its laws." The radio allowed the popular song to become an agent of enchantment, one that never stops urging Americans to "wrap your troubles in dreams" and to "dream when you're feeling blue." Television keeps the citizen literally spellbound, comatose in front of flickering images; and television is controlled by those who have the most vested interest in the Dream. Advertising owns the air, selling the dream of abundance and creating what market consultants Charles Kettering and Allen Orth in 1932 dubbed "the new necessity." They saw that "the simplest way to assure safe production is to keep changing the product—the market for new things is infinitely elastic." Paying lip service to consumer sovereignty, advertising has fostered an easily manipulated public that is prey to novelty.

American has become a society of exciting distractions. The media reinforce the glamour and drama of this pageant of abundance and mobility, charting the personalities, the payoffs, and their positions on the wheel of fortune. Easily charmed, Americans are gourmands of the new. The latest objects have a kind of magical status in a society that confuses the democracy of objects with equality and forgetfulness with hope. It is not simply the driven, obsessive army of businessmen pursuing profit at the expense of conscience, nor their spendthrift wives, who are spellbound. Enchantment is promoted as a desirable state of mind. And much of the average day is spent tuned in to the network of persuasion.

Studs Terkel's *American Dreams: Lost and Found* is inspired by the spellbound. A populist, Terkel has gone in search of the little man with a big story of struggle as an antidote to the enchantment he sees around him. Terkel is specific about the spell:

> Forfeiting their own life experience, their native intelligence, their personal pride, they allow more celebrated surrogates, whose imaginations may be no larger than theirs, to think for them, to speak for them, to *be* for them in the name of the greater good. Conditioned toward being "nobody," they look toward "somebody" for the answer. It is not what the American town meeting was all about.

In his introduction, Terkel quotes Tom Paine's remark that America was "the only spot . . . where the principles of human reformation could begin." Terkel still clings to that hope. *American Dreams* treats the Dream as a fact, but it is an amalgam of fictions. Terkel has chosen his subjects, culled and edited a few hundred interviews, the way a novelist chooses his characters. They may speak for themselves, but they make *his* points. Terkel rightly acknowledges that in his oral history "there is no pretense at statistical truth." But he presents the testimony as evidence that "a long-buried American tradition may be springing back to life," that the "hitherto quiescent are finding voice." This is

Terkel's dream. And in these tales of frustration, demoralization, and occasional success, a strong sense of the Dream-*politik* emerges.

Terkel's book begins as a meditation on winning. Terkel knows about winning and losing; he's a media celebrity who loves both the famous and the underdog. He reminds us that his mother died embittered at having "almost, though never quite, caught the brass ring." The prologue to his book is the voice of a former Miss U.S.A., Emma Knight, soured on her success: a winner who refuses to wear her laurel. It sets a tone of skepticism about the society's obsession with winning, which the book pursues. Even before Book One begins, Terkel goads his audience with a quote from Albert Einstein about man finding meaning "only through devoting himself to society." Terkel wants to reaffirm a spirit of cooperation and community.

In a society where the individual is made to feel that success and survival depend solely on his effort, winning becomes an inevitable obsession. It is a cruel and wasteful ethic. "A dog you feed will not hunt," says one interviewee, a black entrepreneur, S. B. Fuller, damning welfare and celebrating insecurity as a way of life. "Only in America, you're free to eat if you can find something to eat and free to starve if you don't." America makes a myth of competition at the expense of cooperation. Winners acquire magical status. "People don't like failure. It's a real mark, especially in business," says Jann Wenner, the founder and editor of *Rolling Stone,* whose interview shows how competition can make a monster of a man. Crime acts out the dream of winning, the flip side of free enterprise. The issue isn't *how* you win but *that* you win. Discussing his life as a thief, Ken Jackson tells Terkel:

> I was learning the American value system, the Syndicate value system. What you were supposed to do is steal and get involved with the American Dream. You made big money, bought a home, and got away from the niggers. . . . It's a corporation. They're not licensed by the state of New York, but it's a buyer's market. Supply and demand. We supplied, and then we demanded they pay us. It's capitalism at its best.

Competition and the myth of winning are necessary to capitalism. The dream is of other people losing. "The dream is *not losing*," says Stephen Cruz, a successful Mexican-American. "This is the notion pervading America today: Don't lose." Bill Veeck, the president of the Chicago White Sox, is getting at this in his understanding of why Americans crave sports' stage-managed victories:

> For the most part, we're losers. We're losers in a country where winning means you're great, you're beautiful, you're moral. If you don't make a lot of money, you're a loser. The bigness, the machines, the establishment, imbue us with the idea that unless you make a lot of money, you're nothing. Happiness has nothing to do with it . . .

And Terkel talks to Claude Humphrey, a defensive end for the Philadelphia Eagles, who is instructive about how winning often means cultivating hatred and isolation to keep the competitive edge:

> I don't have any friends out there. Even the guys on my own team, really, are the enemy. If I got to work with this guy and he don't do it right, he's taking bread out of my family's mouth. . . . I build up the hate during the course of the week, so by the time Sunday gets there, I really am pissed off at the guy. It's not right to be able to hurt people and not feel anything. . . . You understand what I'm saying? When I'm through with football, all those kind of feelings will be gone.

Industrial capitalism seems to require a belief in personal acquisitiveness as a dream. An agglomeration of self-interests is presented as the common interest. Individual goals have been promoted to prevent an identification of class interests; vertical solidarity serves capitalism better than horizontal solidarity. But the pursuit of happiness, that unique notion written into the Declaration of Independence, originally meant the pursuit of *public* happiness, not private pleasure.

Terkel, who quotes Walt Whitman's "One's-Self I sing, a simple separate person,/Yet utter the word Democratic, the word En-Masse," believes in the wisdom of the ordinary citizen. In contrast to the bland background noises of instant media experts and stars, the guts, commitment, and irresistible vigor of the ordinary American come almost as a shock. It is no longer the Common Man but the Uncommon Man that the American Dream celebrates; not the man in the world but dream figures of fame, who make their separation from society sensational. As Karl Hess, who worked for the White House on special assignment under Eisenhower and later as a speechwriter for Barry Goldwater, tells Terkel:

> You ride with motorcycle escorts. You're zoomin' along in a limousine in all the noise, and you look out on the street and all those people are frozen. You're movin' and they're frozen. That's a powerful lesson. . . . Your whole life is special information, special privilege, separation, and, oh, my, so phony.

Fame isolates as it enchants. Increasingly, the people's representatives have lost touch with the people. "There's no two-way dialogue between senators and their constituents anymore," explains James Abourezk, former Democratic senator from South Dakota. "The guy takes a poll, gets on TV, and runs his media campaign according to the poll. He really doesn't hear from his constituents and the depths of their feelings." Media stars, politicians become "personalities." Instead of serving the public, the politicians play to it. They hold sway not so much by the power of their ideas as by the quality of their public relations. Their impact lies more in exposure than in ideology.

The disparate voices in Terkel's book show how the Dream works to the well-organized advantage of corporate America, which pretends that what is good for business is good for America. The corporation institutionalizes America's dream of self-aggrandizement, selling the notion that self-interest brings about public good. What are taken to be public goods—libraries, welfare, housing, clean air, health care, public transport—are grossly inadequate compared to the ballyhoo about America's high standard of living. The society sanctions social indifference in the name of freedom, and America's dreams of self-fulfillment become a decoy rather than an inspiration.

Terkel's book strains under the weight of frustration at the despotism of big business. James Abourezk is outspoken on the subject:

> We have a government that is ostensibly run by the people, for the people. It's not true. We have a government run by the establishment for the establishment. If there are some droppings left over for the people, well and good. No more than droppings. . . . The ones who run this country are the multinationals, the banks, the *Fortune* 500.

Business preaches the gospel of free enterprise because it manipulates the market. Planning is efficiency inside the board-room and "anti-American" or "socialistic" outside it. "I came to understand," explains Dennis Kucinich, the young former mayor of Cleveland, "that big business has a feudal view of the city, and that City Hall was within their fiefdom." Whether Terkel is talk-ing to the black Mississippi farmer Hartman Turnbow ("We makin' dyin' progress. We makin' progress to dig our grave") or to the old activist–turned–prophet of self-sufficiency Scott Near-ing ("The job is to keep your head above water and to do your share in making the dying society as tolerable as possible"), a great sense of demoralization emerges from these tales. People and resources are outrageously wasted, and the dreaming exacer-bates the despotism even as it tries to assuage it. The despotism of the ruling elite seems to have had the same emotional effect on modern America that de Tocqueville saw in the Ancien Ré-gime of France:

> Love of gain, fondness for business careers, the desire to get rich at all costs, a craving for material comfort and easy living quickly become the ruling passions under despotic government. . . . It is the nature of despotism that it should foster such desire and propagate havoc. Lowering as they do the national morale . . . where equality and tyranny coexist, a steady deterioration of the mental and moral standards of the nation is inevitable.

Terkel's book frequently pits the spirit of American indepen-dence, struggle, and high-mindedness against the despotic forces of industry. Herschel Ligon, fifth generation on his Tennessee farm, struggles to keep going against fierce competition from "agribusiness." Joe and Gaynell Begley fight against the mine owners whose strip-mining has ruined the Appalachian land and impoverished the people. Bob Ziak fights to protect his patch of the Oregon woods from the greed of lumber companies destroying the landscape and wildlife. Jessie de la Cruz, a migrant worker, organizes her friends successfully to obtain proper housing and fair practices from California landowners. Ray Kaepplinger, a Chicago photographer, recounts his one-man search-and-destroy mission against the Chicago political machine. All these stories about unsung citizens who find their identity in their struggle to be heard are thrilling to read but deceptive as bellwethers. "There are signs," Terkel says in his introduction, "unmistakable, of an astonishing increase in the airing of grievances: of private wrongs and public rights." These tales—as Terkel hopes—may augur a shift in the collective national spirit, the arrival of a more cooperative, public-spirited age. But they also may simply add more currency to the old chump change of individualism.

Terkel ends *American Dreams: Lost and Found* with an interview he conducted sitting up all night on a train with a seventy-year-old black man, Clarence Spencer, bound for Martin Luther King, Jr.'s March on Washington in 1963. Spencer tells Terkel: "When this thing started out, I said to my wife: 'This I want to be *in*. I don't want to see it on the television or hear it on the radio. I want to be *in* it. I crave to get into that light.'" Spencer's lyrical monologue spells out Terkel's ambition: to get beyond the shadows of dreaming and the technology of enchantment into the light of action. The enchanted may be content, but they are not free.

12

Walt Whitman

"One's-Self I sing, a simple separate person." With this un-
rhymed, luxuriant line, Walt Whitman's "Song of Myself" ush-
ered the cult of personality into American literature. "I will effuse
egotism and show it underlying all, and I will be the bard of
personality."

The iconography of modern American individualism—the
open road, the free-spirited traveler, the hobo, the daydreaming
democrat, the star, the outlaw prophet—begins with the protean
voices in Whitman's *Leaves of Grass*, the title of his collected
poems, 1855, which would go to nine expanded editions in his
lifetime. Whitman's songs encapsulated American optimism,
hymning the abundance on which it was based, and nurturing a
sense of anticipation.

> Chanter of Personality, outlining what is yet to be,
> I project the history of the future.

Whitman proclaimed "the destiny of me." As Justin Kaplan's
shrewd biography *Walt Whitman: A Life* documents, Whitman was
a cagey impresario of himself. When Henry Thoreau visited
Whitman in 1856 in Brooklyn, he found prints of Hercules, Bac-

chus, and a satyr over his writing desk. A self-styled liberator of the American spirit, Whitman aspired to transform himself into a "Titan." He preached the perfection of Identity, but his own was very vague. He was the first American literary star to rationalize emotional greed in terms of a heroic project. He made a myth of himself. "I desire to hear from your own lips—some story of athletic friendship from which to learn the truth," wrote the English historian and homosexual John Addington Symonds to Whitman, responding to the "Calamus" section of *Leaves of Grass*, which sang of the "manly love of comrades." Whitman replied: ". . . I had six children. . . . Circumstances connected with their benefit and fortune have separated me from intimate relations."

It was a lie. Whitman's pronouncements about perfect sexuality and his own sensual serenity were, in D. H. Lawrence's words, "dead mentalized." He was not the free spirit his poetry claimed. It was one of the many contradictions between the poetic persona and the actual person. Raised in the radical democratic tradition by his carpenter father, Whitman promoted a faith in democracy while being essentially charismatic. He also propounded the romantic fallacy that a man's work is the man himself: "Camerado, this is no book,/Who touches this, touches a man." This delusion has served to obfuscate identity and justify generations of literary self-importance.

Ample in suffering ("I am the man, I suffer'd, I was there") and blessings ("Vivas for those who have fail'd"), the garrulousness of *Leaves of Grass* matched the largesse of the New World. Whitman made a poetic connection between national character and geography. "America demands one Song, at any rate, that is bold, modern, and all-surrounding as she is herself," he wrote in his brazen introduction to the anonymous first edition of his poems. Later, in *Democratic Vistas* (1871), Whitman returned to this central poetic concern. "The United States themselves are essentially the greatest poem," he said, elaborating the wide variety of American life and manners. "[America] awaits the gigantic and generous treatment worthy of it."

Whitman demanded a renegade poetry that departed from the "moth-eaten systems of the old world," and evoked the coarseness and energy, buoyancy and restlessness, individuality and commonality that the frontier had stamped into the American character. He awaited "the great literatus of the modern," and crowned himself with the laurel of poetic greatness long before society did. In print, at least, Whitman was the model of the perfected individual he sought to mold with words: "a great leading representative man, with perfected power, perfect confidence in his power . . . who will make free the American soul." Whitman took the idea of the Union of States and extended it to the emotional possibilities of everyman. "I give the sign of democracy," he chanted in "Song of Myself." His notion of individuality did not propound an elite, but the sacredness of everyman. It is still a radical idea:

> I am not an earth nor an adjunct of an earth,
> I am the mate and companion of people, all just as
>   immortal and fathomless as myself,
> (They do not know how immortal, but I know.)

"An individual is as superb as a nation when he has the qualities which make a superb nation," he had written in the 1855 preface to *Leaves of Grass*. Whitman sang America's greatness, making inventories of its sights and sounds, its smells and citizens as he tried to encompass the whole nation in his poetry. The "endless announcements" of *Leaves of Grass* were about being, not having. The poems counseled independence, action, and self-awareness:

> You shall no longer take things second or third hand
>   nor look,
> Through the eyes of the dead, nor feed on the spectres
>   of books,
> You shall not look through my eyes either nor take
>   things from me,
> You shall listen to all sides and filter them for
>   yourself.

Whitman, who called his poems "The New Bible," and looked to the day when "everyman will be his own priest," saw his poetry

as a strategy for regeneration. "The highly artificial and materialistic bases of modern civilization," he wrote in *Democratic Vistas*,
must "be confronted and met by an equally subtle and tremendous force-infusion for purposes of spiritualisation for the pure
conscience, for genuine aesthetics and for absolute and primal
manliness and womanliness. . . ." Otherwise Whitman foresaw a
destiny equivalent to the "fabled damned." The poetry was
pitched directly to the public: cheering, provoking, cajoling,
promising renewal:

> You will hardly know who I am or what I mean,
> But I shall be good health to you nevertheless,
> And filter and fibre your blood.

Part prophecy, part self-help, part tall talk, *Leaves of Grass* was
chanting for change. It was meant as an antidote to the material-
ism that by the mid-nineteenth century had confounded the
spiritual mission of American democracy. Whitman was outspoken on the subject: "It is as if we were somehow endowed with
a vast and more thoroughly appointed body, and then left with
little or no soul." His poems were an act of faith and transfigura-
tion. "Avoid all the intellectual/subtleties and 'withering doubts'
and 'blasted hopes' and 'unrequited/loves' and 'ennui and
wretchedness' . . . Preserve perfect calmness and sanity," he
wrote in his notes for a second edition. Skepticism was a European vice and optimism not yet an American one:

> I laugh at what you call dissolution
> And I know the amplitude of time.

Leaves of Grass was ecstatic, not analytic; it wanted to create a
sense of new life, not dredge up the decadent old one. "The
Modern Man I sing," wrote Whitman, coaxing him into being. "I
am afoot with my vision." A kind of poetic poltergeist, he imagined himself everywhere ("Speeding through space, speeding
through heaven and the stars/Backing and filling, appearing and
disappearing/I tread day and night such roads"). He wanted
poetry to intoxicate, to infiltrate, to infect, and to heal:

> To make the people rage, weep, hate, desire, with yourself,
> To lead America—to quell America with a great tongue.

In other words, Whitman wanted magic.

Whitman's quest was the shaman's search for the perfect spell.
He studied the great politicos and preachers of his day and found
them lacking: "Logic and sermons never convince/The damp of
the night drives deeper into my soul." To make words potent, he
turned for clues to other masters in the techniques of enchantment. He found a liberation from the metrical, rhymed ballad
style of poetry in the operatic brilliance of the Italian prima
donna Marietta Alboni: "I wonder if the lady will ever know that
her singing, her method, gave the foundations, the start, thirty
years ago, to all my poetic literary efforts since." The personal
magnetism of great performers also fascinated him. The
tragedian Junius Brutus Booth, he wrote, "was to me one of the
grandest revelations of my life . . . a lesson in artistic expression
. . . electric personal idiosyncrasy . . . as in all art-utterance it was
subtle and powerful . . . something special in the individual that
really conquered." In articulating "the destiny of me," it was not
just success but total surrender that Whitman sought through
poetry:

> I am not content now with a mere majority . . . I must have
> the love of all men and all women.
> If there is one left in any country who has no faith in
> me, I will travel to that country and go to that one.

"Speech is the twin of my vision," Whitman said in "Song of
Myself." "It provokes me forever,/It says sarcastically,/ *Walt you
contain enough, why don't you let it out then?*" Whitman broadcast
himself to the world. Naming himself and the world around him
was a magical gesture of regeneration. In his poems, Whitman
reinvented himself and his America. Both were projections of the
future made concrete through the power of language. He was
"Walt Whitman, an American, one of the roughs, a kosmos,/
Disorderly, fleshly and sensual . . . no stander above men and

women or apart from them." Poetry became a technique of ecstasy, a self-hypnotic experience that gave the poet himself a
giddy sense of plenitude: "Seeing, hearing, feeling, are miracles,
and each part and tag of me is a miracle." Speech celebrated
the miracle and renewed it. "What am I after all but a child,
pleas'd with the sound of my own name? repeating it over and
over . . ." Whitman's "ecstasy of statement" was a self-induced
trance—

> a trance, yet with all the senses alert—only a state of high exalted
> musing—the tangible and material with all its shows, the objec-
> tive world suspended or surmounted for a while, & the powers
> in exaltation, freedom, vision—yet the *senses* not lost or counter-
> acted.

Whitman's poems speak in voices, the voices of his American
century. "I am your voice—It was tied in you—In me it began to
talk." The words are simple, direct, American, yet full of mystery.
They were an attempt, he wrote, "to give the spirit, the body, the
man, new words, new potentialities for speech." To Whitman,
words were "metaphysical beings," and they had magic in them:
"A perfect writer would make words sing, dance, kiss, do the
male and female act. . . ." Whitman selected his words to convey
a visionary sense of national and personal identity. "Make no
quotations and no references to other writers," he urged himself
in his notebooks while composing "Song of Myself." "Take no
illustrations whatsoever from the ancients or classics . . . nor from
the royal and aristocratic institutions and forms of Europe. Make
no mention or allusion to them whatever, except as they relate
to the new, present things—to our country—to American character and interests."

Singing stops stuttering; and as Justin Kaplan's biography
illustrates, the poems' greatest magic acted not upon the indifferent general public but upon Whitman himself. Up to 1853, when
Whitman was thirty-four and embarked on his major work, his
writing as a reporter, journeyman editor, novelist, and versifier
had been the literary equivalent of a stutter. *Leaves of Grass* transformed his talent and his past. The book remains a miraculous

literary freak, whose unique eloquence and prescience seem to come from nowhere. Whitman wanted it that way. He ensured the myth of the book and of the man by destroying vast numbers of manuscripts and letters. "Some manuscripts he carefully altered, destroying single pages, changing 'him' to 'her' or a man's initial to a number code," says Kaplan. "By the time he died scarcely a period in his life had not been revised in one way or another." Whitman celebrated the sacredness of self, and his life attested to the fallacy of romantic individualism. He spoke with neither "perfect candor" nor spiritual liberation. He was too self-referring to achieve wisdom. Whitman spent $4,000—twice as much as he paid for his house in Camden, New Jersey—on a mausoleum for himself. Kaplan puts it nicely but misses the point of his pride: "In death, Whitman reunited his scattered family under his granite room and also in a lasting assertion of self, merged their identities into his: the pediment had only one name, 'Walt Whitman,' carved in high relief." By the end of his life, the great voyager of the open American roads was lost.

The shaman is part healer and part con man. Whitman, too, was a great artificer of personality. The poet promoted a cult of identity that, stripped of its spiritual trappings a century later, has its apotheosis in the notion of "perfect individuality" we call stardom. He wanted to regenerate society, not to cash in on it. He didn't have a star's sense of vindictive triumph, but he *did* have a star's sense of emotional imperialism:

> I and mine do not convince by arguments, similes, rhymes
> We convince by our presence.

Kaplan calls Whitman "his own biographer," referring to his much-photographed later years. Whitman sat for Mathew Brady and Thomas Eakins; his face even adorned cigar boxes although he didn't smoke. He had become an American trademark. From the outset of his poetic career, Whitman had styled himself a Democratic Dandy. On the frontispiece of the first edition of *Leaves of Grass,* he presented himself as a brazen, strong, self-confident loafer. Bearded, open-collared, his pelvis thrust forward, Whitman staged himself in dramatic contrast to the dark, stiff, sexless fashions of the day. Later, in his old age, he was to observe about the picture: "I look so damned flamboyant, as if I was hurling bolts at somebody—full of mad oaths—saying defiantly, to hell with you!" By the end of his life, Whitman was adjusting his poetic persona to Christlike dimensions, cultivating an image of sweetness and amplitude. In the 1889 frontispiece to *Leaves of Grass,* Whitman posed himself with a butterfly on his right forefinger—"I've always had a knack of attracting birds and butterflies and other wild critters," he explained about the photo. Later, among his memorabilia, the butterfly turned up. It was cardboard, "with a loop of fine wire attached by means of which it could be fastened to a finger."

Whitman's spiritual preening ("Divine am I inside and out, and I make holy whatever I touch or am touch'd from") had its corollary in publicity. His identity was more fluid than his poetry admitted to. His chants were ways of reasserting a vague sense of self, an inauthenticity that D. H. Lawrence, who knew what he was talking about, detected underneath the poems. "Your mainspring is broken, Walt Whitman. The mainspring of your own individuality. And so you run down with a great whirr, merging with everything. . . ." Whitman promoted his ecstatic sense of self as a means of calming the American restlessness (and himself) and moving Americans beyond their blinkered material concerns. In generalizing the passions of his life, Whitman transformed his own family history of dislocation into a myth of the open road, his homosexual appetites into a dream of the comradely "adhesiveness" of democracy:

> Henceforth I ask no good fortune, I myself am good fortune,
> Henceforth I whimper no more, postpone no more, need
>   nothing,
> Done with indoor complaints, libraries, querulous criticisms,
> Strong and content I travel the open road.

"The proof of a poet is that his country absorbs him as affectionately as he has absorbed it." The remark comes from the famous 1855 introduction to *Leaves of Grass.* Far from being absorbed, Whitman was reviled and ignored by the American public, who were not captivated by the spell of his songs. However, the poet had influential admirers on both sides of the Atlantic. "I find it the most extraordinary piece of wit and wisdom which America has yet contributed," Emerson wrote to him upon receiving the first edition. "I greet you at the beginning of a great career." Whitman shamelessly printed the letter without consent in subsequent editions. Over the years, while Emerson's admiration dwindled ("I expect him to make the songs of the nation but he seems contented to make the inventories"), Whitman found such enthusiastic European readers as Tennyson, the Rossettis, Swinburne, Robert Louis Stevenson, Vincent Van Gogh. But his book had not done its work in the world.

"Whitman's poems in the public reception have fallen stillborn in this country," began an article entitled "Walt Whitman's Actual American Position" in the *West Jersey Press*, 1876. "They have been met, and are met today, with determined denial, disgust and scorn of orthodox American authors, publishers and editors, and in a pecuniary and worldly sense, have certainly wrecked the life of their author." The unsigned article was written by Whitman himself, prepared to make a myth of his suffering as well as his inspiration. Whitman's poems offered the world his best self, but his press agentry showed a truer one. Kaplan's biography doesn't sweep Whitman's self-promoting spirit aside; but he tries to evade the implications of the greed behind it with a little literary hocus-pocus of his own: "This incessant clamor and posturing possessed a certain purity," Kaplan writes. "It was always and ultimately in service of the work, *Leaves of Grass,* not the self." But as Whitman contended again and again, the work was the man. Whitman was brazen in promoting both. As a literary hustler, he was terrific. He lied about sales figures; he reviewed his own work; he wrote articles about himself and the poems, which sympathetic followers signed with their names; he kept the press informed of every turn in his career. "The public is a thick-skinned beast," he said. "You have to keep whacking away on its hide to let it know you're there." But Whitman's stories about himself reminded the American public not so much of his presence as of his omnipresence. In one of his planted articles, Whitman wrote about himself: "It is just as certain that the subtle shadow of him, his fame, has established himself in Europe, and is branching and radiating there in all directions in the most amazing manner. . . ."

By defining the self as man's highest aspiration ("And nothing, not God, is greater to one than one's self is"), Whitman could never truly transcend himself or achieve his vaunted identity. In rebellion against the material aggrandizement of America's industrial revolution ("the depraving influence of riches as well as poverty, the absence of all high ideals in character . . ."), Whitman preached its corollary: spiritual aggrandizement. In this, as in most other aspects of his thought, Whitman was archetypically American. He practiced sympathetic magic and sought for himself the magic of fame, which, however it served the spiritual mission of his poetry, also served his pride. Kaplan assures his readers: "Almost alone among the major American writers, Whitman achieved in his last years radiance, serenity and a generosity of spirit." These were the attributes the poet had been claiming for himself since 1855. But Whitman's collaboration on his biography, the panic in his self-promotion, and the perpetuation of his legend belie claims of wisdom and serenity. Nevertheless, *Leaves of Grass* remains the watershed of nineteenth-century poetry.

Whitman's poetry sang of the rich variety of American life just as technology was beginning to homogenize it: "everywhere turning out new generations of humanity like uniform iron castings." His poems contributed to the debate of democracy but not, as he hoped, to its realization. Then, as now, democracy, as Whitman said, was "a great word whose history, I suppose, has yet to be enacted." Whitman was the pathfinder of modern American poetry, bushwhacking his way beyond the taken routes of meter and content. "It was you that broke the new wood," Ezra Pound wrote of him in the *Cantos*. "Now is the time for carving." Whitman set American writers to mythologizing and exploring their consciousness.

Whitman's "destiny of me" is no longer "an unknown want" but an appetite shared by an entire nation. Burnished by psychologies and every form of spiritual massage, the twentieth-century American sense of selfhood is the ruling obsession of all life. The self is infallible. The media have turned the society into a whispering gallery of identities "doting" on themselves. The perfection of self has become a habit and an industry. "I will report heroism from an American point of view," Whitman announced in "Song of Myself"; but by now, the propagandizing instinct is an ingrained reflex of American individualism. The body and soul of American society have become hopelessly confused. The society functions best not on Whitman's "force-infusions . . . of spiritualization" but on infusions of envy. The society is still as barbarous, promising, and lost as when Whitman first launched his attack on it. The enemy now is not just soulless abundance but the emptiness of individuality that abundance makes possible. The economic opportunities of America have diminished the spiritual ones. The society therefore remains adolescent: a great man-child of a nation, at once willful and irresponsible, with no sense of community or sacrifice, no goal larger than self-improvement. Whitman's brand of harmonious individualism ("completeness in separation . . . the last, best, dependence is to be upon humanity itself and its own inherent, normal full-grown qualities . . .") remains a daydream of America's eternal future promise. Far from redeeming democracy, the great "miracle . . . of me in the centre," which is the first principle of American individualism, has contributed as much to its undoing as its growth. The conflicting interests of American selfhood have led, as Whitman feared, to a society that is "aimless, a cheat, a crash." And for this predicament, songs still remain to be written.

13

Hunter Thompson

Hunter Thompson calls his kind of writing "edge work." Thompson has a compulsive gambler's addiction to raising the stakes. He puts himself in impossible positions for the thrill of seeing if he'll survive them.

Twisted on drugs, or riding with the Hell's Angels, or sneaking out of a hotel after running up a huge tab, the gambits are just Thompson's way to kill boredom and get the adrenalin flowing. "When the strange music starts," he writes about the rush from pushing his motorcycle to the limit in *Hell's Angels* (1966), ". . . you stretch your luck so far that fear becomes exhilaration." The edge is where danger banishes fear, where time stops, where past and future no longer matter.

Thompson's writing steers straight for this crazy no-go area, "a means to an end, a place of definitions." His antics are the typical agitations of an American soul that has found no hope or enduring project in the Land of Plenty. American journalism has had other iconoclasts, but Thompson may be its first wild man.

Having learned his style from the put-ons of Ken Kesey and the brutal mischief of the Hell's Angels in San Francisco during the mid-sixties, Thompson knows how to "lay a jolt on the squares." Although he disputes the term "outlaw" for the spectacle he makes of himself in print, Thompson accepts "freak" (and ran on the Freak Power ticket for sheriff of Aspen, Colorado, in 1971). And as with any freak, the public can't take its eyes off him.

Hunter Thompson is a subject of scandal and concern. His craving for drugs is by now as legendary as H. L. Mencken's for beer. Thompson gives the notion of "conspicuous consumption" a meaning all its own: "I like to just gobble the stuff right out in the open, take my chances, just to stomp on my own accelerator." He has at various times ridden with and been stomped by the Hell's Angels, destroyed his editor's car, shot the windows out of his apartment, Maced a waiter, and planted outrageous fantasies in his political reportage—such as that the former dean of American telecasters, Walter Cronkite, was involved in the white-slave trade, running Vietnamese orphans to East Coast brothels. ("Christ, writing about politics would paralyze my brain if I didn't have a slash of wild humor now and then.")

"Some people," Thompson says in his fine tale about meeting Muhammad Ali at the Leon Spinks–Ali rematch, "Last Tango in Vegas," "write their novels and others roll high enough to live them and some fools try to do both." Thompson is one of those fools. A failed novelist, he hit upon his style while in his native Louisville, Kentucky, covering the Derby in 1970. With his brain scrambled on drugs and facing the desperation of a deadline, Thompson "just started jerking pages out of my notebook and numbering them and sending them to the printer. I was sure it was the last article I was going to do for anybody." The article —"The Kentucky Derby Is Decadent and Depraved"—was praised as some kind of journalistic breakthrough, and Thompson thought: "Holy shit, if I can write like this and get away with it, why should I keep trying to write like the *New York Times*? It was like falling down an elevator shaft and landing in a pool full of mermaids."

Thompson looked into the mirror of his own writing and found himself irresistible. He coined the term "gonzo journalism" for the idiosyncratic shaggy-dog reportage he began to practice. His early journalism (1962–1970), much of which is included in the massive anthology of his reporting, *The Great Shark Hunt: Strange Tales from a Strange Time* (1979), is unexceptional. "I don't think of myself as a reporter," he says. And in the conventional sense, he isn't. He rarely gets the story he's sent to cover. He's not good at analysis; and empathy is not one of his strong points. But he does keep a vigilant eye on his own drug-blitzed consciousness.

When Thompson starts to report from the interior of his frenzied mind, his spiky, loose-talking, macho personality comes through in all its hilarity and ugliness. The style is a strange amalgam of fact and fiction, paranoid fantasy, personal chronicle, and outlandish asides. Beginning as a sportswriter, Thompson found a method of bringing the bow-wow ways of the sports desk to the battles he created around himself. They "wanted action, color, speed, violence"; and Thompson could make himself sensational, even if he was bored by the world around him.

"True gonzo reporting needs the talent of a master journalist, the eye of an artist/photographer and the balls of an actor," Thompson says. Although linked with "new journalists," Thompson is quick to distinguish his act from the others'. "[The new journalists] like Tom Wolfe and Gay Talese re-create stories that have already happened while I get right in the middle of what I'm writing about—as personally involved as possible." Thompson wants to be the light, not shed light. He doesn't reconstruct the event, he *is* the event that he writes about.

Subtitled "A Savage Journey into the Heart of the American Dream," his *Fear and Loathing in Las Vegas* (1972) doesn't go to the heart of anything except Thompson's megalomania. The book is structured like an acid cliff-hanger, where the drug-crazed author is depicted "writing feverishly in a notebook about a nasty situation that I thought I might *not* get away from." How far out on a limb can Thompson go without crashing? It's a game he plays frequently, but with only occasional success.

One such occasion is Thompson's hilarious account of a Mexican fishing tournament where he quickly runs amok. "By the third day of the tournament or maybe it was the fourth, I had lost control of my coverage," he writes in "The Great Shark Hunt." Bored by the fishing assignment, he turns the story into a frenzied account of his hotel escape plot, drug smuggling, and terrorizing the sports fishermen by driving a jeep onto a patio bar during a cocktail party to demand more ice for his drink. " 'You crazy son of a bitch!' someone yelled. 'You just mashed about fifteen trees.' "

In all his gonzo reportage, Thompson acts out the romantic notion of fulfillment through the wreck of consciousness. Twice in his books, he quotes Dr. Johnson's dictum: "He who makes a beast of himself gets rid of the pain of being a man." Thompson doesn't dispel the beast, he cashes in on it.

Thompson savors the pangs of self-loathing. On his Kentucky Derby assignment, he searches with his sidekick, the illustrator Ralph Steadman, for a face that will epitomize the corruption of the scene, and catches sight of the perfect visage in a mirror: "There he was, by God—a puffy, drink-ravaged, disease-ridden caricature—like an awful cartoon version of an old snapshot in some once proud mother's family album. It was the face we'd been looking for—it was, of course, my own."

His perverse romanticism has become a cult in an age that is seduced by those who destroy themselves for meaning. Writing the author's note to *The Great Shark Hunt*, Thompson considers throwing himself out of a New York window and into a fountain twenty-eight floors below: "If I decide to leap for the fountain when I finish this memo, I want to make one thing perfectly clear —I would genuinely love to make that leap, and if I don't I will always consider it a mistake and a failed opportunity." He survived to collect his royalties; and his flirtation with death was yet another walk on the wild side.

Only once in Thompson's accounts does his role as the crazed dark shadow of a mad society become even faintly resonant. He travels on the press plane to San Clemente on the last trip Nixon made as President and then arrives drunk and disorderly at the press conference. "I had a bottle of beer in my hand," he told

Playboy. "My head was painfully constricted by something some-body had put in my drink. . . . Rabbi Korff began a demented rap about Nixon being the most persecuted President in American history. I heard myself shouting, 'Why is that, Rabbi? . . . Why? . . . Tell us why?' He said something like 'I'm only a small-time Rabbi,' and I said, 'Nobody's bigoted here.' "

When Thompson followed the 1972 presidential election for *Rolling Stone,* an assignment that produced his best book, *Fear and Loathing on the Campaign Trail* (1973), his loose talk, humor, and weird ways stood out more vividly in contrast to the grave, buttoned-down and fawning attitudes of the press corps. Whereas most political journalists trade on their reputation as Mr. Insider, Thompson had the copyright on Mr. Outsider.

As the court jester of the campaign, he could speak the un-speakable about the press and the candidates and get away with it. He was the first to see that George McGovern would win the nomination; and long before Watergate or his fine description of Nixon's elaborate tape system, Thompson had vilified Nixon as a criminal: "He speaks to the bully in us: the bully, the predatory shyster who turns into something unspeakable, full of claws and bleeding string-warts, on nights when the moon comes too close. . . ."

The scourge of politicians ("Hubert Humphrey should be castrated") and stewardesses ("You nasty little bitch," he imag-ines saying to one, "I hope your next flight crashes in cannibal country"), Thompson has always been ten thousand miles of bad road. "I was a Hell's Angel in my head for a long time," he told *Playboy.* "Some people just lie down when they lose; these fuckers come back and tear up the whole game. I was a failed writer for ten years and I was always in fights. I'd do things like go into a bar with a 50-pound sack of lime, turn the whole place white and then just take on anyone who came at me. I always got stomped, never won a fight. I lost a lot of my physical aggressiveness when I started to publish what I wrote."

But it wasn't so much lost as refurbished. He could now enter-tain the paying customers with his murderous instincts. "About 20 miles east of Baker I stopped to check the drug bag. The sun was hot and I felt like killing something. Anything. Even a big lizard. Drill the fucker," he writes in *Fear and Loathing in Las Vegas.* And elsewhere in the book: "I liked to shoot guns—especially at night, when the great blue flame would leap out, along with that noise . . . and yes, the bullets, too . . . I meant no harm. I just liked the explosions."

Thompson's gonzo journalism is in the familiar American psychopathic style. Obsessed with action (motorcycles, a campaign, drug adventures), ruthless in pursuit of his journalistic goal ("hammer and tongs and God's mercy on anybody who gets in the way"), Hunter Thompson personifies the restless emptiness of American individualism. He grows big without growing wise.

The last lines of *Fear and Loathing in Las Vegas* epitomize the dead end of America's guiltless pursuit of her own pleasure: "I felt like a monster reincarnation of Horatio Alger. . . . A Man on the Move, and just sick enough to be totally confident." Thompson means to satirize the Las Vegas "greedheads"; but unwittingly it is his own numbed greed he exposes. His credit-card sprees, his drug bills, his high living don't penetrate the American Dream, only indulge it.

Like all psychopaths, Thompson elevates his outrageousness onto a heroic plane. He is a dandy of dementia. As an explanation of gonzo journalism, he quotes Muhammad Ali's "My way of joking is to tell the truth. . . ." But Thompson is neither so truthful, unique, nor unpredictable as he likes to think. His kind of slapstick selfishness gets less of America onto the page than meets the eye. But this hell-for-leather trivialization is inevitable when you cleave like Thompson to the junkie's credo: reality is for people who can't cope with drugs.

14

Joan Didion and John Gregory Dunne

In his book of essays, *Quintana and Friends*, John Gregory Dunne salutes Los Angeles as "the kingdom of self . . . it is the end of the line. The last chance. *Eureka.* I love it." Dunne and his wife, Joan Didion, both best sellers in a community that respects only the numbers, are the Lunts of the Los Angeles literary scene. Each in his own way celebrates the sights and symbols of California, a vacuum making its emptiness sensational. Their writing is typical of California insensibility.

As with the rest of the California middle class who jog, exercise, diet, sunbathe, and search for inner peace and self-awareness, Dunne and Didion are obsessed with themselves. In a society without a mission, they are their own most heroic projects, and this self-absorption manifests itself in style. "I hate to ask questions," Dunne admits, his selfishness very much a part of his journalistic posturing. "In any event I am not interested in the answers. . . . What I do is hang around." This could be called the surfer school of journalism, where the laid-back reporter simply goes with the flow. In beach language, "radical" means "very," as in "rad dads," which are G-string bikinis. Dunne's cool is equally frivolous and diminishing. His wife's style and persona are more cunning. She turns herself into a metaphor of the social malaise, alienation in a twin set.

"We tell ourselves stories in order to live," Joan Didion writes in the much-quoted first line of *The White Album,* essays that span the upheavals of the late 1960s and the becalmed 1970s. But the real story she is telling is that of her own suffering. She has the Brentwood Blues. She meditates on her desolation and makes it elegant. She puts herself in the vanguard of suffering and uses this to set herself apart from the rich, successful, and decadent Los Angeles life she enjoys. She needs the fiction to rationalize the fact that she is part of the problem she analyzes.

The tactic runs in the family. Dunne begins his *Vegas: A Memoir of a Dark Season,* "In the summer of my nervous breakdown . . ." But Didion has no peer in special pleading. Anxiety passes for seriousness. She exploits the drama of her lack of affect, staging it with all the tact and relish of the Ancient Mariner and his tale of woe: "I want you to understand what you are getting: you are getting a woman who for some time now has felt radically sepa-rated from most of the ideas that seem to interest other people" ("The Islands"). Or: "Three, four, sometimes five times a month I spend the day with a headache, almost insensible to the world around me" ("In Bed"). Or: "Quite often during the past several years I have felt myself a sleepwalker. Acquaintances read the *New York Times* and try to tell me the news of the world. I listen to call-in shows" ("The Islands").

Didion is a Hollywood somnambulist. She remembers the famous names she meets along the way. In dramatizing the para-noia of the 1960s, her case history reads like a gossip column of the decade's chaos:

> . . . In this light all connections were equally meaningful, and equally senseless. Try these: on the morning of John Kennedy's death in 1963 I was buying, at Ransohoff's in San Francisco, a short silk dress in which to be married. A few years later this dress of mine was ruined when, at a party in Bel Air, Roman Polanski accidentally spilled red wine on it. Sharon Tate was also a guest at this party, although she and Roman Polanski were not yet married. On July 27, 1970, I went to the Magnin-Hi Shop on

the third floor of I. Magnin in Beverly Hills and picked out, at Linda Kasabian's request, the dress in which she began her testimony about the murders at Sharon Tate Polanski's house on Cielo Drive.

In the aristocracy of success, there are no strangers. This is California radical chic. In the sixties, California gave America many of its celebrated killers (Charles Manson), kingpins (Richard Nixon and his henchmen), and crusaders (the Black Panthers and the Esalen Institute). As a famous writer, Didion has entrée to everyone. She makes an art form out of aimlessness. "The Coast" describes not only the California shoreline, but its state of mind.

When she encounters the movers and shakers of her time, Didion, like her husband, has no questions. What she brings back is not "the story" but tidbits of insiders' gossip that tell us more about her state of mind than the life of those she reports. Eldridge Cleaver made her ring his apartment bell and then stand in the middle of Oak Street in San Francisco before deciding whether to admit her. Then they talked about the advertising budget of *Soul on Ice*. She waited for Jim Morrison of The Doors to arrive at a recording session, and an hour after he made his entrance, he finally said to one of his sidemen, "in a whisper, as if he was wrestling the words from behind some disabling aphasia: 'It's an hour to West Covina. I was thinking maybe we should spend the night out there after we play.' " Didion, of course, was close enough to hear the muffled whisper.

The sense of abundance in California is extraordinary—the beauty of the landscape matched by the apparent material well-being of its middle-class citizens. "Have you hugged your realtor today?" say the bumper stickers, a reminder of the land boom that has filled the pockets of Californians and fed the dream of perfectibility that the landscape inspires. The film industry promotes this sense of abundance, epitomizing the greed that stars make glorious. As occasional screenwriters, Dunne and Didion are members in good standing of the Hollywood establishment. Although they both pretend to be disenchanted by the scene ("I admit a certain impatience with Holly-wood and all its orthodoxies," Dunne says), they are spell-bound by celebrity. Dunne, a groupie by nature and a hustler at heart, moved to California in 1964 and found himself in Heavy-set City. "Why write for films?" he asks in his essay "Tinsel." "Because the money is good . . . and because the other night, after a screening, we went to a party with Mike Nichols and Candice Bergen and Warren Beatty and Barbra Streisand. I never did that at *Time*." Jack Warner once called screenwriters "schmucks with Underwoods." Nothing Dunne boasts about in his film experiences belies this description.

Didion is a much cooler customer; her conservatism is hidden behind her shrewd satire of California high life. Her prose is never more energetic than when she is turning her consumer's eye to the objects of the rich. Detailing the lifestyle of Holly-wood's old guard, she writes: "Dinner guests pick with vermeil forks at broiled fish and limestone lettuce *vinaigrette,* decline des-sert, adjourn to the screening room, and settle down to *The Heartbreak Kid* with a little seltzer in a Baccarat glass." As Mr. and Mrs. Insider, they write most vivaciously about the superficial. Dunne can infiltrate Twentieth Century-Fox to report on the fiasco of filming *Dr. Dolittle* in his entertaining book *The Studio,* and Didion can drop the persona of narcolept and come alive as *grande dame* in her essay "In Hollywood" to explain the customs of the natives to the tourists: "Flirtations between men and women, like drinks after dinner, remain largely the luxury of character actors out from New York, one-shot writers, reviewers being courted by industry people, and others who do not under-stand the *mise* of the local *scène.*"

In their enthusiasm, Dunne's and Didion's descriptions al-ways evade any political nuance or moral position. They defend themselves for this symptomatic myopia by adopting the high-falutin' tone of insider. "Driving the freeway induces a kind of narcosis," Dunne writes in his essay about Los Angeles. "Speed is a virtue, and the speed of the place makes one obsessive, a gambler. The spirit is that of a city on the move. . . . Mobility is their common language, without it, or an appreciation of it, the visitor is illiterate." But the vast, sophisticated network of free-ways—which epitomizes both the ambition and restlessness of the society—also stratifies and blinkers it. Dunne sees the car as a symbol of mobility; it is also the symbol of California's cultural sterilization, keeping each class sanitized from the experience of the others. The freeways, the shopping malls, the drive-ins are all controlled environments that promote evasion, not community. Isolated in their cars, the commuters see and hear only what they want to. Only the poor walk or take buses in California. Yet Dunne is too busy cheering the society's sense of freedom and liberation from "community chauvinism" to see the vicious im-plications of this attitude. A winner in the competition to survive, he takes no notice of its effects on the poor.

Dunne practices his own brand of chauvinism. The punk group Dead Kennedys sings, "California über Alles," and Dunne shouts, *"Eureka.* I love it!"—a phrase that isn't exactly a call to arms. It is as if, as Auden writes of earlier migrants to this disap-pointing Eden, Dunne was touched in the head:

> The tolerant Pacific air
> Makes logic seem so silly, pain
> Subjective . . .

And as if to prove the point, Dunne recently bragged to *Esquire* about being hell on a short fuse:

> I hit a trick-or-treater a couple of years ago. He came to the house—that is, he egged my house. Anyway, I caught this kid and really gave him a whack. Just belted him. Then some man—not this boy's father—was going by the house and he said "You can't hit him." And I said, "The hell I can't." He then kicked me in the nuts and we began going at it in the street in front of my house in fashionable Brentwood Park. . . .

California's spaciousness, the absence of a past in a jerry-built society, the wealth, turned a sixty-pound East Coast weakling into a West Coast he-man. "For eight years on the Upper East Side of Manhattan, I had been a have-not and malcontent. I dreamed of being an adventurer. . . . I can say now what I dared not say then: I was a jerk." California, the eternal present, the world of now and "Have a good day" hymned by sincere pool attendants and cashiers, was Dunne's new world. The laminated skies, the purifying ocean, the manicured lawns, and glassy pools where dirt and guilt seemed to have been abolished, promised him rebirth. Dunne said goodbye not only to the cramping failures of his East Coast/European past, but also to his conscience. The transience and kitsch of California race Dunne's engine: an entire community symbolizing the detritus of Western capitalism.

> To me it was a new world: *the* new world. I watched Los Angeles television, listened to Los Angeles radio, devoured Los Angeles newspapers trying to find the visa that would provide entry. "Go gargle razor blades" advised a local talk show host pleasantly; it was a benediction that seemed to set the tone of the place. Dawn televised live on the Sunset Strip: a minister of the Lord inquired of a stringy-haired nubile what she liked doing best in the world. An unequivocal answer: "Balling." . . . I read of a man living on the rim of Death Valley who walked alone out into the desert, leaving behind a note that he wanted to "talk to God." God apparently talked back: the man was bitten by a rattlesnake and died.

A self-confessed jerk, Dunne found peace at last in the psychopathic styles that pass for "individualism" in Southern California. In fierce defense of his new turf, disdaining outsiders ("the casual visitor"), Dunne can't see the hellishness behind the vulgarity he enjoys. As Bertolt Brecht wrote of Hollywood in "Hollywood Elegies I":

> The village of Hollywood was planned according
>   to the notion
> People in these parts have of heaven. In these parts
> They have come to the conclusion that God,
> Requiring a heaven and hell, didn't need to
> Plan just two establishments but
> Just the one: heaven. It
> Serves the unprosperous, unsuccessful
> As hell.

Didion is no less perverse than her husband, shrewdly selling her anxiety while praising those things in California life that symbolize its sterility. In her essay "In Hollywood," Didion maintains that the driven, megalomaniacal, isolated, and insecure life of the film colony is "the last extant stable society"! At the same time, in the same essay, she rightly observes about the film industry that "the action is everything, more consuming than sex, more immediate than politics; more important, always, than the acquisition of money, which is never, for the gambler, the true point of the exercise." That does not sound like a prescription for stability.

Didion is equally mischievous in her love of shopping malls, which have destroyed local markets and homogenized the suburbs. She sees these malls not only as "equalizers" but as tranquilizers. She welcomes their anonymity and craves their blandness. "In each of them one moves for a while in aqueous suspension not only of light but of judgment and of personality. One meets no acquaintances at The Esplanade. One gets no telephone calls at the Edgewater Plaza." Where Dunne uses "freedom" to rationalize rootlessness and cruel romantic attitudes ("It deepens the sense of self-reliance"), Didion is never so crudely sentimental. Her moral emptiness is cloaked in the neurasthenic performance of victim. Princess of angst, Didion mythologizes an arid world and also its antidote, water. Of course, as she admits in "Holy Water," she has "an obsessive interest not in the politics of water but in the waterworks themselves." Water, emblem of purity and remission, becomes in her imagination an extension of the greed and glut that dominate the pampered landscape through which she moves:

> Some of us who live in arid parts of the world think about water with a reverence others might find excessive. The water I will draw tomorrow from my tap in Malibu is today crossing the Mojave Desert from the Colorado River, and I like to think about exactly where that water is. The water I will drink tonight in a restaurant in Hollywood is by now all down the Los Angeles Aqueduct from the Owens River, and I also think about exactly

where the water is: I particularly like to imagine it as it cascades
down the 45-degree stone steps that aerate Owens water after its
airless passage through the mountain pipes and siphons. . . .

Longing to be refreshed, soothed, nurtured, and calmed, Didion offers an evocative description of water that always reminds
the reader that it, too, is a sedative. She champions the totemic
Hollywood swimming pool against those who have "misap-
prehended" this $10,000 to $50,000 item as a symbol of waste
and affluence. "Actually a pool is for many of us in the West a
symbol not of affluence but of order, of control over the uncontrollable. A pool is water made available and useful and is, as
such, infinitely soothing to the Western eye." Brecht wrote:

> The city is named after the angels
> And you meet angels on every hand
> They smell of oil and wear golden pessaries
> And, with blue rings round their eyes
> Feed the writers in their swimming pools
>   every morning.
>
> ("Hollywood Elegies," III)

California is a state of amateur outdoorsmen—of runners,
swimmers, bikers, sailors, golfers. Here, the surface of life can be
enjoyed without analysis. Amid the sun, surf, and caesar salads,
intellectual stimulation is never a high priority. Dunne and Didion are really pretenders to the throne of High Culture; only a
society indifferent to literature could tolerate their pretensions to
excellence.

But their work does reflect a society seemingly anesthetized
to the implications of the wealth it enjoys. Dunne and Didion
never question the consequences of Los Angeles or the California scene on which they report—the general absence of community, the moral stupor, the greedy self-aggrandizement, and the
emotional impoverishment that characterize and enchant the
place. "We have a sense out here, however specious, of being
alone, of wanting to be alone, of having our own space, a kingdom of self with a two-word motto: 'Fuck off.' " If Dunne runs

off at the mouth like an Irishman who has just kissed the Blarney stone, Didion speaks in a terse, oblique style that is more commanding but no less spurious. Didion's muted prose gives both her life and her writing a sense of elegant unease. She has staked out the dead heart of American life as her territory, but its barbarism claims her. "We were drinking an indifferent bottle of Château Léoville-Poyferre which costs $20 American," she writes of a sojourn in Bogotá, Colombia. The sentence is unworthy, but typical, of that California side of her drawn to brand names and big names. She is obsessed with the moral emptiness around her because she embraces it. The story she tells herself is that her suffering sets her apart. On the contrary, her narcissistic self-absorption, her steadfast refusal to acknowledge a moral position, her indifference to the suffering of others, and her love of luxury make Didion and her husband brilliant mirrors of the California bourgeoisie.

POSTSCRIPT

In 1982, having exploited her private terror in print, Joan Didion was sent for two weeks to El Salvador to exploit other peoples'. Even the book jacket of *Salvador* (1983) treats her as a technician of trauma: ". . . a time and place so terrifying that only Joan Didion could capture it." Didion had used the fictional Central American country of Boca Grande as an exotic locale in her pretentiously arch novel *A Book of Common Prayer* (1973). But with the possibility of real and not imagined death in El Salvador, Didion finds new ways to make fear pay. It concentrates her mind wonderfully. Didion the self-dramatizing, panic-stricken somnambulist discovers a country where "terror is the given of the place," where the details of omnipresent murder induce "an amnesiac fugue," "where the only logic is acquiescence"; a country, in other words, not unlike her own fabled inner landscape.

Face to face with mayhem, Didion's detachment from life is dramatized as the inevitable, even essential way of negotiating the situation. With the adroit use of an impersonal pronoun, she can stage her affectlessness and the death she seems to abhor and make them both sensational:

> In El Salvador one learns that vultures go first for the soft tissue, for the eyes, the exposed genitalia, the open mouth. One learns that an open mouth can be used to make a specific point, can be stuffed with something emblematic: stuffed, say, with a penis. . . .

Didion picks over the carnage, visiting body dumps, the morgue, a rural battle zone. What excites her is the aesthetic of terror ("the exact mechanism of terror") and the atmosphere of death ("I did not forget the sensation of having been in a single instant demoralized, undone, humiliated by fear").

It is not the dead but the living that elude her. El Salvador's turmoil is a peasant revolt. But Didion, astonishingly, speaks to no peasants—except "the Salvadoran woman who works for my husband and me in Los Angeles." The people and the reasons for their enduring sacrifice don't interest her; she gives no sense of their heroic fight, only her own fear. Abroad, Didion keeps the same establishment company she keeps at home—the power brokers of the local scene: the President, bankers, embassy officials, local aristocracy. A policy of law and order favors those who already have privileges; not surprisingly, therefore, Didion equates violence with chaos. "El Salvador has always been a frontier . . . and remains marked by the meanness and discontinuity of all frontier history . . . any situation can turn to terror. The most ordinary errand can go bad." Emphasizing the randomness of violence gives succor to those who have the legitimate monopoly to use it.

Didion's curiosity is for chaos, not justice. Her word picture of the Salvadoran struggle gives the experience of terror without the political context that created it. The real chaos in El Salvador was the pre–civil war situation, which Didion hardly mentions. She has no talent for interpreting the past, only her present. She prefers the shifting ground of nightmare: "In the absence of information (and the presence of disinformation) even the most straightforward event takes on, in El Salvador, elusive shadows, like the fragments of a legend retrieved." But, of course, there is information, just as there is a story—a story of injustice. In 1881, communal land tenure was abolished by the ruling elite, who proceeded to turn the land to their own profit with coffee plantations. Some peasants were allowed to stay on the land as sharecroppers. By 1961, 12 percent of the rural population was landless; but this figure increased dramatically in the 1970s, when even the sharecroppers were dispossessed for the added acreage required for the new cash crops of sugar cane and cotton. By 1980, 80 percent of the Salvadoran peasantry was landless; and the wealth was consolidated into some two hundred families, who owned 60 percent of the land and 90 percent of the country's trade.

History is bleached out of Didion's report. She averts her eyes from rebellion as she does from dangerous street scenes: "I noticed soldiers herding a young civilian into a van, their guns at the boy's back, and I walked straight ahead, not wanting to see anything at all." She sees and doesn't see, she knows and doesn't know. If everything is dramatized as incomprehensible—Salvadoran politics, the "hallucinatory" U.S. claims about "land reform" and "human rights"—then she has only her own sensations to fall back upon. She insists there is no *solución*, only *el problema*, but Didion's problem is *her* solution. Sent to get the pulse of a people, Didion ends up taking her own temperature. Narcissism is the side show of conservatism.

Didion is expert at playing her laconic, high-rent persona against brutal situations. She mediates between the surrealism of Central American terror and the surrealism of American abundance, whose violence she (and her readers) can handle. After sharing a taxi with a Salvadoran woman, she spots a whiff of Arpège in the air. She notes President Magaña "drinking cup after Limoges cup of black coffee." When things get too tense in San Salvador, Didion cools out at the shopping mall: "This being the kind of 'color' I knew how to interpret, the kind of inductive irony, the detail that was supposed to illuminate the story." Although Didion discounts such irony for plumbing the depths of

El Salvador's confusions, she uses it continually and often to brilliant effect. She can winkle out dissonance from the most trivial incident: dropping a Halazone tablet into a pitcher of water; watching Ronald Reagan on her hotel TV screen, dubbed in Spanish, in a baseball movie called *The Winning Team.*

But this style, for which she is widely praised, obfuscates as it persuades. Adept at showing the self-deception of the U.S. involvement in El Salvador, she cannot see her own. Describing lunch in the garden of the American Embassy with her husband and the ambassador, Didion paints a tranquil scene of bounding English sheep dog, of chilled wine drunk from crystal glass, of fish served from porcelain plates and decorated with the insignia of the American eagle. She goes on: "The sheep dog and the crystal and the American eagle, together had on me a certain anaesthetic effect, temporarily deadening the receptivity to the sinister that afflicts everyone in Salvador."

Didion's elegant style gives her, too, "the illusion of plausibility." Her muted, finely tuned words erect a chic screen behind which she hides her shallowness. Her outrage at the U.S. government is at its hypocrisy and ineptness, but not at the U.S. presence in El Salvador in the first place. Didion mocks the fiasco of the Salvadoran election, but she cannot see the absurdity of her own imperial suggestions that the United States should "encourage" broad center-left coalitions and "discourage" the far left. Didion's shock at the violence she finds doesn't stop her from practicing her own variety by eliminating from her account of a civil war the ordinary people who fight on. The jittery, cool ring of her literary voice masquerades as neutral, while giving aid and comfort to the forces of reaction.

15

Notes on Fame

Since Satan is overworked and cannot take care
of the whole world by himself, he relies on the
services of the celebrities.

REBBE NAHMAN, from
Elie Wiesel's *Souls on Fire*

The fascination with fame that has turned America into a whispering gallery also drives it crazy with hope. "Unfortunately in
America today," said Michael Bennett as the newly famous director of *A Chorus Line,* "either you're a star or you're nobody." Or
to put fame's punishing appeal as baldly as *People*'s headline for
its story on Chevy Chase: HE'S HOT AND YOU'RE NOT.

The famous are heroes of free enterprise. They inspire envy
and feed off it. The most observed of all observers, the famous
are prodigious survivors. They set the standards of comparison
in a competitive society trivialized by its pursuit of status. Thor-
stein Veblen called this "invidious comparison." The adulation
is also an alienation. Envy, a passion that creates havoc in
private life, also creates it in public life, contributing to a rest
less, unhappy, violent society more prone to suspicion than
to friendship. The famous hide the vindictiveness behind their
triumphs with studied professional courtesy. But as Barry
Humphries in the guise of Dame Edna Everage teases in her
song "My Public," the success of the famous is meant to be
killing:

The David Hockneys on my wall
The Royal visitors who call
That's what my public's done for me.
All those requests I get to stay
With famous folk in St. Tropez
That's their idea of fun for me.
But they can keep Roman Polanski and Bianca
It's for the company of nobodies *like you* I hanker . . .

Dame Edna leaves no one in doubt that her intimidating victory is at the expense of others. The archetypal "superstar," Dame Edna sees all life as combat. She cannot resist showing off her advantage, which means reminding others ever-so-nicely of their worthlessness:

You need to have a pretty humble attitude
When you see little faces looking up *grotesque*
    with gratitude . . .

The classical idea of fame was reputation based on deeds. It is the classical notion of fame as accomplishment that Milton writes about in "Lycidas":

Fame is the spur that the clear spirit doth raise
(That last infirmity of noble mind)
To scorn delights, and live laborious days.

Fame is changing. Visibility is now an end in itself. A celebrity in our media-dominated age is, in Daniel Boorstin's words, "someone who is famous for being well-known." "Dame Edna" merely announced her stardom, with no apparent talent but a desire to shine and a sure sense of how to hustle the media. Renown now comes from having a media job, not from being good at it. World leaders get in line to talk to Barbara Walters. Politicians become newscasters; newscasters become movie actors; movie actors become politicians. Celebrity turns every serious endeavor into performance. Everything that rises in America must converge on a TV talk show.

Whoever is most visible holds the most sway. Modern politicians (Hitler, Eisenhower, Nixon) have understood this and taken lessons from actors. Inevitably, in a society where exposure is more important than ideological debate, America has found itself with a former actor as President. The unrelenting scrutiny of the TV camera forces everyone into a public turn. For the benefit of the camera, Gloria Steinem tap-dances. State Senator Julian Bond of Georgia ad-libs the role of the first black President, former Governor Lester Maddox performs a cabaret turn with a man he sent to prison, Gore Vidal takes a part in *Mary Hartman, Mary Hartman.* Not only is the modern celebrity visible, he has the power to be *everywhere* at once: a technological solution to the restlessness that marks the American character.

Attention-getting becomes the national style, in which gesture replaces commitment. Since the Hippies made themselves irresistible to the media in the late sixties (Jerry Rubin accepted the "Academy Award of Protest"), political activism has taken on a theatrical flamboyance in response to the *realpolitik* of celebrity: the knowledge that public indifference is certain powerlessness. "Fame is the perversion of the natural human instinct for validation and attention," the English playwright Heathcote Williams has said, describing the psychic impoverishment it creates. "As the media stand now, .001 percent of the population is getting crême brulée every day, and the rest are being ignored." The infantile wish for total attention was epitomized by Stanley Siegel, the former host of *AM New York,* who talked to his psychiatrist on the air in front of millions—"I'd like everyone to spend a little time each day thinking about my problems." Siegel was momentarily famous because he had access to the media. Those who don't are goaded into ever-increasing outlandishness to get attention. "BALTIMORE—A gunman held his wife, seven children and about eleven other people hostage," an AP dispatch reported. "His only demand has been to hold a press conference."

Before he gunned down President Reagan and three others, John Hinckley, Jr., wrote in a poem:

> This gun gives me pornographic power.
> If I wish, the president will fall
> And the world will look at me in disbelief.

And the world did. In that moment, Hinckley's demented act of prowess made him equal in celebrity to the actress Jody Foster, with whom he was infatuated. They were, in his eyes, now in the same business. As Hinckley told psychiatrists, the shootings were "a movie starring me," with President Reagan as featured player and "a cast of doctors, lawyers, and hangers-on." In seeing his life elevated to myth, Hinckley was only aping the stage-managed imperialism of the famous, who are made to seem like the history of the nation. Hinckley even referred to the assassination attempt as a "historical deed." Speaking of his imagined relationship with Jodie Foster, he said: "We are a historical couple." Society gets the murderers its national neurosis encourages.

> Regardless of your lovely life
> I am still here writing in pain

Hinckley wanted to turn Foster's enchanted life "upside down" with a magical solution of his own. In rationalizing the event, Hinckley spoke in the language of popularity that had contributed to his madness. "After I shot President Reagan," he remarked, "his polls went up 20 per cent."

Both criminals and stars make their names with a vengeance and are rewarded for their notoriety with the accoutrements of success. Recently, Ronald Biggs—Britain's fugitive Great Train Robber, now living in Brazil—appeared in an ad touting a good cup of coffee "when you're on the run, like me." Watergate is still a million-dollar industry, the crime transformed by its perpetrators into legend through their novels, autobiographies, and lecture tours. Gary Gilmore went to a murderer's grave with Norman Mailer signed to write his story and the movie rights sold. His producer was among the four intimates who watched him die. Like any star's name, Gilmore's became commerce, emblazoned on T-shirts with his last words, "Let's Do It," and the subject of a punk-rock album, *Gary Gilmore's Eyes*. "Murder," Auden said, "is negative creation." And the killer, by his deed, sacrifices his own life for a chance—however brief—to know the only life American society seems to value: celebrity. As Hinckley wrote in a poem published in *Time*:

I have become what I wanted
To be all along, a psychopathic poet

Jackie, Marlon, Liza, Liz, Tennessee, Elvis, Mick, Marilyn, Groucho, Bing, Raquel. "To make your name," "to see your name in lights," "to be a household name" has always been part of the culture's mythology of success. To establish "a name" in a nation of immigrants (many of whose names were lost at the port of entry) assuages the trauma of being uprooted and proves to the newcomer that he is here, here in the place where people are eager to lose their old names in the hope of making an even bigger one: Archie Leach (Cary Grant), Ruby Stevens (Barbara Stanwyck), Bernie Schwartz (Tony Curtis), Doris von Kappelhoff (Doris Day). The famous keep alive the romance of individualism, for fame is democracy's vindictive triumph over equality: the name illuminated, the name rewarded, the name tyrannical.

Americans do not live easily with the idea of scarcity. The cult of the famous has burgeoned as the nation comprehends that the looming energy crisis, increasing unemployment, industrial and urban stagnation deny the dream of limitless material prosperity. Winners in a competitive society, multinational corporations of one, the famous are flaunted so that the system can be seen to work. With class distinctions in America replaced by cash distinctions, the famous have the power to turn everything into capital: every acquaintance, every job, even every failure serve to make their name and their asking price bigger. ("The recipient is advised to save this memorandum," it says at the bottom of "Dame Edna's" creator, Barry Humphries's notepaper, "as it could well become a very valuable collector's item.")

The occasional refusal of the famous to be visible (Howard Hughes, Greta Garbo) creates its own mystique because technology abhors a secret. The famous make self-interest legendary. As Ethel Merman explained her star status: "When I do a show, the whole show revolves around *me,* and if I don't show up, they can forget it!" These displays of power create a sense of well-being and possibility. They make American life seem like a blessing. As a result, fame has become America's greatest export, re-creating in modern materialistic terms the exciting illusion of perfectibility that first drew Europeans to the New World.

But the Dream is a tyranny. While the famous aspire to be the perfect product, pleasurable and addictive, the public, hooked on fame's contact high, craves new connections. As with all addiction, an ever-larger dose is needed to get the same rush. Having created the need, the machinery of celebrity must produce bigger and better celebrities. Like commercial American tomatoes, people are "forced" in fame's artificial light to gigantic size while their unique flavor shrinks.

The ranks of the famous swell. Yet "stars" are insecure in the firmament of the public imagination, often burning out from overexposure. (Even those whose careers have been lost still retain the cachet of being once well known.) "Power passes so quickly from hand to hand," de Tocqueville wrote of America, "that none need despair of catching it in turn." In modern American life the turnover is dizzying. The media's overload of celebrity prompted Andy Warhol to observe sardonically: "In the future everybody will be famous for fifteen minutes."

Warhol showed the business of celebrity for what it is: the celebrity of business. He cashed in. His studio is "The Factory," where he has put his stamp on paintings, books, films, a newspaper (Interview), a rock group (The Velvet Underground), as well as a whole social scene that grew up around these enterprises. Warhol understood the media and how to make surface sensational. In Warhol's aura of celebrity, the speed-freaks, thieves, psychopaths, dropouts worked up "their problems into entertaining routines" and became "superstars" with instant entrée to every establishment. "Start thinking rich. Start being grand," Warhol told one of his "superstars." "You're Entertainment: don't give it away. People like things more when they have to *pay* for them." Candy Darling, Jackie Curtiss, Ondine, Viva, Ingrid Superstar, Vera Cruise, Joe America, Nico—all became part of the small change of contemporary celebrity. By putting on film the stories of these sexual and social outsiders, Warhol did for a subculture of America what he had done for its commercial detritus in his paintings of Campbell Soup cans. It was Pop's vision of democratic stardom: "Everybody was part of the same culture now. Pop references let people know that *they* were the happening, that they didn't have to *read* a book to be part of culture—all they had to do was *buy* it."

Fame, as Warhol realized, was now just getting and holding attention. "Tell the story of your life," Warhol told one of his actors in *Chelsea Girls*, "and somewhere along the line take off your pants." The Pop credo "was to do the easiest thing"; and making a spectacle of yourself was easier than making art. Warhol turned himself and his entourage into a media happening. At one Philadelphia exhibit, the crush to see Warhol and his crew was so great that the pictures had to be taken off the walls. "We weren't just at the exhibit," Warhol writes in *POPism*, "we *were* the exhibit." Personality had replaced output as the measure of fame. Through his entourage, Warhol could multiply himself. Using his name, Silver George gave telephone interviews ("I wear what everybody else wears at The Factory. A striped T-shirt—a little too short—over another T-shirt . . ."). Paul Morissey, his hair sprayed silver like Andy's, did an art lecture in Utah as Warhol. And when Warhol made TV appearances, he would usually let one of his gang, like Viva, speak while he sat silently taping the proceedings. What did it matter? Warhol was a brand name.

Warhol feeds and parodies the culture's craving for celebrity. Each newly minted "superstar" is a reminder of the conspicuous waste of talent—the dark side of American abundance—where, exploited and exhausted by the voracious media, careers are "gloriously" made and "spectacularly" lost. The public relishes each fall of a star as a sacrifice that brings renewed fertility in the shape of someone yet richer and more glamorous. *People* offers its readers a "Sequel" section: "Ever Wondered What Happened to So-and-So?" More than two thousand men, women, and children appeared in *People*'s pages during 1976. Many were celebrities and will be for a long time; others were anonymous, revealed for a moment in the spotlight, then fading back into the crowd. The famous, who make a myth of accomplishment, become pseudoevents, turning the public gaze from the real to the ideal. They substitute for a historical consciousness. Desperate cultural efforts have been made to "enshrine" individual accomplishment in Halls of Fame. Pantheons for strippers, baseball players, statesmen, cowboys, dog mushers, animal actors—nearly 750 Halls of Fame have been established (only three outside America) in a crude attempt to fix points of reference and cultural values.

The famous embody the twin American obsessions of restlessness and commerce. Mention of a star is rarely made without a price, a product, or a purchase. Feeling the surge of momentum and fearing its loss, the famous hurry to keep their appointment with destiny. They have achieved success, but they cannot rest in it. In pursuit of their immortality they are compelled to explore power, test it, extend it. They must work at being famous. In skating on thin ice, the safety of the famous lies in speed.

Fame is America's Faustian bargain: a passport to the good life that belittles human endeavor while seeming to epitomize it. The famous gain excitement and activity, only to lose concentration and calm. A sense of acceleration spins the wheels of their imagination and seizes their life. Their momentum becomes their existence.

At a certain velocity, all things disintegrate. Presidents and performers have tried to ease the pressure with drink and drugs; but the awesomeness of their omnipotence and their schedules is unbalancing. "Competition," according to Bertrand Russell, "considered as the main thing in life is too grim, too tenuous, too much a matter of taut muscles and intent will, to make a possible basis of life for more than one or two generations. After that length of time, it must produce nervous fatigue, and various phenomena of escape . . . and in the end the disappearance of the stock through sterility." Russell, who himself feared "being worn out and broken by the time I'm thirty," prophesied in 1932 the state of fatigue to come, in which competition would poison not only work but also leisure, since relaxing would become impossible—"There is bound to be a continual acceleration of which the natural termination would be drugs and collapse." American social history is littered with the legends of fame's walking wounded: Richard Nixon, Judy Garland, Marilyn Monroe, Tennessee Williams, Janis Joplin, John Berryman—all had their breakdowns in public and turned even their ruination into myth. (It was the fiercely competitive Berryman, whose 77 *Dream Songs* won the Pulitzer Prize for Poetry in 1964, who, on hearing of Robert Frost's death, exclaimed: "Who's number one? Who's number one?")

Perhaps the most grotesque recent example of the competitive strain on the famous is Elvis Presley. "Every dream I ever dreamed," Elvis said, accepting the Junior Chamber of Commerce Award as one of the ten most outstanding men in America, "has come true a hundred times." That was the problem. When he died at the age of forty-two in 1977, the king of rock 'n' roll was a 255-pound junkie, an incontinent recluse with a court of keepers and cooks on twenty-four-hour call to keep him cleaned, stroked, and fed. Presley was the *reductio ad absurdum* of fame's greed. He died of chronic boredom. Presley called his Memphis estate Graceland—his adult life had been spent in that American state of grace called Fame.

Fame legitimizes the tyrannical will, and it doomed Elvis to a perpetual adolescence. He was trapped in an endless exhibition of his power. Elvis had a permanent staff of good ole boys to keep him company and do his bidding. He was never alone. Sometimes he would compare himself to Jesus breaking bread with his disciples as he and the gang chowed down to the greasy Southern cooking he loved. Then the good ole boys would sing "What a Friend We Have in Elvis." He once bought thirteen Cadillacs in a day and gave one to a passing black woman. A law-and-order nut who packed three guns in his later years and kept one on the table while he ate, Elvis thought nothing of running up an $85,000 gun bill. He also thought nothing of drawing a gun on people who crossed him, or blasting away at a television set when the program annoyed him. Elvis was the Enforcer (he collected sheriffs' badges like football cards and had a stoned interview with President Nixon, who made him a narcotics agent). And when Presley's will was seriously challenged, he could go into murderous tantrums. He had one of his flunkies take out a Mafia contract on the man for whom his wife had left him. At the end of his life, Elvis's live-in girl friends read him his favorite Bible stories, hand-fed him, and talked in baby-talk to the King. In his hog heaven, Elvis had returned to the security of the womb.

Fame creates its own caste system. The famous keep and extend their power by association with the famous for, like most Americans, they socialize by métier. Elvis had only to drop a note to the White House to get President Nixon to put aside the Vietnam War and other matters of state to see him; and when Presley died, Caroline Kennedy was the only one outside the family allowed to gaze on the King's face at the private memorial service. When Cher called Washington "the crime capital of the world" on television in the mid-seventies, President Carter got on the phone to disabuse her. And recently, when Nancy Reagan wrote a song, Frank Sinatra came along to the White House steps to sing it with her. In an insecure society, the mere presence of the famous serves as a totem to the public that the gods are with it. Sherman Billingsley, the restaurateur who conceived one of the legendary American celebrity hangouts, the Stork Club, understood this: "I found out that a flock of celebrities made a café popular. People will pay more to look at each other than for food, drink and service." The exclusiveness of the famous is even built into manners. Amy Vanderbilt cautions her readers: "To ask a really important person to sign an autograph pad full of the names of nobodies is to insult him."

The glare of public attention limits the experience of the famous while widening their range of connections. Instead of having experience, they have experience provided for them. Fame homogenizes life; and this inevitably brings its own creative impoverishment. "The effect of power and publicity on all men," wrote Henry Adams at a time before the media made the problem epidemic, "is the aggravation of self, a sort of tumor that ends up killing the victim's sympathies." The star is aware of himself not just as a person but as a "personality." He becomes self-conscious. "When you become relatively well-known," says George C. Scott, "you lose one of the great tools an actor has—observing human nature in other people. It's like a painter—you translate what you see and you do it. But the sad thing is that you become so self-conscious against your will that you lose that ability to appraise, evaluate and file away other people. You're repulsed by what's happened to you, but as hard as you try, you really can't quite get back to the situation you were in before."

As the lives of the famous become slowly, irremediably thinner, so does their work. Discussing fame, Gabriel García Márquez said: "It reminds me of something Graham Greene wrote about bombing. 'The trouble is, after you've been hit, it still goes on.' " Perhaps the American novelist is the best bellwether of the problem: Truman Capote retails the gossip of his fashionable friends; Erica Jong rehashes her sudden success, unable to escape in fiction the banality of her inflated self; Norman Mailer mythologizes himself in the third person and grandstands for the crowd. Writing is an act of penetration, celebrity of presentation. The two are often at odds. In America, the writer strives to develop his singularity *and* his popularity—an impossible task because fame, which demands conformity to the standardized rituals of success, is promiscuous with talent. In the haste to go public, the novelist too often rushes into print. "The worst thing, I should say, that can happen to a writer is to become a Writer," Mary McCarthy says in her shrewd essay "The Fact of Fiction." Noting the absence of texture and fact in the modern novel, she sees the problem of the novel as partly the social predicament of the novelist. The contemporary writer who breaks through to public notoriety expands his royalty statement and shrinks his world. When he promotes his work, he traverses America in first-class hops between hotel and television studio. When he socializes, he finds himself amid people with the same aspirations, the same histories of success, the same cultural references. "Esteem," as Veblen said, "is awarded on evidence"; and the famous company a star keeps is evidence to himself and to others of his status. He is surrounded in his private life by people who either support his success or refract it. Having sought to win public opinion, the famous writer becomes enslaved by it.

The writer is made to see himself as a commercial unit; and, like any commodity, he is pushed to be a brand name. The writer's advances, his publicity, his sales are in proportion to the public's awareness of *him*. In this climate the writer must become his own product. If the product is to stay before the public, so too must the writer. No wonder then that instead of broadcasting ideas, best sellers like E. L. Doctorow, Jerzy Kosinski, John Irving, Norman Mailer, Truman Capote turn up on the movie screen broadcasting themselves. The novel means "news"—and the big news is no longer the writer's prose, but his or her presence. Instead of living with his characters in mind, the famous writer lives with the idea of other people. The result is trivializing: "Robert Penn Warren Loves Eleanor Clark: With three books out, the preeminent U.S. literary couple copes with her growing blindness" *(People)*.

Every society has its particular kind of acceptable neurosis; and fame is America's cultural defense. America has co-opted fame for its own needs. By making it desirable, the culture disguises it as a defense. Fame's pageant of ambition is therefore more important to the society than the individuals who achieve it. Fame dramatizes vindictiveness as drive, megalomania as commitment, hysteria as action, greed as just reward. Idealized accomplishment is forced to gigantic proportions, a situation in which size replaces substance as a barometer of success. "It doesn't matter if you fail," explained the producer of *Dr. Dolittle,* which lost $28 million for Twentieth Century-Fox, "as long as you fail *big.*" The famous are like dinosaurs whose behemoth size is at once their glory and their downfall. They cannot adapt; but by dint of their power, they force life to adapt to them. When it won't or can't, they perish.

America's Dream has always been more important to it than its reality; and the famous are living proof of the Dream come true. As the society flounders without a lofty mission, its institutions in disarray, the machinery of celebrity works even harder to produce a sense of the culture's greatness. Celebrity proliferates in proportion to the society's fear of decline. To achieve fame is to risk dying scorned rather than rejected. But the society seems undaunted. It is not reason but faith that Americans seek. In their glittering immediacy, the famous celebrate the gratifications of the moment but discourage the values of protracted effort, wisdom, permanence, and calm on which greatness is built.

The news is so swollen with non-event that the citizen can't see the sky through the stars. "Fame—" sings David Bowie, who should know, "what you get is no tomorrow." In the hubbub of celebrity, the public loses its sense of historical proportion, unable realistically to assess either its past or future. The material gains of the famous are so large, the technology that promotes them so pervasive, that the neurotic pattern cannot be broken except by disaster, which makes prestige irrelevant and lifts man's sights beyond himself to the survival of the species. Meanwhile the rigid ethic of individualism leads to stagnation. Fame standardizes the goals and the measures of achievement. The result is a frenzied yet monotonous society, smug in its stage-managed sense of greatness, where the names of the actors change but the show remains the same.

Index